D1605921

Honorable Bandit

Terrace Books, a trade imprint of the University of Wisconsin Press,
takes its name from the Memorial Union Terrace, located at
the University of Wisconsin–Madison. Since its inception in 1907,
the Wisconsin Union has provided a venue for students, faculty, staff,
and alumni to debate art, music, politics, and the issues of the day.
It is a place where theater, music, drama, literature, dance, outdoor activities,
and major speakers are made available to the campus and the community.

Honorable Bandit

A Walk across Corsica

Brian Bouldrey

Terrace Books
A trade imprint of the University of Wisconsin Press

Terrace Books
A trade imprint of the University of Wisconsin Press
1930 Monroe Street, 3rd Floor
Madison, Wisconsin 53711-2059

3 Henrietta Street
London WC2E 8LU, England

Copyright © 2007
The Board of Regents of the University of Wisconsin System
All rights reserved

Printed in the United States of America

The poem "A Man Leaves the Sea" at the beginning of chapter 3
is used with the permission of Will Butler.

ISBN-13: 978-0-299-22320-5

This book is for

Petra

and her new daughter,

Julia Johanna

—upon you both I heap all possible blessings.
Ultreya, babies!

Contents

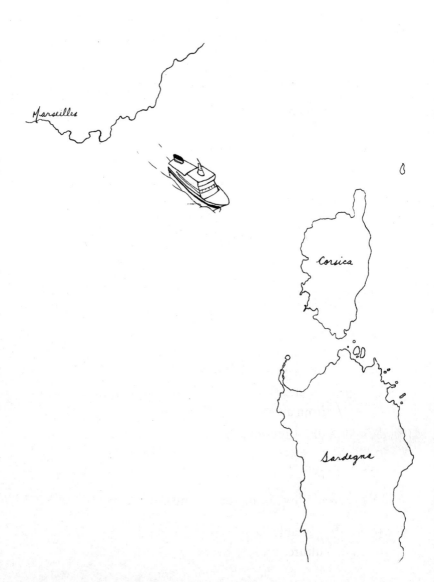

Marseilles

Corsica

Sardegna

Author's Note

There once was a lady of Corsica
Who purchased a little brown saucy cur
Which she fed upon ham
And hot raspberry jam
That expensive young lady of Corsica.
                                            Edward Lear

Corsica is an island 5,233 square miles in size, floating like a stone ship in the Mediterranean (this area of that great European bathtub is specifically called the Tuscan Sea), closest to the Italian city of Genoa (some eighty miles east) but politically and problematically part of France. Sardegna is only ten miles from the southern tip of Corsica, and on a clear day it looks quite swimmable. Corsica is a short boat ride from anywhere, and over the centuries every culture within swimming distance has made a point of invading it: Etruscans, Vandals, Goths, Saracens, Genoese, Aragonese, and French. Corsica was attacked so many times that if any town were not reduced to rubble along the coast (and many of the towns in the interior, as well) it is because it made of itself not just a town but a walled citadel. How remarkable it is, then, that the country has its own specific, pungent culture, with its singular cuisine, musical tradition, language, and stories, and also that mad, operatic history of the *vendetta*—bloody family feuds that last centuries.

This is a book whose two intentions push and pull at each other. I wanted to write about a month-long travel experience, mostly on foot, crossing the island of Corsica. I also wanted to consider, as if to imitate the meandering of a walker's mind, why it is that I spend so much of my spare time with a backpack strapped over my shoulders in order to hike, nearly every year, hundreds of miles—and why others might do it, too.

And so the travelogue you read here, a straightforward hike from north to south across that island, imitates a novel's through-line, a forward momentum, the fairytale's "and then" and "and then" and "and then" that propels you through any number of (mis)adventures, while my meditations on walking are intended to slow that progression, suspend you from an actual or figurative cliff, and even, Lord help you, back up a bit, in order to ruminate on rambling.

But that's what walking is like: a tramp through landscape carrying a change of clothes and a brainbox full of jostled gears and screws, and in the evening, if you're lucky, time to wash socks and rewind the gears, to rest and think about what just happened over the past twenty miles.

There's a danger here. My meditative chapters, considering over and over again "Why I Walk," while perhaps casting little stuporous spells, might jar you out of that sweet dreamy sorcery of the journey. And while a dream within a dream might sound, well, *dreamy,* it might also need to be paid for by a never-ending rousing. That's me, blowing a bugle reveille over your head every twenty pages or so. And that's what walking is like, too.

The road, then, is not direct, and as I have unfailingly found in my real and reckless walks, the way is sometimes lost. Plato called it "aporia," a purposeful loss of reason's linear thread, a getting lost in order to be found, eventually.

I hang the structure of my own story—the "and then this town, and then that town"—on this astonishing island, from a trail that cuts across it. It is a camino officially created in 1972 by the French, which, in all of its land and possessions, manages some 72,000 miles of well-marked trails as part of the *sentier de grande randonnee*—the GRs, for short. They are numbered like highways for cars (I have enjoyed walking on several of these, most notably the portion of the pilgrim way to Santiago de Compostela that stretches over France and crosses the Pyrenees, known among hikers as the GR65), and the trail that follows a rough diagonal from the northwest to southeast corners of Corsica is called the GR20.

It usually takes a dozen days to stomp your way over the GR20, and walkers can stay in or near *gîtes d'étape,* small shelters maintained by a more or less friendly *gardien* who keeps things organized, offers a few supplies (a sausage or an egg, perhaps; baguettes, overpriced Mars bars, and wine, always wine), and sometimes does a little cooking. This is not a simple walk in the park: the GR20 follows Corsica's spine of granite peaks. Every day requires the assay of a mountain or two, so that most of the trek is spent in a series of climbs and descents—exhausting but offering a wildly different view every few minutes at every switchback and precipice. That is, wonderful views for those possessing the wherewithal to press on. Whether I had the wherewithal to execute the GR20 is the subject of this book.

BRIAN BOULDREY

Norton Island, Maine
August 2005

Acknowledgments

My thanks to Michael Cook, John Bliss, Tony Rella, Anthony Veerkamp, Jean-Philippe Casutt, Petra Wellemsen, Mary Kinzie, Reginald Gibbons, Marta Maretich, John Beckman, Kelly Luchtman, Gwenan Wilbur, Jill Olson, Larry Wood, Jennifer Locke, Toby Sullivan, Mary Sutherland, Wayne Sheldrake, Charley Thomson, Doug Moore, and Will Butler, that Guy from the Arcade Fire. Thank you, Brenna Killeen, for your mapmaking skills.

My most sincere and warm thanks to Stephen Dunn and the Eastern Frontier Society's Norton Island Residency Program. How lucky I've been to write about an island on an island. This book never would have been completed without that colony's peaceful precincts, jolly colleagues, and massive lobsters, both the quick and the cooked.

Honorable Bandit

I

Why I Walk

Imagining the Maquis

> The sight of a burned maquis is enough to make a man
> fancy he has been transported into midwinter in some
> northern clime, and the contrast between the barrenness
> of the ground over which the flames have passed, with the
> luxuriant vegetation around it, heightens this appearance
> of sadness and desolation.
>
> Prosper Mérimée, Colomba

I had never seen a burned maquis, but back in 1991, from our south
San Francisco cottage, my partner, Jeff, and I could see the Oakland
Hills blaze away. We were having a party in the garden, and it was
too late to call it off on account of bad taste, so we all stood among
the gerber daisies, nasturtium, Mexican sage, agapanthas, hydrangeas, and calla lilies (perhaps we *should* have called off the party for

bad taste!) and watched the sky turn orange, hazy with smoke. There's nothing like a wildfire to kill off cocktail conversation: we turned up the radio and listened to woeful interviews with stumped firemen, and reports of people hosing down their siding (hoping to keep their homes from becoming tinder) and of the mass exodus of wildlife scampering into the roads (out of the frying pan, into the line of fire).

And once the sky turned from orange to green, that's when the ashes, wafted over the bay, began to snow into our drinks. And that's when I saw, no kidding, a large flaky sheath of ash that I could just make out as it rested on some paving stones, a chiaroscuro of glossy black on flat black, "Apex #32 Roofing Supply." It wasn't very cold that day, but I'm sure I shivered a bit.

But conflagration has never made people like me steer away from prime real estate. Soon after, Jeff found himself well-employed as a carpenter and electrician rebuilding all those incinerated homes on Grizzly Peak, which kept us in cheesecakes and rent money throughout the winter. The color of the garden hydrangea changed from blue to red after all the soot changed the nutrients in the soil.

And ten years later, even though I had read that some portion of the Corsican maquis was constantly on fire nearly every month of the year, I bought a ticket and packed my backpack and made my plans to walk across the island, over mountains and through the maquis. I needed to get out.

I consider myself to be, like certain Sherwin-Williams paints, an indoor-outdoor kind of guy. I am both city mouse and country mouse, prefer the extremes of urban living and the wilds of open terrain, the asphalt jungle and the, uh, jungle. Equal easy access to the felicities of espresso beans and blue curaçao and to the austerities of mountainside coffee plantations and the blue waters around Curaçao. I want trails to the lonesome pine and rare books; quick wit and cricket chirp.

But at the moment I know I'm going to be gone, when the backpack is packed and the shuttle to the airport has been arranged, I begin to feel unglued, a label peeling from its bottle. The mail is cut off, the message on the answering machine wards off any friendly callers, and all the friendly callers think I'm already gone. I have time to take the dog out for one last round before taking her over to the friends who watch her.

I moved from San Francisco to Chicago two years ago, yet another choice I've made that brought my sanity under scrutiny, but that is no country for old men. I live now, quite happily, across from Winnemac, a midsized park flanked by a grade school and a high school. There are more than half a dozen baseball diamonds and a football field, and when my window is open I get the sound of urban domesticity—ringing tardy bells, players chanting "hey batteh-batteh-batteh," cheerleaders taunting, "Wegot spirit, howbout *choo?*" In the spring, birds don't sing so much as scream—oh, how the robin insists on that same refrain from his favorite Gilbert and Sullivan operetta: "Cheerily! Merrily! Cheerily! Merrily!" We're in the flight pattern of O'Hare airport, and overhead you can always see a handful of planes begin to extend their landing gear, too high to generate noise pollution. Even now, in late summer, there's salsa music on a jerry-rigged stage. In recent years, under the Green Mayor, the Chicago Park District set aside huge tracts to native grasslands and plants, and while I've heard the occasional neighbor grumble about such a lot of money thrown at the cultivation of weeds, I, for one, am overjoyed. They call the stuff "prairie grasses."

We take our turn, in no hurry here at the end, for my dog, Grace, is, like me, a walker, not a runner. We run into Eileen, who, with her rheumatoid arthritis, is not likely to run, either. She recognizes me, that crazy guy with a poky dog on a bootless leash, the ones who wander in the weeds with a little green *Audubon Field Guide to North American Wildflowers,* trying to identify the glorious quotidian:

brome, rye, flax, mallow, yarrow, coneflower, hawkweed, quackgrass, bachelor's button, Johnny Jump-Up, and don't forget forget-me-nots. No more the garish gerber or the fickle hydrangea; I've traded those for the plain jane of Black-Eyed Susan and Queen Anne's lace. In the evening, evening primrose, the gold in goldenrod, crimson clover, over and over.

At the Mezquite of Cordoba, historically, you entered through an orchard of orange trees planted at the same intervals as the many hundreds of columns of the mosque, so that you didn't know at what point you had moved from the outdoors indoors. So it goes with my little patch of wild: there are, all around Grace and me, great brick chimneys, remnants of the industrial era, preserved and smokeless; in fact, one of them has a tree growing out of the top of it, and the one toot-tooting from the high school shelters a family of barn owls. Their upright strength stands in my line of vision, along with the sycamores and oaks lining the prairie plot. My backbone straightens accordingly.

"I thought you were already gone," says Eileen. Her scruffy old bear of a dog, Cleo, sniffs Grace, and they acknowledge each other, two golden girls among packs of dogs from Dawson's Creek.

In my peeling-label state, hours before a many-legged flight connecting Chicago to Paris and Paris to Marseilles, I already miss where I already am. I linger until dusk, until fireflies rise up out of the prairie. On evenings like this, when everything is at some sort of central turning point, when night is falling but everything else is going up, up, birds and fireflies and smokestacks and sycamores and heat, there also rises a specific scent, a combination of all those native grasses. Eileen says goodbye again, "no, *really*," and moseys to her brick two-flat. And then it gets dark, and the scent disperses, and something else seems lost, and I'm just a little alone, a little depressed.

My friend Michael has dealt with depression since before Prozac was even born. He hates, as any sane person would, to be filled with all those medicines, although he knows they help, but he's been able to supplement a less-lethal dose by taking up a number of soothing cottage industries. When we visit, he may be finishing the knitting on the sleeve of a sweater, or checking the glaze on some ceramics. Michael has, as well, a small candle-making business, and invented his own line of special scents. I love the combinations he's come up with: the tame "Pear Butter" (pear and vanilla extracts) and "Easter Parade" (malt and bubble gum and the softened whiffs of jelly beans and sugar); there are other, rowdier scents like "Father Figure," with its bold cedar odor punched up by tobacco, patchouli, leather, and just a touch of CK-One; and "Mom's Purse," based on Father's leather and tobacco but bolstered with spearmint and peppermint.

Sometimes when Michael busies himself knitting and purling, I rummage around in his tackle box full of little brown bottles in which he's captured all sorts of smells. I pull out swizzle-stick-shaped cardboard paddles, write down the names of the scents, then dip them into various extracts: orange, musk, magnolia, pine, balsam, bergamot, ginger. Sometimes companies manufacture blends and give them their own suggestive names, like "snow" and "rain" and "ocean spray." I'd rather get my own hit of a hot driveway, thunderstorm-doused, the hissing wet that brings the earthworms up on asphalt: petrichor on a paddle; I'll mix attar and earth and lily of the valley, of all things, for that flower has a scent as close to spring rain as I have found. I want to approximate, somehow, the native grasslands patch in the park. There's no brown bottle labeled quackgrass or mallow, but "daisies" will work for Black-Eyed Susans, and I can always pretend there's some "lupine" out in my patch, although I haven't seen it.

The more I work and sniff, however, the less sensitive my nose becomes. It's all one big perfume in the room, and I lose my aromatic way. Even after shutting down the olfactory factory for the rest of the day, I get the occasional whiff now and then, some suggestion of something lost right under my nose.

When you Google the word "maquis," the first listings are from a bunch of Star Trek fans devoted to a group of defiant rebels that never liked the peace treaty between the Federation and the Cardassians. Trekkies borrowed the word, I'll guess, from the actual Résistance of World War II, "the Maquis," the French patriots who fought against the Nazi-controlled Vichy government. They, in turn, took their name from Corsica, for a "Maquisard" was one of the "honorable bandits" who hid in the unmappable scrub of the island, hiding from authorities after committing what they considered crimes of nobility. The maquis is, for bandits and patriots, nothing but a boon.

And the maquis that concerns me is, reportedly, a bane to walkers, made up of low, spiny scrub that grows quickly over any trail you might blaze. The maquis is the ultimate indoor-outdoor stuff; it provides firewood to Corsicans and shelter to its honorable bandits as well as to wild boar, a favorite dish. But it is also impenetrable and flammable. Hikers are often trapped for days because of maquis burns.

Corsicans say you can smell the maquis wafting over the Mediterranean when you approach the island in a boat. Napoleon, in exile in a prison on Elba, said he could catch wafts of it from his cell, fifty-some miles to the west, and the perfume of it brought him to tears.

Every guidebook about Corsica describes a different combination of plants that constitute the maquis. "Myrtle, thyme, rock rose, rosemary," claims one. "Juniper, lavender, and heather," another. Chestnuts, strawberry trees, wild marjoram, bay. The wrinkled pink flower called cistus is common, too, and is the source of myrrh, that ancient oil. Corsicans usually get their myrrh by harvesting it off the beards of their goats.

Certainly, if one were to make a "maquis" perfume with Michael's aroma collection, store-bought myrrh would do the trick. But can one imitate the funk of the sort of myrrh gleaned from the beard of a goat? Could we add a crumb of chevre cheese? Honey is not simply honey, after all; bees that produce localized honeys are trained to gather only the right sorts of clover, or chestnuts, or wildflowers. And what of the hottentot fig, which grows on Corsica and may not be the main ingredient of the maquis but certainly has its role in the scentual makeup, tiny and necessary, like homeopathy or a pinch of cumin?

I'm reminded of stories of Italian matriarchies that, generation after generation, pass down their spaghetti sauce recipes but leave one item out, putting it to the children to revitalize the sauce with something new or to let it thin out, die out. But the metaphor doesn't quite work because, as of now, the now of this chapter, I have never smelled, first-hand, the maquis. It's all theoretical. I have a Rashomon potpourri of conflicting accounts, and when I try to add them all together, I get soup. "India is not a mystery," said E. M. Forster, "it is a muddle."

I am romanticizing the maquis, trying to make it a mystery rather than the muddle it is. In a similar way, writers of the nineteenth century romanticized the maquis, the maquisard, and many things Corsican, like the honorable bandits that committed murder through the tradition of vendetta and ran into the flammable wilderness. Writers like Dumas and Mérimée came looking for those outlaws, made up torrid stories about their adventures that come off far more dramatic and exciting than the actual life of a maquisard. But then, the maquisard read these tarted-up stories and reimagined themselves and the maquis they hid in, and ironically set a new standard—a code of bandit honor. The legends fed on the facts, and the facts, legends.

The previous year, on the eve of my departure for a foot pilgrimage to Santiago that took me eight hundred miles across France and Spain, Michael stopped by to wish me a good journey. My backpack was packed, my passport in order, my dog with the family she stays with so often that she showed up in their holiday card photo. I had only three forlorn Pepsi Ones in the fridge, so we drank two. The air conditioner was off and I had the window open, so we could both smell the prairie grasses in the early summer heat.

"I envy you," Michael sighed, "being able to just pick up and go like this."

It's nice to be envied, although not everything about my life is enviable. I told him so. I also told him, or at least I hope I told him, that I envied his ability to sit still, a quality valued by monks, mothers, and barbers, three admirable professions.

He pulled out a paper sack and offered it to me. He had made three votive candles to bring to the cathedral in Santiago, all scented with "Mom's Purse," or a minor variation that included a little rosemary, too, the symbol of gypsy peregrination.

I carried those three votives at the bottom of my pack, along with the other things I wouldn't need very often—the winter fleece, powdered meals in packets, condoms. The thing is, as I plunged deeper and deeper into the pilgrimage, surrounded by an ever-growing entourage of fellow pilgrims, it became more and more difficult to stay clean. Mildew grows on T-shirts that never quite dry after washing, pig and cow crap get kicked into socks along the trail, and you contend with sweat and mud and smelly cheese you packed for a lunch in a field. All the pilgrims keep to themselves because only other pilgrims can tolerate their stench. A goat would be a better sleeping companion, at least one that were myrrh-made.

But I, oddly enough, did not smell (as) bad. Michael's candles kept my backpack anointed, and there was a touch of the suspicious among the other walkers. Is this guy a pretender? A fake pilgrim? I had a hard time explaining why my pack was as fresh as your mother's pocketbook as she clicked it open at the clasp and offered you a stick of Wrigley's Doublemint.

Too bad, then, that at the end of the journey, I learned that the cathedral of Santiago did not allow live flame. Because it caters to daily rounds of thousands of fanatical faithful, it makes sense to ban candles, though Santiago could have benefited from the domesticating influence of Michael's good scents. I ended up lighting the three votives at a street corner shrine to the Virgin Mary, but that's another good story, and stories, like aromas, don't always belong in the mix.

TRAVELERS DESTROY WHAT THEY SEEK. A few years ago, I saw a bumper sticker with this slogan. I hated reading it, the way I hated hearing that there might not really be a God the first time somebody said it. It's a punch to the solar plexus. But then I suspected the source, after spending some time with callow youth, youth being that period when one actually fixes bumper stickers to bumpers and buttons to backpacks. That period when one confuses solemnity with profundity, prefers drama to intimacy, and mistakes brutality for honesty. Nevertheless, there was a scorching idea at the bottom, and once I got past its mean-spirited bitchery, I recognized its truth. Here I am, wondering how to extract scents. I am able to see the irony of bringing back the smell of the maquis, as opposed to lab-created fragrances like "Mom's Purse." Corsica is tough and attracts tough customers. I have in my possession a little monograph called *The Scented Isle: A Parallel Between Corsica and the Scottish Highlands* by Joseph Chiari. Printed for a flinty Glasgow audience, Chiari's favorite parallels are the rather macho ones, a familiarity bred by mutual contempt, for its bandits and wars and the grouchy, taciturn nature of the people. He compares the maquis to his native heather and waxes poetic: "I shall not die in a bedroom / With a priest and a lawyer beside me / I shall perish in a terrible ravine / With a mass of wild ivy to hide me." "Terrible ravine" is Glaswegian for "ditch," I wager, and my mother always warned me about ending up in a ditch. Ditches, I had thought, were bad.

I find it odd that the mass of wild ivy is fragrant and florid, and Corsica's one capitulation to weakness. But Corsicans and their admirers don't dwell on the scent. They prefer to discuss the thornier issues, for only the wily can dwell among the spines of Br'er Rabbit's briar patch.

And every account of the maquis is yet another tank of fuel for my imagination. I'm going to Corsica, not with Michael's Mom's Purse votives but with a jar of oil in which I will collect up specimens of the maquis. My friend has taught me how to extract the scents from flowers, and I am going to be a new kind of bandit in the maquis, pillaging Corsica the way the Vandals and Etruscans and Aragonese have done before me, destroying what I seek.

My intention is to comfort the future me, the one who will return from Corsica, the one you'll meet in the final chapter. The intention of taking souvenirs is to aid memory. What, then, is the opposite of memory? How am I approximating the smell of the maquis here, now? Through the guidebooks, yes, and oddly enough, the prairie grasses flowering in the park across the street. But I really don't know what a hottentot fig smells like (okay—figlike, but still). And besides, it may not even be the smell of the maquis that I will remember most. My memory will probably dwell on the part where I get lost in it, or cut myself on it, or watch it burn and rain ashes down upon me, leaving behind a field of white soot, like snow.

My friends never think I'm foolish to go on these treks, although they're puzzled about why one would crap outdoors or forego basic cable. Many people do think I'm foolish, or have nothing but disdain for the arduous sweaty act of carrying all of one's belongings over a lumpy terrain and calling it a vacation, or enjoyment. Vacation means beaches for most, or shopping in Paris, maybe, or having The Help bring food and bath salts to a luxury hotel room. All of these I have done myself, but I am soon bored. While my friends baste under a hot sun, I pace the beach, and usually step on broken glass or a sea urchin's spine half-buried in the sand. "Want to go camping?" I asked a new friend one time. He nervously said that he probably might manage that.

"You don't really want to go," I said, letting him off the hook.

"Well," he said, with some relief, "where would I put my contact lenses?"

Risking one's life, generating bodily discomfort, courting disaster—these are hard to justify. The nagging bothersome question of the bumper-sticker reproach is: What exactly is it that I seek and wish to destroy? Something genuine? Something earned through suffering? It is difficult for me to find a succinct answer when somebody mocks the "high adventure" hikes I make, for they don't seem to make any sense at all; I can't give such people the canned responses (exercise, proof of courage, encouragement of deep existential thought, chicks dig scars), for they're not useful or true for me. So each time I go off, I find myself stumbling along the piste, asking this question over and over again, because the answer is different with every journey, and until I stumble upon the answer, I'm feeling foolish when I'm not feeling completely unselved by the experience.

Some might call me foolish to walk in the park at night; this is the big bad city, after all, full of another kind of wild animal. But when nature calls, a dog must walk, and by dog, I mean Grace, *my* dog. The police cruiser always passes me by no matter what o'clock in the morning it is, as long as I've got a dog with me—a dog in a park is carte blanche. I will not say I haven't seen any trouble there, because I've come across drug paraphernalia and, just a few months ago, a fellow dog-walker showed me a zipper of stitches along the inside of her arm where some unrestrained pit bull took a bite out of her.

But sometimes I'll look out my window and see four or five pre-teen baggy-pants'd boys who have decided, the way my friends used to decide to put on a play in the garage, to start a gang; I watch them practice hand signals, and even I know that they are doing the signals wrong, and if they can't get the hand signals right, then they aren't really capable of, say, leveling the World Trade Center or wrecking the economy. In light of this, I don't fret too much, since I am a forty-year-old man and accompanied by a dog and have seen more of the dark hearts of people than they can ever hope to generate.

Okay, true: the night before I left for Corsica, I was walking late and my heart leaped to find another shadowy figure in the high prairie grass. His face aglow from the sulfur lights of the high school, he said, even before "Hello," "Can I ask you something?" and I thought for sure my luck had run out, and I was about to be beaten and robbed. But then he said, "Where is a good place to have a bachelor party?" I told him I didn't know. "I just proposed to my best friend's sister, and I'm gonna buy her a ring. I love her more than anything ever in my life," he rambled, in the way only drunks and bad poets can, "and she wants a bouquet of her birth flower. She says her birth flower grows here. Do you know which one it is?" Not knowing the horoscope or birth flowers, I told him I couldn't help him. He let me walk away but kept proclaiming his love, and his wish to make her happy, and his hopes to hold down his job with the city so that he could get her a ring, and so forth.

It can seem very wild there, in that contained space; sometimes the prairie rye is pressed down, as if wild animals had been sleeping in it. I doubt that anything like feral boars would ever find their way to my park, but it was a phenomenon unexpected by the Chicago Park District when killdeer, that prairie bird that, for lack of branches, learned to nest on the ground and protect its young by standing between the nest and a predator (my very urban Grace, for example) and drag its wing as if it were wounded in order to lead the danger away. Dogs are their only foes, I'd guess, unless a barn cat found its way in; mostly, they're tormented by oversexed teenagers who are, no doubt, the ones who roll in the hay like rutting boars and restless fawns.

Michael gave me one more gift: a leather-bound journal, because, for all of his homebound preferences, he knows exactly what to pack for a long trip. "What are you going to write about?" he asked.

"I don't know," I said, "I don't yet know what is going to go wrong." The pages of the journal will be perfect, too, for pressing the leaves and blooms of the plants in the maquis.

I am going out to conquer Corsica, overcome it in some way, the traveler destroying what he seeks by removing its mystery. Or perhaps not. There are infinite ways of construing the world, and the land is ever shifting. What might be true now won't be so in a month or year. We lose a key ingredient to mom's spaghetti sauce. The bee goes to a different glade to make his honey. Even maps become outdated.

For one thing, I am traveling in the off season, something I try to do as often as I can. Of course, it's cheap in August, as Graham Greene puts it, but it's not just savings I'm after. I once chose to stay on the nearby island of Burano when visiting Venice and found, on the vaporetto trip home, that all the locals had come out in the evening, after hiding all day from the hoards with cameras and guidebooks. I got a chance to pretend, if only for an hour or two as the light failed, that I was part of the landscape, having a chance to see the *real* Venice. I am attracted to travel that is unfashionable, risking bad weather and closed facilities in exchange for the way a place will return to its true self when not faking out the tourists, for the spooky, abandoned way towns look after the party is over, like a closed-down carnival.

The problem, of course, is when I come back and try to recommend my travels to people, people who tend to go when the place is at high season, my travels are nothing like theirs. One would seem to need a different map, a different guide. Can anything—a place, a people, even a scent (especially a scent!)—be captured and specified?

It was only recently that I came into an area of my park's prairie-grass area where suspicious teenagers had been doing a bit of lazy damage; a bundle of ox-eye daisies had been tied off with stalks of wheat but still remained planted, tipped. It was the first time it ever came into my head that these wildflowers might be plucked and put into a vase of my dining room table. Not only did I quickly dismiss the possibility (I thought of all the bugs crawling out of the leaves), but I felt dirty, obscene, for having such a thought.

In the maquis, the bandits have gone, but there are still a handful of dangers. Fire, beasties, scratches gone septic. There are occasional reports of Corsican nationalists kidnapping tourists for a little publicity. On the other hand, I think of Winnemac Park and the dangers it can offer. At night, sometimes, I'll hear a rustling in some thicket, and even the insects will stop their deathless burr, startled, preferring to hide. It still smells like the familiar perfume of the mesic prairie grasses. But other smells come out with the critters of the night: the gunpowder from old bottle rockets, the fermenting tang of overripe unpicked mulberries, the last beer at the bottom of a can, piss pong and dog doo. Even these emblems of our crafty indoor culture run wild again when spilled on the open prairie. Run wild, or are reclaimed: "Apex #32 Roofing Supply." And every once in a while, of an evening, I'll bend down, stretch over, and reach my hand into the dark, mysterious cricket-black place that is not, for a moment, my safe home. That's where the imagination can't always lead the way. That's reason enough for going to Corsica, at least for the moment.

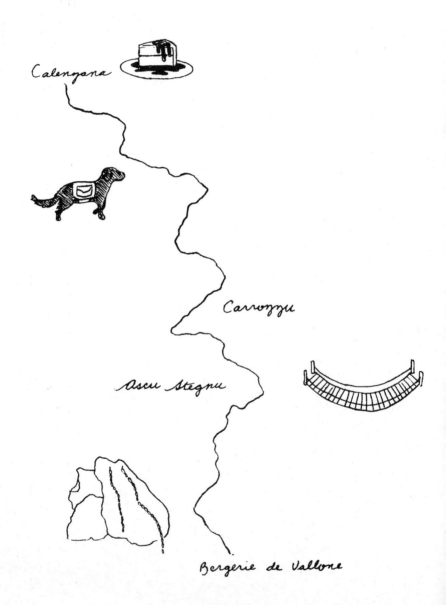

Calenzana

Carrozzu

Ascu Stegnu

Bergerie de Vallone

2

Jet Lag

Marseilles to Ajaccio to Calvi

The Port of Marseilles! *Putaine de merde!* Everybody along the quay looks like a pirate or a prisoner! Ruffians and lowlifes! Con artists and cheapskates! Five o'clock shadows at eleven in the morning! Beer fifteen minutes after that! And that's just the babies, crying out for unfiltered cigarettes from their carriages.

But it is I who must look demented to the other passengers aboard the *Danielle Casanova,* our ferry that sails out from Marseilles to the island of Corsica. I can do my best at trying not to look like a tourist. I can hide (or, more likely in my case, forget) the maps, I can wear the local sports team colors, I can eat the entrails of animals (my people—and by my people, I mean English speakers—call such stuff "offal," and aurally, that's an apt word, while "sweetmeats," no, is not) with a good helping of wine. But my outsider nature reveals itself at inopportune moments: learning to unclasp the latch on the Metro at my train stop, for instance, that first struggle, throwing too much strength and attention into the mechanics of what is, for a local, habitual gesture. I reveal my foreignness the way a person who doesn't have a baby holds a baby and proves childlessness, or who never smokes does so pretending he's always smoked, while everybody can plainly see that he's never smoked—even nonsmokers.

Here, on deck, I lean far over the prow and try to get a whiff of the maquis. Instead, I get a noseful of exhaust and grease. A young French couple, perhaps honeymooners, eye me and step away: I am, even among tourists, an outsider. And the bumper sticker starts to haunt me again like a snatch of annoying tune that you can't get out of your head: TRAVELERS DESTROY WHAT THEY SEEK. Travelers are bad guys, of sorts—if not villains, at least antagonists, not invested in this community, not fully aware of the laws and ways of the locals, not doing, despite the good advice of it, what the Romans do.

Back in Marseilles, I had sat for a long time in Terminal 2, wondering whether I'd had the wrong time printed on my ticket. The waiting room had an exoticism, even in its drab municipal colors (aqua and dirty green), as if the terminal had slept in its clothes, hadn't had time to shave. In a corner an equally rumpled man lounged in a little booth with a sign: ECRIVAIN PUBLIC SERVICE GRATUIT. A person to write official letters for you, free of charge if you were illiterate or perhaps didn't speak the language. On the scuffed walls, I read warnings to travelers headed for Algeria; there's some nasty flu afoot. And under glass, a wanted poster for a Corsican terrorist, armed and dangerous. I decided from the photo that this guy really did sleep in his clothes.

I felt like I'd slept in my clothes, too, and always do until the first cup of coffee, which seemed far away. But the lackadaisy of the terminal alarmed me, and alarm can do the work of good coffee. The big board, with its embarkation points and times spelled out with roll-dexes of metal letters and numbers that tickered into place periodically, sounding like pigeons spooked into flight from a city roof, told me our stopping place was Bastia, on the northern cap of Corsica. But my friend Petra, already on the island, was meeting me in Ajaccio, on the west coast. And where were the damn ticket agents?

Another ferry boat, the *Napoleon Bonaparte,* landed and disgorged hundreds of Corsican visitors to the mainland. The *Bonaparte* was big. It dispelled my notions about ferries being nothing more than glorified rafts or upgraded tugboats just sufficient enough to cross a wide river. The people disembarking had had a boat for sleeping. There were lots of families, children, the infirm. I knew my boat, the *Casanova,* had, at best, "comfort seats," so I'd be getting more of a working class—and yes, *smoky*—crowd. But what people I saw waiting with me (not many) were Northern African types in hiqabs, hijabs, and kaftans. The public writer would have made a killing for all his work if his *service* weren't *gratuit.*

After another hour of nervous pacing, I captured the pity of a girl in the information booth out on the street who saw me wander by once too often, and asked in a French even I could understand: "Where are you going *now*?" I was in the wrong terminal, it seemed. She did everything but take me by the hand when she walked me to the proper one, and in my defense, it was also called "Terminal 2." "Attention shoppers. If anybody is missing a little boy named Brian, please meet him in the other Terminal 2." But nobody was missing a little boy named Brian. Had my boat been on time, I would have missed it.

But it was fashionably late, and I was grateful. It must be remembered, it seems, that however villainous we travelers are, we are of the bigger-than-life sort, the snake, The Dissembler, and we have shed our home like a skin. In the book of Job, God asks Satan, "Where have you been?" He shrugs the answer off: "Traveling about in the world." Seeing the sights. Still capable of malice and sidewinding in unexpected directions, he is also a bit vulnerable, pokeable; when the weather gets cold, his heartbeat nearly stops.

I waved goodbye to Info Girl; all the heroes of my life remain strangers. This crowd, in The Other Terminal 2, was much more like me: a bit more tonsorial attention and One-Hour Martinizing, engaged in the reading of newspapers and mass market paperbacks, nobody seemed to be shipping massive carts full of cheap goods. For a single euro, I finally got my coffee, strong and sold with an adorable little disposable filter. MTV pabulum'd through a half-dozen video monitors, and the dirty green paint was replaced by two zippy aqua stripes that raced each other around the white walls.

I sized up my fellow travelers the way they sized up me. There seem to be two kinds of travelers in general: the jobless twenty-year-olds ready to rough it with little cash and just a handful of belongings, and the fifty-year-old couple, their nest emptied, who'd earned some time, who'd have nothing to do with travel but luxury (no surprises, thank you). Both parties looked upon me with suspicion. My gay friends back home, who sometimes have enough money and time, even though they're not yet fifty, are also fairly horrified by my preferred manner of travel. My next door neighbor in Chicago, Jim, retired and content working and worrying his lawn and garden, turned to me after hearing my hiking plans and asked, "What *are* you, sixteen?"

I am a stranger to this place, and by this place, I mean everywhere. I let the landlord show my apartment to a guy debating whether to take the identical one below me; when the potential tenant saw the piles of books and shelves full of more texts, he said, as if he'd found the Unabomber among us, "This is an awful lot of books." My desires are inscrutable to most people, slick and effete and diabolical (Claus Von Bulow: "You tortured your own wife?" Menendez brothers: "You killed your own parents?" Bouldrey: "What *are* you, sixteen?"). And when I get to the place where the walking across Corsica begins, I will be a stranger again. I've brought with me the strangest ideas: I want ice in my Coke at the café, have no pressing need for fresh bread, and I eat spinach in a salad uncooked.

It was more than two hours later that we heard a reassuringly smooth voice, fluent in at least five languages, announce that our boat was ready for boarding.

The couple in the fore of the *Danielle Casanova* back away from me, and I look up at what I've been sniffing at: two of the ten smoke-stacks belch thick black smoke into the blue Marseillaise sky. It looks like squid ink bleeding into Mediterranean water, almost fake, a stage show for our benefit, so we can make believe this is the industrial age and the primary transport mode. The Tricolor is wrapped so many times around the flagpole it may as well be the Swiss banner, for all we know. Or the Corsican bandera. The Dramamine I took was also inutile: we're too big to bob.

The Mediterranean—what *is* that color? It's wine-dark, Homer was right, but what kind of wine is that? I'm not afraid of swimming or sailing in the Mediterranean, and I ought to be. It's a shipwreck-ridden sea, and two days from now, Petra and I will jump headlong into it, and I will bark my shin something fierce against a rock when a big wave batters me, and I'll scrape most of the skin off the bottom of one foot, and a finger as well. I spend so much time worried about various imagined accidents that might nix a long hike (getting mugged in the park after dark, the floor-polishing Zamboni at the Gare Ste. Charles, a missed stair in the cathedral, a big rusty sign blowing down on me, rejected credit cards, thugs) that the obvious danger, at hand, is never heeded. It's not scree but sea that will make me limp through my first day along our trail. But I'm getting ahead of myself.

I chose to take a boat to Corsica, rather than fly into the island, for several reasons, all of which didn't really work out. For example, it was supposed to have been more convenient for Petra, arriving on her own speed from Vienna, where she lives. She had planned to fly into Ajaccio, but then found a cheaper ticket into that northern town of Bastia (in which case, the Original Terminal 2 would have worked out just fine). Also, I am not fond of jet travel, or rather, not fond of all its components: the anxious and generic fermata of airports, the cramped, too-social seating of the plane, and jet lag, which is the closest thing regular folks have, I'm betting, to the feeling of drug addiction, as the body is pulled farther and farther away from its normal rhythms and told that this new, unnatural set is correct, when it is not. Freud said that if a person can work, love, and sleep, then he is healthy. Freud never experienced jet lag.

And, as usual, jet lag didn't come over me until the second night, when my guard was down. I always make arrangements on the first day for being tired, for forcing myself to stay up as late as possible. That's why I spent two days in Marseilles, to sample bouillabaisse and sleep, and not sleep, in a genuine *habitation* built by Corbusier (something like living in a shoebox with a veranda), working out the jet lag–drug addict withdrawal. By the evening of the second day, I felt normally tired, and I went to sleep.

And awakened, bolt upright, at 2 a.m. Ravenously hungry.

The journey back to sleep, indeed, is one akin to the journey of the recovering addict, except there is something natural to fight as well. The addict must know things are wrong. It seems wrong, for example, to be fighting this alert state. In me, it creates a strange corporeal hallucination: I see things behind my eyelids, and the misfiring hormonal secretions generate all manner of pink elephants. And the struggle back to sleep is comical and impossible. In my

Corbusier habitation, I could hear the cheap clock I bought in the Marseilles bazaar ticking like a bomb; a single Renault roared past like a Mack truck.

And I had deep thoughts in the dead of night, alone in that remote hotel room. Could the early explorers divine the change in time with sextant, astrolabe, or telescope, I wonder? It didn't matter, I supposed; all that slow going made it easy to adjust to the earth's time differences. When did it start to matter? What came first: alarm clocks or stress? When did we first start to trick nature, both mother and human? Was it my imagination, or did the minute hand on my cheap, noisy clock move backwards?

And somehow, I survived jet lag's second night, that horrid witch's Sabbath. The second morning after the second night, the jet lag manifested itself in a memento mori of creaky shoulder bones, bunched muscles, and raw eyes. And the desire for a six-course dinner for breakfast. Was this the glamour of shuttle diplomacy, as Henry Kissinger made it his way? I'd heard of one solution for jet lag called the "Pentagon Diet," an unholy regimen of meats and hard alcohol and starches and coffee. Separately, each of these food groups is a favorite of mine, but (and despite my love for stews), in the case of curing jet lag, this seemed a bad mix, the stuff you might dig out of a fairgrounds dumpster after the carnival had shut down.

Before the continental adjustment, emotional states become arbitrary, or freestanding, uprooted, unearned, without their attendant narrative arc. I can look up at the in-flight movie at a random moment and burst into tears while hardly knowing the context of what is usually a dreadful second-rate film.

Being on a boat hasn't really solved jet lag's uprooting. Three hours into the six-hour ride to Corsica, I come out on deck after sobbing through a French-dubbed edition of a Harry Potter movie (though the French even managed to muddle the context that I can usually divine when I don't rent headphones on a plane and further confused me, I cried anyway), trying to catch that first whiff of the maquis. The smokestacks that were earlier squirting night into the day now seem only able to eke out weak black, the annoying stuff that gets into the blue of a watercolors set. With this much blue above and below, the smokestack black could never hope to besmirch it. No sign of land yet, but is that a floral scent? No, no; it's an old woman standing upwind, her old woman perfume. My collar points whip little hickey marks into my neck, and handsome Corsican soldier boys loiter about.

No first scent of the maquis, and no solution to the problem of compartmentalized travel, really. Jet lag is just one symptom of the way I feel snapped off, without a proper beginning or end—not just in body and mind but in the rise and ebb of emotions and memory. Perhaps what's happening during this thing called, too generally, "jet lag," is the ability to travel so quickly from one place to a hugely different other place, and the mind's desire to be with the body, which it simply cannot. It is the mind stretching, or shrinking, or maybe searching, or all three, to pick up what got left behind. For the entire six-hour ride, I never surrender my wish to sniff up some maquis but only huff the smell of food from vents along the side of the boat.

And then: approach. I look up at the horizon and realize that what I thought were clouds were actually Corsican mountains, rows of spines, like those on a horny-backed toad. In this same way, I decide that I don't quite know, finally, what it is I've been sniffing for.

As we sail closer to the old port town of Ajaccio, the sky over it grows dark. The boat is two hours behind schedule, and we won't land until half past nine in the night. Along the shore, the regularly spaced streetlamps look like tiki party lanterns swinging on a string; they twinkle from heat and atmosphere. Ajaccio is having a party!

On a Monday night! Of course it is—this is a resort island and a landing spot for tourists.

There are several towns along the coast of Corsica that are resorts, with their perfect sand and delicious Mediterranean waves. But resorts have a rather cruel feel to me, the pretty lady who likes to have you at her party—although if you didn't show up she knows the party will be just as successful.

On any island whose sand is worth its salt, the town with the beaches will be the least typical of the place's real self. Beach towns are for discotheques and suntan lotion, and are interchangeable that way. Even so, there are ways in which economic opportunity brings a bit of the genuine down to the waterfront. I have learned on islands like Italian Ponza or Spanish Mallorca that frumpy housekeeping peasant women will come into town to mix incongruously with the chic and fabulous in order to lure adventurous sorts without hotel reservations from the ferry to the little rooms they let in their home.

Sometimes these rooms can be a bargain, if you aren't the sort that wigs out by living with a family, usually extended, and all its clutter of inherited and repaired furniture and one or two Down's-syndrome child-adults that must be cared for until death. This is often the way of backpacking in my style, and I've gotten good at knowing what to look for in quality, when it comes to these lady hawkers down on the beach. For example: check the ankles. If their ankles have red splotches all over them, that would probably be bedbug bites. Decidedly, two-star accommodations.

But the closer we get to Ajaccio, the more it seems silent, even abandoned. No men in sunglasses with trophy wives on their arms, no ice-cream seller or boat renters or ladies in housecoats, with or without bedbug-bit ankles. A bell rings out the hour. No maquis here, just the smell of town: motor oil, garbage, bait bilge from the fishermen, fried food. I walk down the gangplank far ahead of the others, because I travel light and fast with just a backpack. Everybody else aboard is encumbered with blocky luggage and blockhead children. For thirty seconds, I have Ajaccio all to myself.

And there is Petra, and she *is* a party. We have known each other for nearly ten years now, met on the pilgrim's way to Santiago de Compostela, another long walk, when she was still married to a civil engineer named Matthias and lived as a cloistered housewife in the suburbs of Munich. Matthias fooled around with an Ethiopian Jehovah's Witness, or no, not fooled around, for the only thing the Ethiop did, being strictly religious, was trade love letters to Matthias, and so he got nothing, in the end, from either woman.

Petra has bloomed since their divorce, become something of a high-powered executive for Siemens, taken up with a handsome young Austrian med student, and moved to Vienna. We get together at least once a year, here or there, and do a bit of walking together. She and I have an idiosyncratic and, we think, civilized way of doing this: hard work with a backpack all day, a shower and a glass of wine in the evening and, preferably, a modest hotel room at a modest price. We aren't unwilling to rough it, but if one doesn't have to, why should one? Petra carries in her backpack dresses, a bikini, lipstick. I have nothing but respect for her.

"Bienvenue!" she says and kisses me the way foreigners do. Her French is impeccable, another reason never to let her leave my sight on La Corse. Oh, Petra, I love your hair that way; are you getting younger instead of older as the years go by? "Sorry I'm late," I say, instead, as if I were the one holding up the boat.

We have a long drive ahead of us, from Ajaccio to Calvi. She whisks me off into the interior of the island in a rented red Clio. *Now* is the time I wish I had taken the Dramamine, careening up narrow, winding mountain roads. If my mind had caught up with my body on the trundling ferry ride, it is left behind again, perhaps tucked into a seat pocket on the boat, along with what turns out to be one of my guidebooks.

It feels late, because I have only been on Corsica in the dark. But it's only a little past ten. We stop in some village (I don't know its name; I am only along for the ride) and find a restaurant with several candlelit tables outside, with a magnificent view of my first forest fire. I am excited by this, having heard so much about fires in the maquis.

"It's like living in a Mérimée story," I tell Petra.

But she is unimpressed by the distant flames, or takes them in along with the constellations of the night sky. She has been here for a couple of days, so she is *over* the fire thing. "I got in trouble in Vienna last week," she tells me over a little wine, to change the subject. "I went with some colleagues from the office to a champagne bar and then we went to a disco club and they asked me to dance on the bar, so I did," she explains.

"Well, if they asked you," I say, "then you shouldn't get into trouble."

"But I didn't want to get down!" says Petra. "The professional go-go girl started tap-tap-tapping on my ankle and I had to lean down to hear her and she said to me, 'You have to get down so I can do my job!'"

I've visited Petra in Vienna, that Byzantine city made of, apparently, rolled fondant. Its bricks seem made of leftover pieces of wedding cake people forgot to take out of the freezer on the first anniversary, or because the marriage failed. The streets seemed filled with Miss Havishams. "You got in trouble because you live in a city of sixty-year-olds," I console Petra. I look around our restaurant, nearly abandoned except for one of those extended families, retarded menchildren included, grazing at a table at the other end of the patio. They may just be the owners, actually. I am nothing but an expansive, overmoneyed American tonight. "Dinner is on me," I tell her.

29

Petra tells me, as we receive our menus, of the German tradition of the *Damenkarte,* the menu given to a young lady when she is being taken out by a man. A Damenkarte is the same menu, only the prices aren't listed. She says she is disappointed not to receive such a menu at our table. "You always know that chicken will be cheap," I tell her.

She looks at me in disbelief. "You think I will order the chicken?"

Here, we order pastas and a fish smeared with *oursin,* which is delicious in a secret sauce sort of way, and only later do I find out that *oursin* is sea urchin paste. And while we wait, we sip more wine and look above us at the unobstructed stars, and I don't recognize any of the familiar summer constellations. Are they arranged differently on this side of the world? I used to know them all so well, but living in the city, with all the light pollution, they've not been so vital to me, until I come out deep into the dark. This is the month of a year in which Mars will swing closer to Earth than it has at any other time in some absurd period, like sixty thousand years or something.

"Cavemen saw it happen," I tell Petra.

But she's not much more impressed with this than she was with the forest fire. "Cavemen didn't know what Mars was," she says, but I'm not so sure of that.

"Cavemen didn't have it so bad," I say, because for the next two weeks, we are going to be living, to a certain extent, like cavemen. Cavemen didn't have to deal with freakin' jet lag.

Our waiter brings yet two glasses more of the wine we've been sipping, a strong rough red from the Sartene, a region in the south of the island. I say we are sipping, but that is a lie. We quaff. Petra takes a gulp and plunks it down on the table with satisfaction. "Cavemen never knew how good this tastes." The wine kicks in. My mind catches up with my body, and jet lag is no longer a problem.

I awaken the next morning in the modest hotel (no family squabbles, no retarded man-child, no bedbugs; just a noisy pool cleaner out the window) Petra has arranged for us. The pool seems redundant, for just beyond it spectacular surf crashes at the citadel walls of Calvi. Calvi is a grand fortress of a town. Its stone walls are a pigskin color (and by pigskin I mean football), and along the quay where the boats are moored you can get a view of everything that makes Corsica specific. Granite mountains practically rising straight from the Mediterranean.

The shape of Corsica is something like a fisted hand holding up its index finger. Not a "We're Number One!" ballpark novelty foam hand sort of raised finger, but more of a "How many times have I got to tell you kids that this island is free and independent?" raised finger, a scolding finger. There has always been among incendiary nationalist types, whether they are ETA or Catalan or the local Front Corse Nationaliste Liberation, a rather schoolmarmish, corrective feel to the desire for statehood.

Of all the places I will visit on Corsica, Calvi, on the northwest corner of the island and a handful of kilometers from the start of our hike on the GR20, seems to maintain its Corsicanitude and avoid being a generic beach resort, and in its own right, also seems less of a scold. Guidebooks disagree with me, but Calvi feels more like a port town than Ajaccio, more like those naughty places like Marseilles or Odessa or New Orleans or Shanghai or San Francisco, full of leniencies and exceptions, where the rules get bent a lot because the borders are so porous.

Calvi, too, is our own point of launch, even though we're going inland rather than out to sea, and it's the town of our last hoorah before facing the rough road ahead. While studying our maps one last time and wearing our street shoes and dress shirts, we wallow in overpriced imported newspapers (the French journals are consumed with the loss of Charles Bronson, that greatest of American actors—"Adieu, l'ami!"), filling out postcards showing all the places we visited, looking just a little better than they actually did, slurping espressos, and (not in our street shoes) taking a dip into the sea.

Yes, perhaps I should be more frightened of the Mediterranean, because it does not bode well that our first-aid kit is broken open even before we start walking. It is now that I scrape myself on the coral reefs while swimming. I owe it to my mistaken belief that the Mediterranean is tame, or tamed, delineated, unwild, cultivated like an acre of land, all done so by stories as well as history. Swimming in it does not inspire fear, but carelessness, and that's why I bleed. It's also the warmth of the water, I think, along with its pleasant painterly color, not snot-green nor scrotum-tightening, so that its dangers reside in its comforts. For this and many other reasons, I've come to understand that that which is slightly uncomfortable is safer. My skin, after I get out, is powdered with salt, almost dry, almost wet, as if I were lubricated with graphite. Oh wait: that's blood. The antibiotic cream I smear across myself has nothing over the cauterizing salt of the sea, though it burns a little; the cause and cure are one and the same.

The pain comes later. That night, after I repack my backpack and bury these street clothes at the very bottom, I dream I am floating, being pulled out by waves, looking up at the fortress town of Calvi and the mountains behind it; I lower my ears in the water and hear the click-clicking of mussels.

Calenzana to Carrozzu

We sit trapped, after only six kilometers of hiking from Calenzana, at the top of a hill in the forest of Bonifatu. We have been stopped abruptly by a very serious park ranger because of (surprise!) a massive fire in the maquis. Petra and I hope to wait around by the ranger station in order to start later, but in the meantime, we take a day hike with just a day pack and find some strange rocks that look as if they've been worn away by ocean waves pounding. They belong on the beach, but here they are inland; only wind and rain could have done this work. Evidence of all kinds of violence—geological, meteorological, conflagratory, political, alcoholic, bilious—meet us at every turn on Corsica, and all of it is just barely softened by a thin layer of moss and lichen.

I have time while we cool our heels (mine still sea-scratched from our reckless swim, the real consequences of which I am just noting today) in a parkside restaurant, eating an excellent *omelette forestiere* (mushrooms and ham) and a tomato salad. For dessert, the local specialty, chestnut cake immersed in warm chocolate sauce.

Chestnuts have gone the way of the Corsican vendetta: south. They were once vital to the local economy, but already, we have encountered several trees that were clearly well tended and now seem, troublingly, ignored. I say "troublingly" not because trees seemed sickly but because of their overly robust state. It chills me the way it might chill a traveler finding a field of tomatoes rotting on the vine or overripe apples breaking the branches in an unharvested orchard. I imagine that the entire population of the towns nearby were wiped out by plague or mass suicide.

Everything on Corsica used to be made out of sweet chestnuts, and there are hoary old trees everywhere we go on the island. They were planted five hundred years ago by the ruling Genoans to mill flour from the nuts, but as we would discover in our explorations over the next month, the trees were dying of their own fecundity, or falling apart, or rotting away, still fattening feral pigs yet forlorn and abandoned, as so many islands sometimes seem.

Perhaps the fires that hold us up are a kind of mercy killing. Just days before, I'd been dazzled by the fires in the mountains, spectacular as holiday fireworks. Now it occurs to me that half the Corsican men are employed as *pompiers,* fitted into dashing deep blue fireman uniforms, trucking across vast stretches to douse the maquis, the pine forests, the scrub alders. Even the cows, it would seem, spontaneously combust.

And apparently, there's a scam going on. "Les faux eleveurs," they call them, "the false stockbreeders," the cattle shepherds who have been known to burn the woods and maquis to create grassland for the cows so they don't have to spend the allotment of money given to them, for cattle feed, by the European Union. The government and the EU discovered skullduggery and put an end to the allotments, and the number of fires dropped dramatically. In a country with high unemployment, however, fires create overtime pay for a lot of handsome pompiers, so nobody seems to mind, much, the flammable, inflammatory nature of inland Corsica. Except for Petra and me, who sit and wait for our journey to begin, truly.

The omelette is nice, though.

We are just about to give up and pitch our tent outside the little café for the night, when the ranger suddenly, almost capriciously, tells us we are out of danger and can go into the trail again. And before we know it, we are climbing straight into the stratosphere toward the refuge Carrozzu. "I think he was testing us," Petra says. She has, usually correctly, distrusted men on our journeys together.

In a rather cliché turn, the moment we pass beyond civilization's grease (both motor and cooking), the way, which might be a meadow anyplace else, offers up my first bona fide experience with that elusive thing: the Maquis. I take out my notebook and start to write, but I'm quickly frustrated—it's as inscrutable as civilization's grease.

"What were you expecting," Petra asks, conciliatory, sincere, "a bouquet of wildflowers?"

When I lean down to pick a little, I'm pricked a little. I'm disappointed a little, too, for I've felt these pricks before, without paying a thousand-buck plane ticket for them. In my midwestern backyard are all sorts of berry brambles and wild rose thorns and leaflets three, though I'd rather not let them be. I hate to steal a Corsican's thunder, but where I'm from, baby's first words are often, "vicious seed dispersal systems." Okay, yes, the maquis smells nice when the sun beats down on it and draws out its perfumes, but when the sun is beating down on it, it is beating down on me, and I, be-backpack'd, sweat, and smell, and smell more strongly than the maquis, and I can't smell the maquis, and then when I grow tired, there's no place to sit but on this, the devil's broadloom, the maquis.

I tell Petra something like this, only with less punctuation. She says she broke up with her husband for similar reasons.

We trudge on, and I find another excuse to moan.

"What thing is it now?" Petra asks. I can tell when she is more exasperated than usual when she speaks to me in an English with the bones of German construction still in it.

"We've been walking all day, and I can still see Calvi like it's just down the hill."

"It *is* just down the hill," says Petra, who is never afraid to tell a true thing at the wrong time. This is why she gets on so well in France.

Along the way, signs nailed to the trees ask us whether we've seen a lost British boy. It's here, while attempting my first climb over rocks rather than an actual dirt trail, that I try to distract us by joking about the British boy. If we come across a discarded map littering the piste, I point to it stentoriously and look at Petra with overweening significance: "Little dead British boy's map."

"Little dead British boy's cigarette butt."

"Little dead British boy's rain poncho."

"Little dead British boy's upcoming accordion festival poster."

"Shut up, stupid American guy."

I do, because I have to concentrate. It's here, while attempting my first climb over rocks rather than an actual dirt trail, that I realize this is a different sort of walking altogether. Let us call it a *more difficult* sort of walking. As we trudge into the Refuge Carrozzu I notice, once I've stopped bending over with my hands on my knees catching my breath in the thinning air, that the Basque flag oddly flies over the sour gardien's hut; this gardien always gets the worst of the traffic on the GR20 because so many people start their journey in the north and are terribly unprepared for it (not me! No, no, not me), and they arrive on his doorstep, more damaged goods. I see him glower over the bleeding feet of a Danish girl as he tapes them up, and this is probably the wrong moment to ask him whether he is Basque, but I do.

Rather than tell me that he is, which he is, he asks in French, "Are you an American?"

Perhaps it is the thin air that makes me a little dizzy. Perhaps the gardien and I are both trying to launch a Platonic dialogue, and both of us want to be Plato. But when an air of expectation descends over the four of us (even the bloody damaged Danish girl waits), I say, "No," giving Petra a glance: back me up here, girlfriend: "I'm Canadian." The cock crows for the first time.

Whether he believes me or not, there are more wounded lying in the streets of Atlanta, so we purchase from him a small camping site in the overcrowded grounds around his hut. Another thing different from other sorts of walks is that there is a very finite number of places where hikers are allowed to stop for the night. One cannot go pitching a tent all willy-nilly when there are problems with forest fires, food and water supply limitations, and flash thunderstorms that come up over a mountain in a moment.

"Canadian," Petra snickers, as we unroll the too-clean tent (clean tents are not cool among seasoned trekkers).

"Shut up, stupid German girl," I hiss.

"I am not German," Petra says, standing up, and suddenly we are striking a deal: "I am Austrian."

I am more than happy to shake on it. "Shut up, stupid Austrian girl."

It's not so awful to be in the camp city, at least not today. We dine and sleep with glorious views of the mountain, and three wiry French boys next door, their noses, feet, and hands bigger than the rest of their bodies, like puppies. Aching a bit, but grateful to be allowed to pass through the forest fire, I am also grateful that Petra brought instant soup.

As the light wanes and I prove useless in the task of flirting the French boys into lending us one of their slick aluminum collapsible pots, I try to provide the entertainment by placing the flashlight under my face in order to create a spooky grimace and tell Petra a story about Bigfoot, a folk legend of my (Canadian) people.

"You do not have to use the light to make your face scary," she tells me. "You do not even have to tell me a story about Bigfoot to make your face scary." She goes to talk with the French pups—and they like her. I rub my hands together in gratitude: hot soup tonight! I'm hungry: pimping, as a folk saying of my people goes, ain't easy.

I mused, as I walked this first day, that I was made for walking. I'm a pack mule, and I tell Petra that I plan to start a travel magazine called *Stubborn Pack Mule Monthly* and show all these extreme sports guys what for.

"Will you tell them how to pack the special cooking utensils?"

"Clearly, we didn't need them," I say, and move my hands over the cute French guys' aluminum pot Petra has charmed them out of, full of our soup—or rather, the soup Petra carried.

The funny thing is, I've done so much of the extreme trails by blundering onto them. The *Via della Bochette,* for instance, in the Italian Dolomites, "The Way of the Ladders," to translate, or, to add a note of prosaic accuracy, "The Way of the Rusty Ladders Precariously Nailed into Sheer Cliff Walls Half a Century Ago and in Great Need of Repair." After sauntering onto this walk several years back with only a day pack and some sandals, I found an article in *Men's Journal* about the locus of my alpine madness, which requires hikers be outfitted in crampons and ropes.

I say, any trail that requires crampons and ropes is a trail not worth doing. My overcautious guidebook says I ought to have a compass here in Corsica, but it also says I should carry a snorkel and mask. I know what I am doing. And thank you, Petra; yes, I will have a bowl of our soup.

Carrozzu to Ascu Stegnu

The false start is spoiling the narrative of our journey. If there is an abrupt sense here of lurching into a journey without a good deep breath or a gradual sense of gaining momentum, if there is no grand climactic sense of the start of the walk proper, it is because, well, none of these things are possible, thanks to the "hurry up and wait" setback of the fires. The truth is, any walk seems without overture or announcement. One does not so much cry "all aboard!" over a bullhorn as slink away, slip away, escape. Which is another reason why I like to walk. It doesn't seem as if anything monumental is taking place.

And yet, here I am panting again, leaning against a big piece of granite at the edge of a precipice, looking at another hour's walk to a chalet hotel below. It has been a day of sheer ups and downs. We are exhausted. Even an hour's walk seems overwhelming at the moment. In the ever-present present tense of walking, time ironically collapses into nothing, so that the hiking we will do tomorrow (and the day after that, and so forth) all piles on top of itself, so that it seems we must make two weeks' worth of exertion all at once, and the thought of that makes me panic for a moment. I am used to making fifteen- to seventeen-mile walks in an average day of backpacking, but here on Corsica I discover another way in which the GR20 is new business. We will call it a long stretch if we manage to make seven miles between stations. The effort is put into ascent and descent, switchbacks and zigzags, and the trail never, ever, rides ramrod straight but molds itself to unyielding granite.

The next day we'll be assaying the dreaded Cirque de la Solitude, but this day seems harder, perhaps because we didn't psychologically prepare for it and I didn't have the finest night's sleep in my little, yet incredible, tent. I don't have a soft mat to separate me from the granite ground. I scoff at the need for such a thing, the way I scoff at the snorkel, at the compass.

The walk this day, again, has been spectacular, first crossing the Sentier de Spasimata over a swinging suspension footbridge connecting a precarious chasm's lips. In the early part of summer hikers swing over a raging river torrent, but now, it's just something deep and dry to fall into. A young French-Basque couple who live near the Pyrenees hike alongside us with a black Labrador; he carries his own things in a little doggy saddlepack. He is all energy and curiosity, and trots far ahead and comes back to master and mistress, so that in all, by my reckoning, he is walking the GR20 twice. On the suspension bridge, however, he is a terrified pup, so frightened we have to pitch in to help him. By taking off my own pack and going out to lend a hand, I am able to discover his name, which is Lula; by "his," I mean "hers."

The French kids are nice, although the French guy kid is looking me up and down. Yikes, he's clocked the Yankee. Is it in the shape of my head, or my haircut? Can they tell from my brand of socks or nibbled fingernails? But his eyes lock on my feet, and I realize he's looking at my shoes, and he's not the first to do so on this trip. "Pas de probleme?" he asks.

"No problem at all," I respond. I don't usually wear big clunky hiking boots, although I have a pair. I prefer a tough pair of walking shoes, instead, which means my ankles are weaker but my ability to maneuver my feet is expanded. Besides, when I wear my hiking boots, I often suffer blisters. I never do with walking shoes. With all this upping and downing, however, I am starting to wonder whether things might be different this time.

Lula recovers, but I quail on the steep stuff that leads into a spectacular batch of mountains, including the highest one on the island, Monte Cinto. Monte Cinto: symbol of Corsican spiritual autonomy. One always requires a big heap of stone to reinforce nationalism: Gibraltar, Canigau, Mount Rushmore. Monte Cinto is a spectacular lumpy mass that reveals itself just as you breach a pass along the way to the next stop along the trail, Ascu Stegnu. It's the reward you get for the day's labor, made of a strange orange-red stone that contrasts with the other granite, mostly gray, all of it covered from foot to pinnacle in lichen, so that in the morning it looks flocked, like a Christmas tree sprayed down with fake snow tinted crème-de-menthe green, and at sunset, it blazes bright, unmasked, as if we have only just arrived on a completely different island, or gotten it *all wrong*.

Then we descend. Descending is not my favorite thing to do, especially with extreme sports guys overtaking me at every step, appraising my nationality and my shoes as they pass. More of a torture for Petra are the uphills. Jack Spratt could eat no fat, and his wife could eat no lean. But we know this about each other, and we take our weaknesses in stride and cheer each other to the completion of our individual onerous tasks.

We are cheered, also, by the local cheese when lunchtime rolls around. Along the trail, an enterprising shepherd has converted his mountainside hut into a little shop, The Rennet Barn. We sample the Corsican *brocciu* and the smelly aged version of it (there's a big joke in one of the Asterix and Obelisk comic books about this cheese, used as a powerful destructive weapon against enemies). These cheeses are made from *ewes,* ewes specifically. It seems important when the shepherd who sold it to us told it to us. It seems important in my guidebook, as well: ewes, only ewes. Thank heavens none of the local giraffes were involved.

I stand up, ready to deal with the last leg of our day's walk. I notice that "Francesi Fora!" is sprayed on the rock I've been resting on,

"French Get Out!" I am not sure why, but my growing understanding of the Corsican disgust for the French relieves some of the pressure on me, American me. This is the eve of George Bush's invasion of Iraq, and despite the world's resistance to the United States' plan to "rid the world of Saddam Hussein's weapons of mass destruction," we all know war is inevitable. Here on Corsica, I am ashamed, I am resistant, I am Canadian—I am everything but able to carry on a conversation about my leader's catastrophic intent.

"Francesi Fora!" "French Get Out!"—Corsica is a possession or, to use the American euphemism when speaking of Guam or Puerto Rico, a protectorate of France, and not all the Corsicans want to be protected. France doesn't seem to see the problem here; they rain millions of tourist euros annually on the island, so what's the big deal? I wonder whether the French, like most Americans, even know what "Francesi Fora!" means. Is the demand lost on those for whom it is written? In Calvi, I saw a broadcast of the ubiquitous CNN in which a nice lady from California criticized the French resistance to the American invasion of Iraq: "I can't believe how *unpatriotic* the French are!" In my country, many patriots are boycotting French wine and french fries. "Francesi Fora!"

It may be here, on this afternoon, that the maquis loses the last of its romance for me; now that I have seen that it's packaged for tourists in plastic bags in Calvi (a city that, until late afternoon on this third day of walking, I could still see, and about which I say so to Petra every few hundred meters, until she tells me to "Shut up, stupid American guy," which is a veiled threat to "out" me, Not Very Canadian Me. I heed the threat.), and having fallen in its briars and prickers a couple of times. Now I prefer the saxifrage, gentle and luscious, appearing in pink and white. Also, ginebra, and some version of it in red. Liquor bushes!

Ascending once again, we find ourselves in that exhausted state on the granite precipice, and, though I can no longer see Calvi, I can see the ski lodge in the valley below us, the one where we will spend the night, and it is not close. Another hour, by the guidebook's reckoning.

Petra comforts me by initiating a conversation about sex. It works. We walk another half-kilometer straight downward, and I have to grab trees, occasionally, to slow my momentum. At some point, we hear some Bavarian hikers yodeling. No joke. It is a lovely moment, and that's what gets me the rest of the way into the valley. Little things like these, the delights, are what often revitalize me. "Regardez!" yells a French hiker above us, seeing the valley from our little precipice, and the word seems more appropriate for a fine view than, "Lookie!"

Still, "The French don't understand a decent shower apparatus, nor, apparently, can they make a ski village look nice," I tell Petra once we check into our simple hotel room and I step out of the bathroom clean, and wrecked.

"This is no longer a ski village," Petra laments, because the German guidebooks always tell you just a little bit more. It seems that global warming, or at least European warming, has made the once flourishing ski villages in these mountains useless—and the rusty machinery in its wake, its own junkyard, with pulleys, flywheels, wires, and gears, all rusted out. Once again, I get the sense that I am wandering in an abandoned carnival, as if vacation leisure were an artifact. "I can still see Calvi," I say from our little balcony. Petra is as exhausted as I am, but she makes a point of getting off the bed, stepping up beside me on the balcony, and kicking me in the shin. We ought to be in love.

After a handful of regrouping tasks (washing clothes, shaving, getting a pot of tea) I call my friend Doug back home. He is watering my plants and gathering the mail. He is in the middle of a house call for work, and he'd be surprised to know that, although the Dow Jones Industrial Average is plummeting (making my dollars powerless against the invigorated euro) and the president is one step closer to getting his way with a war in Iraq, the most surprising thing Doug tells me is that today is Thursday. What a strange idea. The specificity of time, of days, seems lifted away. Cavemen felt like this, I'm sure.

I regroup, too, by studying the guidebook before the day's trip. For a change. I tend to like guidebooks for walkers because they are usually more frank and less likely to embellish. In *Trekking in Corsica,* of the present location in Ascu Stegnu, the author writes this about the unfinished refuge: "many [campsites] have been spoiled by people shitting in the building beside them. Turds also litter the unfinished rooms on the ground floor." Less earthy yet equally deflating is the review of our dinner soon to be available at the lodge this evening: "This will allow you to order their steak-frites, which"—he can't help but throw a wet blanket on the steak party—"(somewhat undeservingly it has to be said) enjoy near legendary status on the GR20." I do not order the steak-frites, but a pork chop, chestnut-fed.

On the other hand, the guides seem to cater to those extreme sports dudes who are always mocking my walking shoes, for the appellation "difficult" for the walk today seems a bit overblown. "Difficult" in extreme-sports-guidebookese really means, "You have to go slow." Trekkers hate to go slow. It's a dreadful task, full of awful things like *grand vistas* and *common courtesy* and *conversation.* Those boys breeze by so much: I read, on the balcony, of tomorrow's pass through the Cirque de la Solitude, which should slow them down a bit, too. The guidebooks promise a lot of scree and scrambles. I'd rub my hands together with relish—the same relish-rubbing I used to compliment Petra's dance of the seven veils when she extracted the cooking pot from the French boys—but I wonder how well I'll be able to handle that granite pass myself. It is dawning on me this evening: this is harder than I ever thought it would be.

And the next morning, when checking out of the ski lodge, a terrible accident happens: the young French couple who own Lula the

Lab are standing just behind me while the concierge hands back my passport, kept to assure payment, I wager. I hand over a handful of euro notes, and she plops the telling blue-and-gold booklet down on her desk. I can hardly expect anybody to mistake the big truculent eagle, clutching the slings and arrows of a forthcoming outrageous war, for a candy-apple-red maple leaf. French guy is no longer studying my shoes, but my non-Canadian passport. I wish he would look at my shoes.

Ascu Stegnu to Bergerie de Vallone

Sunburned and still sea-scratched all the way down one leg, maquis-mauled on the other: somebody has run me across the zester side of a kitchen grater. A perfect day for walking. Or running, if you are like any red-blooded American who has been caught lying about his nationality and is seeking the proper, moral thing to do.

While it took days to shake the view of Calvi, it is only fifteen minutes after I've been exposed as *un-Americain* to the Pyrenean couple before we lose sight of the old ski lodge—and the Pyrenean couple. It might have taken twenty minutes if I had not begged Petra to run for her/my life. We are surrounded by strawberry trees and a droopy kind of holly hanging in the live oaks. A filter of steely smoke clouds blue the sky. Pine needles fall from the tall pines down onto smaller trees, their upside-down V-bifurcated needles, like wispy clothespins, catch on the branches, and I am reminded of the cuckoo planting its eggs within another bird's nest: the trees are in disguise.

And such mountains. The only thing that can get me to stand up straight anymore, besides the challenging burden of a backpack, is the good example of a tall mountain. I think my body instinctively tries to peer over them. The peaks soar, and so does my heart, a combination of breathlessness, spent energy, and eyefuls of vista. Rhythm and song rise up once I'm in full flight.

Walking has a prosody: when I walk downhill, the legs do dactyls (for the unschooled: one long stride, two doorstop jambs, a stressed syllable and two unstressed: "dithering," "wearying"—"Corsica"). The ancient poets considered dactyls a stately rhythm. When walking down steep slopes, I notice how my feet are slowing the body against gravity, the gravity that needs to be slowed, and so the body generates a controlled energy, even a worrisome caution ("This is the forest primeval, the murmuring pines and the hemlocks"), an intrepid, stuck-up discipline that's not nearly as fun and freewheeling as the wild galloping afforded during uphill anapests (the dactyl's three-beated opposite: two quick steps for a running leap: "on the loose," "unabridged," "to the moon!") that make you feel unleashed ("The Assyrian came down like the wolf on the fold"). But like the barreling burst of the anapest, charging uphill can be difficult to sustain. Just ask Petra.

Metered poetry and songs get caught in the brain when I'm walking, and that can be a gift or a torture. Today I am blessed with endless rounds of the old Blake hymn "Jerusalem," the one asking whether Jesus didn't go wandering around Great Britain: "And did those feet in ancient times / Walk upon England's mountains green?" Yesterday I wasn't so lucky: "I know an old woman who swallowed a fly" wouldn't stop coming out of my mouth, and the day before, I suffered, awfully, Elton John's "Island Girl." I never can leave well enough alone, and spend many kilometers analyzing the song I'm singing: that grandma could eat flies, spiders, birds, goats—but a horse would be considered *beyond the pale:* "She died, of course." Well, *no kidding.*

Here is where I differ, again, with most hikers, who will tell you that they do their best thinking while on the trail. Rousseau made an entire book about what he thought about while on his walks, and kept a walk/thought journal the way people keep dream journals nowadays, and he even called them "Reveries." Rimbaud seems to think walking saved his sick artistic soul. "I have walked myself into my best thoughts," said Søren Kierkegaard, "and I know of no thought so burdensome that one cannot walk away from it."

But in solitude, while walking, the same dunderheaded thought seems shackled to my ankle, and I rattle it, over and over: "Where is a water source? / God, am I thirsty. / Where is a water source? / That guy has one of those high-tech canteens. / Did I mention I was thirsty?" or, "Why does that Belgian need two walking sticks and why is he making all that clicking noise with them? / Why that annoying clicking? / The clicking! / That damnable clicking! Now I must kill somebody!" or, "I never should have dated him. / He told me he wasn't a good boyfriend. / Oh, the existential nausea! Death and anxiety! / It's all his fault." I do my best thinking in crowds, oddly enough, at the symphony or during a play. Dull plays are best for thinking. My playbill is always coated with notes scrawled in the dark concert hall or theater, sad inscrutable scribble, and useless once the lights come up. When walking, the only thing that can save me from my own shallow thoughts is civilized conversation with a fellow walker.

"Shut up, stupid German girl."

"Shut up, stupid American boy."

Two freakin' philosophers, warding off the fear and trembling and sickness unto death. Petra and I climb above the tree-line to discover that the stone of the mountain seems green, though red by nature, because they're wet enough to sustain huge amounts of moss. Later, I'll find old sheep bones that, where not polished white, are flocked with more moss.

Flocked, too, the skies seem, with smoke from fires all about us. It is as if we have been wearing sunglasses all day, and certain cones and rods have been burned out. I'm concerned for all the neglected trees, chestnut and otherwise. (I am not concerned for the maquis at all any more, since I am nearly an open sore from its nagging, scratching persistence, despite all fires, natural and un-. Please, I'm beggin yeh, I'm runnin' around yeh dogwise—*please* don't throw me in that briar patch!) The trees thin out rather quickly as we climb, until the pines give way to birch, aspen, maybe even peach, the kind of trees that have bark arranged horizontally rather than vertically, wrapping themselves for colder air the way mother wraps a scarf around and around your naked neck in winter. The aspen has weensy little pine cones that flake away to nothing between your fingers, like tobacco come loose from an untamped cigarette.

Against a vivid blue sky at the pass, above the smoke, even, the peaks, craggy, look cut with an X-acto knife. Thanks to Petra's sup- plies (dried noodles in packets) and the borrowed cooking pot from the three handsome French boys (not yet returned; we keep thinking we'll see them in the refuge each night, but they were in no hurry, judging from the amount of wine they drank in Carrozzu, and the way they were still sleeping when we cleared out late the next morn- ing), I've been rescued from starving to death; and when we near the valley Spasimata, I run out of steam.

Petra sits down next to me and begins to pull things out of her backpack I have never seen before: a five-day-old German news- paper purchased in Calvi, a tube of expensive lipstick, two walking sticks of the high-tech sort, expandable (I am forgiving the Belgians already), and *traubenzucker,* tablets made from powdered grape juice, which tastes like and has the texture of Pez, and is, as Petra tells me, "given to children before they take a test." I love Petra, full of specifics. And traubenzucker. She gives me three. I am ready for my Spasimata test.

I had hoped for a source of water somewhere along the way, hav- ing scarfed more charcuterie and cheese at lunch. I may as well have sucked on tablets of *traubensell*—salt. Petra's usually dependable guidebook promises a natural spring in five hundred meters, but it is early autumn, and that's why the English word for spring is "spring." At the place where we are supposed to refill our canteens, she spots a crevice in a rock where the moss is a little thicker. I hold my water bottle in proof and appeal, so Petra can see the droplets of condensation remaining inside.

"Je suis désolée," Petra says, using French rather than one of our languages because there is something a little disingenuous in the way the French say, in a singsong taunt, "I am sorry! No water."

I can't blame Petra or her lying guidebook. I've eaten all that briny food myself. I have done this once before, just before attending the four-plus-hour "Die Walküre" at the opera, sucking down the aperitif olives and nuts and cheeses, then settling into cramped hot theater seats while my tongue and feet swelled up inside my mouth and shoes. "Sometimes," I tell Petra, putting the canteen in its special sleeve and scratching my sea-scraped leg, "I think I want this sort of thing to happen to me."

Petra hands me one of her two spiffy walking sticks. "Oh, the stones and the sea want only to get you." She takes the bandanna from her neck to wipe the glow away. She's a solid woman, but with delicate features, lovely blonde locks, and a cold-cream-white skin that does not make SPF 30 sunblock seem a necrophiliac's freak show. Whenever I want to send Petra a gift for her birthday or the holidays, I fight the urge to send face powder, lipsticks with names like "gypsy" and "cabaret" and "harlot," and silver combs. She adds now, "No matter how much you think you have conquered a foreign place, it is always savage and intends to collect your head for her belt, like Kali." I am always wondering, when she rattles out these sorts of odd-duck particularities, whether they might be clichés in her native German.

It is here I must say, before Petra begins to sound like too much of a cliché herself, that so much of her Damenkarte capriciousness is an act. We have known each other for years, and I have seen her overcome every manner of hardship, from a dangerous mountain pass to a painful divorce. She is hard-working, courteous, charming, and funny. She is the first to stop and look at a beautiful vista and the last to give up when the situation seems impossible. I ask her, here, why she likes this business of walking, why she always consents to join my nutty schemes. "But this walking," she says, "it is traveling in the right speed for the soul and your thoughts. You can let your thoughts come, and get the spirit of the nature, your eyes and nose are feeded. Feeded?"

"Fed," I gently correct, though I like feeded.

"It is the best way to travel. When we are walking up the mountains, on the way up I have all those bad thoughts like, I have to tell so and so this! Or I will tell them all! But on the top of the mountain, the thoughts are not that deep anymore, and even when I return home, I have to laugh and think, 'who cares.'"

She philosophizes while leaning against the long trunk of a tree, blasted hollow by frequent furious lightning storms. Storms fly down among the many canyons without warning, and beleaguer hikers like us. The pine's insides have been burned hollow, and people passing through the GR20 have slowly filled up the hollow with granite scree. Perhaps we are stalling here, and the filled-up tree trunk is proof that others have dawdled at this point, too, to avoid the big plunge into the overanticipated Cirque de la Solitude.

Scree—loose stone and sand—slides under my foot and makes me fall again and again. I'm trying to be careful, in case I might hit a walker just below. Singsong cries of "Oop-la!" from silly underprepared French women just above me barely preface a shower of scree on my head as we descend, parched, into the Cirque. *Oop-la* is what the French Academie admitted into their language to represent "oops." *Oop-la.* There is something disingenuous about nearly everything said in French.

When Petra and I finally come to the lip of the canyon we are about to climb into, the first thing we notice is the heavy chains secured deep in the rock, with which we must go rappelling. Somehow, some officious person who helps maintain the GR20 has lowered himself down the cliff walls and painted very sarcastic trail markings—the universal red-and-white double-stripe of the *grande randonnée,* as if it were a walk in the park, as if it were walkable, as if anybody would get lost falling straight down into a chasm.

I look at Petra. Petra looks at me. Already, behind us, people are starting to bunch up. Only one person can descend this rock face at a time, and we are going to cause a traffic jam if we hesitate any longer. The irony (situational irony, not dramatic) of all of the wild GR20 is that the people who walk on it are herded into narrow passages most of the time, and forced to sleep in a handful of regulated camps; I've never seen the outdoors look so crowded as I do on this thin gray trail of the Cirque de la Solitude. And over there in the distance, where the trail leads up out of the amphitheater-shaped basin: all those hikers who have been walking their way across Corsica from the opposite direction. I look at Petra again: you go first.

And this is what she does: she reaches over her shoulder into a little pocket on her backpack, next to where she keeps her maps and guide and traubenzucker, and pulls out that lipstick. Then she opens it, lets its crimson nubbin carousel up and out. And then—listen up, all of you extreme sports dudes and *Men's Journal* and *Stubborn Pack Mule Monthly* readers, for this is important—*she applies the lipstick.*

She puts on two or three layers, in fact, because this is the outdoors, and it is windy and she might have to bite it off her own lips in concentration for the next few hours. But she takes the time to blot a little with a Kleenex, and then she smiles, and she begins her descent into the chasm.

And that is why I go, too.

Yesterday, clouds chugged by in rows like boxcars. They've thinned out here, just south of the Ascu Stegnu. The mackerel sky hangs like a painting overhead, curdled, tired, maybe exhausted by throwing all this weather at us. This is how we enter the toughest leg of the walk, at least as it is reported by most guidebooks (save mine, this).

I behold the ironic outcome of earth's mighty restlessness, which seems a thing of stillness and permanence. Yes, yes, the ferocious beauty of towering granite pillars, the phantasmagoric deep stony abyss ("Little dead British boy's lipstick," I say between gasps, but Petra can't hear me), and, okay, yeah, the lunar loneliness of treeless valleys. But this is not walking. This is spelunking, this is rappelling, this is not even a walk when it is a walk—it is what they call in the business a "scramble," which is a word that sounds like what it is.

The Cirque de la Solitude is also perhaps the most famous passage of the journey, yet our own experience with it seems more like Cirque du Soleil, with clowns and monkeys along with the acrobats and trapeze artists. Day-trippers and lightweight thrill-seekers come into the GR20 from a service road only to walk this one part, making it crowded and noisy with the yammer of "Oop-la!" and scree, scree, always with the scree. Which is also a word that sounds like what it is.

Physically, the Cirque is a steep concave valley, navigated by sheer walls like that of an amphitheater (think of the gallery balcony high up in a large opera house). I suppose if you are an experienced mountain climber, you have no need for the lengths of chain and metal ladders hammered into the clifflike rock faces, but I am grateful for this help, especially since the stone is covered with slippery moist lichen. Solitude is a physical misnomer here, as it's the most popular section of the GR20, and we are surrounded by dozens of walkers of varying abilities. The thrashing of heavy chain against granite undoes any lingering notion that we are the sole proprietors of this bit of trail. But one thing is true: a walker is utterly alone with the ability to execute this bit of troublesome terrain.

It is during this lowering down the sheer rock faces that I learn how to do what most mountain climbers are taught to do in safe laboratories lined with big prefab fiberglass rock faces: how to be a mountain climber. By watching others, the ones who know what they are doing, I see the wisdom of going down a rock face backwards. Hiking backwards tends to limit the ability to enjoy beautiful views, but when holding onto a little bit of stone and lodging your foot in the crevasse between two other bits of stone in order to avoid having your own weight as well as the weight of your backpack pull you off a cliff, I give up a little sightseeing.

The Cirque may be the most difficult stretch of traveling I ever do, I thought, even in the middle of doing it. Do people in the middle of historical battles every have such thoughts? I am climbing over sheer rock faces with ladders and chains and a backpack swinging around, pulling down behind me, and the only way I think I can get by is by imagining somebody telling the story of my doing it, and hoping I don't look bad when the story is being told. Not the best motivation for physical or moral certitude, but today, it will have to do.

I like my guidebook writers the way I like women: sassy, contrary, and sometimes dead wrong (but willing to take that chance). However, the author of *Trekking in Corsica,* David Abram, tried to downplay this circuit, and it didn't help matters. Rappelling down chains with a thirty-five-pound backpack pulling you back into an abyss, a monkey on your back! As I let go of a length of rusty wire and drop onto a section of the trail that is relatively flat, I put my hands on my hips like somebody who knows what he's doing. After all, what a sense of accomplishment I feel, only halfway through the circuit of solitude.

I see Petra, who has climbed up on a big smooth rock and is taking pictures of mountain goats on a ledge below us. I smell bad. I know this because Lula the goofy black Lab is avoiding me, and unless she also mistrusts Americans, I'd guess it is the adrenaline, which

I rarely have to secrete. Yes, yes, the couple from the Pyrenees have shown up (or caught up) again, like a bad centime—we all do on this trail, disappearing for hours or even days, but turning up at the end of a day or along a ledge just when you or they want to pass. And how did Lula get down here without opposable thumbs? She is wagging her tail and barking at the goats below and kites above, as if nothing ever happened. Petra's lipstick looks fresh. She says, "I can still see Calvi." In my moment of weakness, I have let her steal one of my jokes. I vow never to let this happen again.

I want to collapse, but I can see Lula's owners approach from two or three precipices above us. We must flee, for I am pursued by the Furies. It is difficult to "flee"—a word that has built into it speed and sleek aerodynamic design—with a huge pack weighing you down. I do what I can.

And I am rescued from an even less surefooted ascent that day when I get lodged halfway up a crevice by a boy from Berlin (Petra says she can recognize the accent) whose ears are also sunburned purple. He is one of those who has been taking the road from the south, starting at our ending place in Conça, so, though he is just beginning the circuit of solitude, he is just a few days from the end. I realize that I envy him.

Petra snickers. Then, "Stupid German boy," she mutters.

"Why is he stupid?"

"Because he thinks he is such a man for walking all this way, but he never takes care of his skin and his ears will fall off and he will die of the cancer before he even finishes the walking."

I see her point. Day by day, we compromise on certain standards, let ourselves go little by little, and together, so that only an outsider can see the truth, the madness: the boy looks like a homeless drug addict.

"Why didn't we start in the south and go north?" I ask Petra, once we are completely out of the Cirque and walking side by side on a switchback trail. "Then we would not have had to worry about forest fires near Calenzana." I speak in this stilted way to avoid the confusion English's contractions generate. It usually takes weeks before I revert to idiomatic slangy American English when I return from these long junkets to Europe, and the reversion is facilitated only by the kidding of my friends.

"Nobody does such a thing," Petra says dismissively, despite the hobo Berlin lifesaver. For her, it isn't really a business to wonder about. I quickly agree. It seems right, in our Northern-Hemisphere'd brains, that one would head south always, as if by doing so one were going downhill, which might make it feel easier. Treebeard of the Ents makes just such an observation in Tolkien's books. The fact is, the vast majority of hikers on the GR20 and nearly every other major walkway in the world (with the possible exception of the Appalachian Trail) go from north to south: it's the way. I feel, for a moment, like a lemming.

I look back and watch that boy from Berlin move up through the Cirque against the flow of traffic, battling like a salmon upstream. That doesn't seem like much fun.

But I am grateful for his existence, not just for dislodging me from my granite wedgie, but because he is one of those walkers who help spread news up and down trails. We can hear from hikers who have forged ahead, or if we have fallen behind; messages can be conveyed. We pass on rumors of good meals and dangerous passages, friendly shepherds and communist monks. Except that he didn't and we didn't. We should have asked him to tell the handsome French boys we still have their cooking pot; he didn't tell us anything about how his ears turned purple, for he was just annoyed that his way was blocked.

Only a half a kilometer past the Cirque is the official GR refuge. It is huge. It might as well be a strip mall. It has been built to accommodate all the day-trippers, and as we round the bend, a group of

French husbands are waiting to applaud their French wives ("Oop-la!") who took a little longer executing the circuit. We unbuckle our backpacks next to the well, and I slake the thirst that has haunted me since lunchtime, and with the plop of my pack, the "Bravo!"s rise up for the ladies.

Petra looks at me and shakes her head: we are not staying at this zoo. My legs are trembling, they are so tired, but before I can even organize a protest, I see Lula and her people mope up behind the French wives, and my backpack is back on; there is another place to stay just another kilometer down the trail, if I can summon the energy.

I grouch through the entire length of the thousand meters to punish Petra, my willful, lipstick-loving dominatrix. I want to sit. I'm tired. I have to go to the bathroom. How many more meters?

By the time the sun sets, we set up our tent outside the Bergerie de Vallone, *bergerie* being the Frenchified word for a shepherd's hut, and a shepherd and his son make us Corsican soup and nothing much more complicated than a spaghetti ragout, but it does have wild boar in it, and it is delicious, with that strong rough red wine and the sheep's cheese called *brebis*. It, too, is homemade.

The father runs the joint, and he's as friendly as a way-out-West madam. He wears the blue coveralls emblematic of the paysano, the peasant worker. I like to walk through a small European town and chance upon a row of blue shirts and coveralls on a front yard wash line hanging to dry; they change, in the sun, from a dark to light blue, the way paint does when it has dried. His son runs the bar, flirts, wears camouflage pants with a reinforced crotch and a T-shirt with the many unbordered nations of the world represented by their flags: Basque, Quebecois, Catalan, Puerto Rican, Corsican, Tibetan.

The room of the bergerie is warmer than any we've come across before, and by warmer, I mean friendlier; the people who walk this extra few kilometers beyond the main gîte d'étape seem more of the independent sort, and there's irony there, too; independent sorts are much more likely to gather and gab in the evening, after the tents are pitched. There are only ten tents here, if that. I thank Petra for forbidding us to stay at the strip-mall gîte.

It is always the case, always a lesson I have to relearn: if I push myself just a little bit farther, walk for one half hour longer, there is a reward far more valuable than the actual effort.

As others finish their meals and head outside to their tents, I peek into the back room of the bergerie and spy a small kitchen. The mother is cooking her ass off. "Where are you from?" asks the boy with the nationalist T-shirt. I look straight into the flag of Puerto Rico, think of the training bases on the island of Vieques, where I love to take my sorry Yankee tourist carcass for snorkeling. Petra looks at me: she's waiting to see what I say this time.

"Les Etats-Unis," I say, because there are only six or seven people left in the bergerie, and maybe only a third of them speak French, and by saying the United States in another language, it doesn't sound as bad; it seems less crass for me to say "merde" than "shit." Two or three heads do bob up from tables close by, but then they return to the game of cards or leftover boar.

And if the paysano boy's annoyed, he hides it well. He tells me that not many walkers come from the States. Lots of English, but few Americans (stop saying that word, I want to tell him, can't you see I'm trying to run away from home?). He pulls from a shelf behind him a big bottle and four small glasses, for himself, his father, Petra, and me.

I look out the window at the mountain peaks in the fading light. The stone here, the granite, is a shocking red, as if animals have been killing little rodents and eating them as their blood spilled over the rocks. After several drinks and a long talk it will take days and many aspirin to recollect, the shepherd lets me take yesterday's newspaper back to our campsite. I drift off, deciphering the news from Corsican, an Italian-Tuscan dialect. The front page of the Corsican newspaper is full of forest fires and nationalist urgencies, and at the bottom, "below the fold," a quarter-page advertisement for hunting gear. Nothing about Iraq, nothing about weapons of mass destruction.

3

Why I Walk
Walk-Off

Lonesome, I will be no longer
Tied to you. You need a stronger
Hand than mine to slap your face.
When I do it, I leave no trace.
Will Butler, "A Man Leaves the Sea"

I come from an agreeable family. That seems both a bit of damning with faint praise and a little coy, but I am nothing, considering the disappointments and terrible possibilities of the world, if not grateful. Nobody in my bloodline is psychologically wicked, or wrecked, though my mother has thus diagnosed every one of us—father, two brothers, me, individually—at one time or another. "Christ," is how she puts it, "it's like you've got a *screw loose*."

There is a prison in my hometown that has maintained through-out my life the dubious distinction of being the largest in the world. I never thought much about it at the time, although it had so many subtle effects (and by subtle I sometimes mean unsubtle) on the way I think and live. The prison, when I first consider it, stands for for-giveness, atonement, a chance to "work it off," emphasis on the work.

My uncle and my father played baseball against the prison team when they were promising minor leaguers in southern Michigan. They never did well against the prison team, for that adversary al-ways had, as my father grumbled, the home team advantage. My uncle Mike remembers a third basemen on the opposing team yell-ing at him, "Come on, we haven't got all day!" (they didn't: a whistle blew, and the lockdown would commence). But Uncle Mike, sharp-tongued as well as fleet of foot, bellowed back, "I figure you've got a couple of years!" The third baseman hurtled toward my uncle, who was sure that he was in for it. "Thanks, Jack," the prisoner said, in-stead, "the judge said it was life!" Ron LeFleur, a beloved Detroit Tiger, played many a time against my father on the diamond with the high, high home-run wall. My father, from whom I have inher-ited a weakness for the obvious statement, tells us they were playing to a captive audience.

Living downwind of the world's largest prison (largest *walled* prison, the natives of Jackson will specify, so that you knew we were protected) didn't necessarily generate a gallows humor so much as a shaggy-dog-story patience: we did have all day, if not three to five years, if not life.

Nobody ever complained about the prison. It was on the out-skirts of town, out of sight, out of "do you mind?" and it provided more jobs than the ever-failing car industry factories in Detroit's orbit. Every time somebody got laid off from the Goodyear tire plant, they were usually able to find work at Southern Michigan Penitentiary. My brother is now a guard there, or more than a guard, something of a boot camp trainer for nonviolent criminals; he is, approaching forty, in tip-top shape, so the prison has kept him young and put food on his family's table. I know an inordinate number of dentists and hygienists who work with the teeth of prisoners there, and that sometimes gives me pause: experiments?

Too, we benefited from the cottage industries of the prison. License plates, yes, and no end to the municipal signs that had to be made and remade that read, "Welcome to Jackson We Like It Here," because so many were stolen or altered, and that's all I'll say about it. They had, and still have as far as I know, a publishing house for the production of Braille books. When I was in high school, some of my juvenilia, a handful of dreadful poems, were "translated" into Braille, the only work I've written aside from a bit of smut I wrote for an anthology, now available to a lucky but limited German audience, that has been translated into anything other than Times New Roman. So you see, having a prison in your town supports an economy and arguably assists municipal life, science, and even art. I have a houseplant that I feed only bitter, black, cold coffee and its grounds. It is green; it has to be cut back regularly.

How does having such a structure in my life affect the way I look at things? What must I have taken from that early time that I haven't been aware of? Things that wouldn't seem too much "reading into" the business? A love of safe spaces, sure. A distaste for the color orange, the official color of inmate overalls. A judging personality? A need to live at the tops of apartment buildings to have the sentry's view? One's habits are indeed affected by circumstances. A man living alone, I clutch, at regular intervals, for the clanking bunching that is my house keys in my front pocket, and grasp my ass at the other intervals to feel the persistence of my wallet.

I know there are ways in which the women of my town seem more fearless, brassier. One surname on my father's side of the family is "Hauser," and when the women of that clan, my mother included, get a little liquor'd-up together, they are not to be messed with. They are called by the men of the family, with some affection and a little concern, the "Hauser Broads." When I graduated from high school, they took over the folding tables closest to the beer keg at the party thrown in honor of my diploma, and my English teacher heard them so identified, and she said, "Hauserbroad? Is that your mother's maiden name?"

So Aunt Charmayne and my mother discussed this fearless family trait with me while snowbirding it on Jekyll Island off the coast of Georgia last winter, during the "Finders Keepers" ball, where I was the youngest buck by at least two dozen years. Half my family spends winter on that island, golfing and learning how to navigate southern lingo ("Would you like some assed tay?") and living with gators (on the golf course, my father recommends zigzagging to throw them off). The "Finders Keepers" ball was held on February 20, so they were able to get a lot of leftover Valentine's Day candy conversation hearts ("Hubba Hubba," "Oh You Kid") for cheap, to scatter across the tables. The real draw was the promise of "heavy hors d'oeuvres," upon which I think my parents live exclusively through those short-day'd months. The ladies dressed in "glamour" tops, Lawrence Welkish chiffon, and mannerist turtlenecks to comfortably dance to the live big band tunes, and their menfolk hustled to keep up with them, all cardigans and cartilage. I stood in line behind an intimidating octogenarian with skin that had been tanned and retanned into a patterned, seasoned leather the pigskin color of the Corsican citadel Calvi (and by the color of Calvi, I mean a football), watching her scrape half a smoked salmon off its salver into her matching purse, and when I glared, she glared back, and what I thought was: Zigzag. Zigzag.

But there was plenty of prime rib at the other food station, and I listened to my father and Uncle Doug, a career man on the train line, talk about hornets' nests and various methods for clearing them out (drilling, duct tape, flames). I, intermittently bored and then terrified (the way a prisoner might experience the doing of time), looked over at the Calvi-colored salmon-stealer and thought, hornets are ornery.

My mother and Aunt Charmayne, at the other side of the table, talked golf that week. The latest scandal had to do with a regular in their set who went golfing the day after her husband's death. They both agreed that they were on *her* side (so was I), and then they moved on to the subject of *real* rudeness on golf courses, and this included the gators—some business here about "false charges."

"Aren't you afraid of the gators?" I asked, finally. Weren't there mistakes, on both sides, about eggs and balls, and sand traps and water hazards?

"Oh, hell no, Brian," my mother said. "They mind their business and we mind ours." Minding your own business is also considered a virtue in my hometown.

"Besides," Aunt Charmayne added, slapping her own thigh, which she does for any sort of emphasis, having to make herself understood to a long line of rowdy boys and wayward dogs and geese, that, as I remembered from childhood, boldly came up off the lake where they lived and crapped on her porch, "after you've played golf at Jackson Country Club, you're not much afraid of anything."

By this, Aunt Charmayne meant the golf course right at the edge of the Southern Michigan Prison grounds, and specifically, an event that's part of family history. Perhaps in a coup of bad planning, the Jackson Country Club put its farthest holes closest to the prison farms, the minimum security facilities for recovering sorts who were never much of a trouble in the first place and perhaps only needed to learn a trade in order to become decent members of society. More on that in a moment.

Some of them, however, discovered that they had no handcuffs on, no chains or bars or large wall keeping them down on those farms. They realized that they could just walk away from their confinement, and they were called, if you can believe it, "Walk-Offs."

On a fateful day before the advent of cell phones, a certain prisoner decided he'd endured enough of his sentence and this was a day to earn the title "Walk-Off." And off he walked, straight through the golf course. Aunt Charmayne might have been the first to see him, if she had seen him, because the farms were right on the ninth hole, the hole farthest afield at the country club. This also seems to have influenced me, this reckless placing of pleasure next to punishment; imagine being confined to a small room with just a sink and a stinky roommate for years, and the only view outside your barred-up window was a lot of people taking their leisure, hitting golf balls at the country club. In Jackson, you know, we don't even have gators to zigzag away from. Placing punishment and reward so close together, I think, the two may have started to blur together for me, pain and pleasure, stupid and bad.

Aunt Charmayne was upset, but only after she was back home and found out about the event she never knew had happened to her. Post-trauma panic: this, too, I may have picked up from my prison days. To her dismay, Uncle Doug responded, "Oh, for cripe's sake, ma, you had golf clubs! You're a Hauserbroad!"

Yes, I think the prison had a toughening influence over women, and softer creatures, too, such as myself. A decade ago, my brother Chris, who works hard for the prison, married Michelle, a quiet daughter from more northerly climes (the upper peninsula of Michigan, where people are raised to be more reserved, so that one does not need to slap one's knee in order to get a goose's attention, or that of a rowdy boy). I first met her when I came home for Thanksgiving the winter after they got hitched. She was pretty, fair-skinned, happy to offer a gracious smile. I had confidence in her even then, but I do recall that this was also the first Thanksgiving after our Uncle Dick, a man famous for large appetites, with the carriage of a mature

Brando and the ability to smoke through five packs a day, had finally succumbed to desire. His emphysema near the end of his life confined him to an oxygen tank. But he smoked anyway.

As the turkey and trimmings were passed around the table among my grandparents and us three brothers and their families, we all welcomed Michelle into the fold by acting normally, which is to say, the way one acts when one lives in a town with the world's largest prison. "Well, Uncle Dick did slow down his smoking a little bit near the end there," Scott, the youngest of the three of us, informed me. I lived in California then; I needed filling in. "He'd get up in the morning, you know, and light up the first cig in the bathroom, to get his motor rolling, if you know what I mean." I looked down the table to see whether Michelle knew what he meant. She was very interested in the cranberry sauce: grandma always mixes carrot shavings into it, to give it "that finished look" we value so in the Midwest. This "finished look" has kept the paprika industry thriving back in Hungary, for without it, deviled eggs would never have "that finished look."

Scott went on, "So he was smoking away, flicking the ashes between his legs into the toilet and," and now even Scott was wondering about Michelle, but it was too late now, it was time for him to fish or cut bait. "And," he went on, a new resolve pushing the story forward, "Well, he'd gotten pretty heavy there in the last days, so that he didn't realize at first that one of the ashes landed, you know, down there, and had started, you know," one last glance toward our new sister-in-law, "a brush fire. Pass the gravy."

"Christ," my mother diagnosed: "it's like you kids have a screw loose." And then we blessed Uncle Dick and wished him well, free from the bonds of this earth and no doubt enjoying all the cigarettes the afterlife allows. Michelle was ever a gracious thing, then, and smiled, I think, though what I noticed most was the high coloring in her cheeks. It must have gone all right, because she is still part of the family—more than I am, in certain ways.

And on the tenth anniversary of that Thanksgiving, we sat down at that same table, with nearly the same cast, gaining a few children, losing an adult here and there. By then Chris, her husband, had become very much involved with the prison, and I asked him, as the cranberries and carrots went around, what it was like to work in the world's largest walled prison.

"Aw, Brian," he said, hashing turkey into tiny bits for his daughter, "you don't go to prison for being bad, you go to prison for being stupid." Initially, this statement made the bristles of my politically correct nape stand on end, but now I don't think of the race issues tangled up in his observation, or the problem of this nation in which more people than anywhere else in the world cool their heels in a jail cell. I think instead how this is roughly how people see the world in my town: you are not punished for being bad, you are punished for being stupid, getting caught. "You've got your four levels in the prison," Chris explained. "Your ones and twos, they're not so bad, drugs and that. Then there's the real problem, your level threes, and they've done felonies, violent stuff, and they need a lot more supervision, and yet they give all this attention to the level fours, and they're more quiet-like, like that one guy, Reggie what's-his-name."

I was supposed to know of some notorious criminal from our town, but I'd been away a while. Michelle, his once-timid wife, piped up, "Oh, Reggie, that guy who owned a restaurant and killed his wife and deboned her?" You see? She's a Hauserbroad now.

Me too, or perhaps I have become too cavalier when in the presence of danger. I have watched too many forms of safety and precaution fail—hard hats on job sites, survival suits in Alaskan waters, proofreading, airbags, condoms, maps—and now I am the proverbial fool, rushing in. Living close to a clutch of convicted armed robbers, rapists, and thugs, it seemed only a matter of time before they'd spring themselves.

And they did. I was a page at the public library, and have a vivid memory of shelving books from the top story, and looking out beyond the town's boundaries to see the prisoners rioting. Trouble showed itself in a long black plume of smoke; later, I'd see the same black smoke rise out of the Corsican ferry smokestacks, and in the camps of gypsies, that forever-wandering nation that kept itself momentarily comfortable on abandoned sofas and choking, billowing, smoking fires stoked on plastic bags and garbage. There was talk in the normally sedate library, but nobody panicked, nobody left. I had books to shelve, and there's always time to run.

And one more thing: what the prison might also have done to the character of my hometown has to do with art. The prison gift shop, always a fun excursion for the family, was stocked with all sorts of objects *hecho-a-mano* by inmates: leather goods and rather paint-by-numbers-like paintings, but also Popsicle-stick lamps, purses made from gum wrappers, tin can briefcases. Hobo art. The act of making things, especially elaborate things, was associated with confinement, sitting around, having nothing better to do with your time. Not, as it were, with being a productive member of society. What must painters and poets and musicians seem to most of the people in my town?

Islands are historically perfect places to put prisons, to "keep" people. Think of Alcatraz. Islands were used to keep people away from power. Able was Napoleon ere he saw Elba. Supervillains, too, get put on islands in the comic books, and for that their immortality and fame are secure, and after a while, one wants to see how Lex Luthor or the Joker will manage to get away one more time. Said the suffragist Carrie Nation, "If you steal a loaf of bread, you go to jail; if you steal a railroad, you're a senator."

Things of the world that are apt to perish, like politicians or poetry, "keep" on islands, as if packed in salt or ice. There is purity.

Puerto Ricans breed a horse called *paso fino* that runs with the two left legs forward together, then two right, rather than the mix and match, creating a "fine gait," a real ballet. They've been bred this way and stay pure in their island isolation. To see the paso fino in action is to see something from fairyland, more surprising than a unicorn. Another example: linguists consider the rough, grouchy Catalan spoken on Mallorca closer to the way the language was originally spoken long ago than the Catalan spoken in mainland, big-city Barcelona. I blame Anne of Green Gables' incorruptible purity, if not her undiagnosed Attention Deficit Disorder, on the gorgeous unspoiled miniworld that is Prince Edward Island.

An island, for the great, was a place to save one's self, and to languish. Ovid, making his elaborate word things, took his chill pill on Capri. Seneca was stuck on Corsica. These poets, to please their patrons once back in power and out of island exile, might defame the islands, as Seneca did of Corsica in his pastorals, taking a swipe at the quality of the island's honey. The honey, as it turns out, is rather a source of pride among Corsicans, since the bees sip off all those plants in the maquis.

No, I think, instead, that I didn't feel influenced by wardens and guards and cops so much as by prisoners. Southern Michigan Penitentiary maintained that string of low-security prison farms to rehabilitate nonviolent criminals, like the one that menaced Aunt Charmayne lo these many years ago. We could see them from the state highway, and to me, they resembled a profane monastery, where the inmates, like monks, grew their own fruits and vegetables and maintained a certain level of self-sufficiency. One of my earliest memories was watching trustees cut ice on the lake for their low-tech iceboxes.

And from those farms, quite naturally, there were those "Walk-Offs," the prisoners who simply, unwatched, walked away from their punishment. There were signs all along the roads leading in and out of Jackson County—manufactured in the prison workshops—warning us in paint a shade of municipal, fire-alarm red, or maybe blood, "Do Not Pick Up Hitchhikers."

Walking—and perhaps here I am, like my father, pointing out the obvious—seems to be both a monastic eschewing and an escape of the prison-break sort. Although I've never been a prisoner, neither actual nor mental, I've never quite felt at home anywhere but in motion, on the lam. I've pretty much come to accept that I'm alone with that feeling. To discover it feels strange, more monasticism, more escape—and, of course, more of a sense of being one of them—bad-guys. What is a bad guy if not a person whose desires and goals are utterly foreign to everybody else?

Once a bad guy is caught and put in prison, his desire to make others suffer (let's call it "sadism") turns into a desire to suffer (that's "masochism"). Only the stupid go to prison, says my brother.

While walking to Santiago that first time with Petra, I spent three days hiking along with five Belgian men, who mostly kept their distance in the evenings, but who were very talkative during the day's hike. I got to know Pietr well, one of the three who were taking orders from the other two. Every morning, the two order-giving ones, both short, blond, and taciturn, would say in Belgian (therefore I approximate), "Okay, you guys, time to get up, let's get moving." Pietr and I talked for three days about our mutual interests—opera, literature, travel, good wine.

We passed by Irache, a vintner famous for giving free wine to pilgrims. You simply filled your travel cup with as much as you could drink, just as long as you didn't steal. Unfortunately, we'd arrived at nine in the morning. This didn't stop most of us. But when Pietr reached for his tin cup, one of the two phlegmatic blondes said, "No, stay away." Pietr frowned, but obeyed.

I furrowed my brow and asked Pietr, "Why are you always taking orders from those guys?"

Pietr smiled. "Well, you see, I am a prisoner."

A prisoner? So were the other two men who were taking commands. No shackles, no firearms, who could tell? They were "walk-offs." It seems a Belgian law that dates back to medieval days allows criminals to be punished by sending them to Santiago. My fellow Belgian pilgrims were doing penance, with the added chore of fixing church doors along the way.

"What did you do?" I asked Pietr.

He never told me explicitly, although I heard farther down the trail that all three were embezzlers. "White-collar crime," is all he told me.

"So," I thought it out, "if Pietr is walking to Santiago as a punishment, why am I walking?" And I sank into days of asking myself this question, wondering how ridiculous I must seem, thinking more about what I seek than what I destroyed.

Those jabbering, questioning, mental Boolean threads can only be stopped by two things: jabbering with another walker or the arduous, masochistic physical effort of the trek. The second option is the more effective, because the self, or the selfish, retreats deep into the body because it must go into hibernation. No guilt-ridden voice speaks then, no chain of awful memories surface in reflection. No pie-in-the-sky ambition can flourish, only the one that gets you through the next zigzag scramble over scree. Physical exertion is usefully belittling: all of the character attributes of which I am proud of myself mean jack, for apparently, I am not bright enough, not profound enough—even my own hubris is worthless to the task of self-reliance. There is only silence and sensation, and many of those sensations are searingly painful.

It's not all self-inflicted pain, not the process. When you see those people running in triathlons and the sports-show cameras capture them in a mask of wretched pain, you do not know about the other stuff, the endorphins running through the body, the druglike high created by dehydration and apoplexy. How can I make people believe that being silenced, feeling tiny, being sick, even, feels *good* after making it to the top of a peak, or the bottom of a chasm?

"You're an animal!" a girl fruitlessly compliments me, when she is told how many miles I walk in an average summer. Bones heal, chicks dig scars. I'm not fishing for compliments, and it's funny how mocking disdain can turn, on a dime, to awe-struck glorification. If you eat a half a pint of ice cream, you are a *pig*. If you eat the whole pint, directly from the container, you're an *animal*.

And you know what? At the top of a peak, looking across at the other mountains that must be traversed, every one of them a shark's tooth, and then looking down into a deep glacial lake, and looking over at Petra, who has been here for ten minutes and whose tinfoil from her power bar has whipped off in the wind and slices by me, while Lula the Lab bounds effortlessly in front of me as I gasp in the thin air like a large-mouthed bass at the bottom of a bilged-out boat, and the sunblock has gone liquid again with my sweat and runs directly into my eyes and makes me weep, and my ears are burned purple from prolonged exposure, and my backpack seems to have been filled with granite and my ankles ache and the extreme-sports boys roar past me once again, I feel like an escaped convict, a walk-off, not bad but stupid, stupid but divine, the holy fool in some Russian novel—*Raskolnikov,* happy to be free at this moment—though in the next I may be in shackles again.

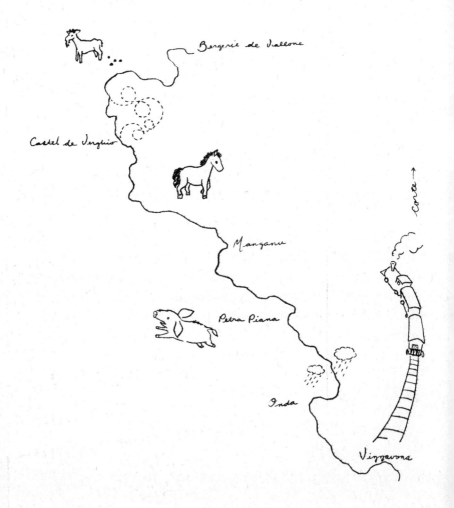

Bergerie de Vallone

Castel de Verghio

Corte →

Manganu

Petra Piana

Onda

Vizzavona

4

Bandit l'Honneur

Bergerie de Vallone to Castel de Verghio

The father shepherd, Paulo, has risen and taken his two pack mules into town for supplies and returned again before we have taken down our tent and showered. It is a gorgeous morning to enjoy, with plenty of coffee for which I am perfectly happy to pay a premium, and Petra takes her time packing. Whatever headstart we had on all the strip-mall types at the gîte a kilometer behind us is gone now. I recognize some of the French husbands and wives as they walk right through the camping area. Lula now recognizes me, though I swear I never gave her a handout, and if I had forgotten about the consequences of being a known American (I keep thinking of these words, "known," "admitted," words usually proceeded by "homosexual" or "communist," and how "American" fits just as well, here), I'm reminded when I see the young couple, fresh as morning dew, stepping like gazelles down the GR20. Is that how my eye sockets got to be feeling this way? From all these walkers stepping on them? No, no; it was that stuff shepherd-boy served us the night before in that unmarked bottle.

We had ended up tying one on, and because Corsicans believe in the hair of the dog as well as several other superstitions, all described over our drunken conversation after dinner, Paulo wakes us up with a complimentary shot of this homemade liquor he makes from myrtle, something I would get much more of as we go deeper into the country, and something I will take home with me to remind me of the things Corsica offers that no other place can.

To arms, to arms! Petra finishes her own preparations. With this little bit of liquor in us, our conversation as we break down the tent turns to all things deluxe. We are in need of a good restaurant. I describe the American tradition of "dine and dash" (slipping out of a restaurant without paying the bill), which renders worthless the German tradition of the Damenkarte. Petra never shows any sort of outrage about bad American behavior, although she is appalled about mass shootings at high schools and the concept of twenty-four-hour grocery stores. "You Americans have no morals," she says, to this second thing. "What shall I do with the herring?"

For a moment, I'm afraid that I did something rash while in my cups the night before, and bought fish from a shepherd. But she is holding up the tent stakes and I'm sober enough now to figure out that "herring" is the German word for them. Like a fish.

"Because they are shiny and quick that way, if they are any good at all," says Petra.

But starting off the day's hike with alcohol doesn't suit our types, Northern European types. We like to feel good and then drift off to sleep, or pass out, another kind of feeling good. We like our sensual pleasures one at a time. As the myrtle liquor wears off, we slip into lousy moods. A buckle on my backpack, not even an important one, has broken off, and I fret about fixing it. Petra complains about the immediate uphill tilt of the trail. I try to use the same sort of encouragement she uses on me during the downhill assaults by misquoting my guidebook: "Only half a kilometer to go!" I say, even though there are, in reality, more than two, almost three kilometers of this. She isn't a stupid German girl. She isn't even a stupid Austrian girl. She studies the guidebooks much more closely than I do.

Heather, and hellebore, and the malodorous—what is that?—it's alder! How is it that I have to go to a remote island to discover that alder is stinky? Cool streams trickle down. More scrambles, the sour of Petra's bad mood (and by Petra's bad mood, I mean my bad mood, or hers dovetailing to mine as we finally get to the downhill segment). I come upon another plant that smells like sterile gauze.

It strikes me that the histories always talk about bandits, good and bad, "giving themselves up" after a long run and hide. A bandit can't go too far on Corsica without seeing the sea, or Calvi; it must make a fugitive feel circumscribed, and I suppose they'd despair after a while, "give up" rather than give the self up. I walk far ahead of Petra for a while to minimize our disuse to each other. I am a little sorry about doing so when I come to a cliff that looks down into Lac de Capitello, one of several glacial fjords that is beautiful to peer down into and so clean and clear that even from this great height above I can see deep into its depths, and know that its depths are astonishing.

I keep waiting for Petra to join me in admiring the view. A good view is like a funny movie or an elaborate meal, not nearly as pleasant when experienced alone, unless you are some poser existentialist, and poseurs are no fun to be around anyway, anytime. And the longer I sit, the more I wish anybody would join me in admiring the view. After the previous day's traffic jam in the ironically named Solitude Circuit, today, I have not seen another walker in hours. I panic for a moment, thinking that perhaps I've taken a wrong turn, but it only takes a moment to let my eyes dart about before I spot that double stripe of red and white paint to prove that I am on the trail. Does nobody else wish to linger over this view of the fjord?

I decide to myself that when Petra catches up, I will stay near her and keep my black mood on a leash. This is one of the things I pull apart in my mind as I plod along alone, and just as my guidebook tells me I am nearing the end of the day's wandering, Petra and I find ourselves reunited in a long, lovely valley along the Golo River.

"There you are, stupid American boy."

"I missed you, stupid German girl."

Her index finger shoots to her lips to hush me. "Stupid *Austrian* girl."

We are so happy to see each other and near the end of our day's walking, so we lollygag, stop for a skinny-dip, and enjoy the vistas. Shamelessly naked, we cavort and wave at several hikers who are finally catching up with us. We recognize many of them from previous étapes. There's an aging, overly fit couple from Quebec who, on the first night in Carrozzu, were annoyed by the French party boys; he was going to shout at them, but when his wife saw that we had their cooking pot, she figured we must have been friends, and I remember her putting one of those tanned hands of hers over his equally tanned paw, and I saw she had a gold wedding band worn so thin it seemed as if it might snap in two at any moment. The three Australians, two women and one man, who have been arguing since they hit the GR20. The pipe-smoking ex-military man from Scotland (maybe), and his two energetic sons. Those two older French macho guys who can't seem to keep their shirts on and who pace in front of the gîte each night as if they were roosters guarding a henhouse. The chain-smoking Italian, liable to ignite the maquis with his butts at any moment. That annoying Belgian couple with their clicky clicky sticks, and matching outfits, and ridiculous splatter-art spandex leggings. The strapping German boy and his new girlfriend.

(I want to be friends with them, but Petra wants to keep a distance from them the way I want to avoid the English speakers. And besides, the girlfriend has announced her sense of being underwhelmed by this trek in many languages, including my own, so that the boyfriend, after trying every form of placation, from scorn to unctuous conciliation to a sloppy liplock, all with the same ratcheted-up result, now makes of his face the blank emotionless beam of some giant plush beast on a children's television show, with eyes all pupil and made of felt and a mouth that's a sewn cloth strip devoid of expression, for any emotional manifestation tends to set her off. I start to call them Herr and Frau Dancing Bear.) And finally, there comes, last up the road, the dumpy guy from France who seems to be walking alone, which sometimes concerns me because, judging from the way I see him put on his hiking socks each morning, so that the reinforced diamond that belongs at the heel rides the top of his foot, he is even more out of his depth than I am. They are all on parade, and they are all looking at our naked bods.

But almost none of them wave back, although they frown at our fun. Nobody looks interested in joining us. And the water is fine!

After letting the sun dry us on smoothed granite, we put on our packs and head toward the promise of a shabby but large hotel (my guidebook gripes but reports that they sell postcards, so it must have some other modern amenities, too). We dare each other to jog to the hotel, probably just over that hill.

No, that hill.

And just across that meadow and over that scramble of boulders. Yonder.

We have been lulled into a false sense of ease, it seems, because both the English and German guidebooks have lied to each of us at the same time. Okay, they didn't lie to us, but they made it mighty easy for us to misread them. "That's not the waterfall they were referring to," we realize, the one we skinny-dipped in, but this one, here, the one we find two hours later. We are two hours behind our minds' notion of when this day's walk would end. This sort of notion is the sort that generates terrible feelings.

By the time we reach a rundown goat-shepherd's hut (scree can be used to hold down roofing tile, too, apparently), the Bergerie Radule, we are as unmanned as the hut. No friendly Paulo or his easy-on-the-eye son serving wee and unwee drams. Just dozens and dozens of charming but trail-blocking goats (my God, I gasp in discovery, chèvre cheese smells like goats! Goats, they smell like goats!). Petra would like to drop despondently onto a rock to pout, but you have to look before you sit, because there are goat doodies everywhere, which makes spontaneous gestures of frustration look just as theatrical and artificial as they are. But I am right with you, girl.

After I give both of us time to have inner tantrums, I say, "that hotel might be busy because it's Saturday, and the French sure do love 'le weekend.'" I am suggesting that she take up her trusty cell phone, the one that gets reception anywhere, even at the bottom of a remote mountain pass on a remote island in the remote Mediterranean, thanks to her employment at Siemens. Petra gives (and gets) good phone. It gives me a false sense of comfort at all times; I remember the stories of guys stuck in a blizzard on Everest, calling their wives to say goodbye. It's nice that modern technology has made it possible to say goodbye from your terrible accident. That's what I call progress. Cavemen never got to call home after getting gored by a mammoth.

Petra, as sapped of energy as I am (I swear she was the one who dared us to jog to the hotel), pulls her phone out. Yup. The reception is so good, even I can hear the singsong voice of the patroness taunt, "Je suis désolée," not sorry at all, really, "Complet!" Filled up. No room at the inn.

I fly into a tailspin of anger, doodies be damned, and stomp through the goats and into the woods, blinded by that lethal combination of fatigue and rage (it's a kind of enchantment; I think it's what witches visit upon their princess victims in the fairy tales). Petra cannot, or does not follow; her pack is off her shoulders, and by now, she knows when to stand back. I'd do the same for her.

I take a very wrong turn, and then another, and another, and the red-and-white stripes demarking the GR20 turn into the yellow markings of a local wayside trail, and they turn into an occasional pile of rocks, until I am following what is probably a goat path, and now is maybe a goat path if I am lucky, and now I am lost.

I try to backtrack, and hunt for the right trail, but there are so many forks and tridents and intersections made by goats who don't seem to give a damn where they are going, and after an hour, the sun is starting to set and I am starting to panic. My acerbic guidebook warns that every year, walkers on the GR20 have to be helicoptered out because they get lost, and here I am, done with the compass, done with the charts, and not in the port, no, not even remotely.

By now, it may come as no surprise that while walking, I've gotten myself lost on several occasions. I scoff at the number of times we've seen the red-and-white stripes of the GR20 (it ought to be a nationalist flag itself, since it often appears every five feet or so), but if they didn't paint them so close together, I am the one likely to wander off on some side trail and starve to death half a kilometer from a restaurant. I have little sense of direction, especially when among mountains that block the sun's actual location.

I have friends who have impeccable directional sense, something I envy as much as I envy the phrase "divides his time between" in a biographical note, or sensitive nipples, or a full head of hair. "It's like I have this map of where I am, in the bigger sense, below me, and it shifts around as I shift," says my friend Pete. I imagine his brain swimming and swiveling about inside his skull like one of those liquid-filled compasses that you install on your car's dashboard. Birds are said to have tiny magnets in their heads to help them know south. Cats and dogs, too. The lower orders. I sit on a rock from which I wish I had to brush goat doodies, but even they are not stupid enough to get this far back in the woods. I console myself by thinking that my profound lack of directional sense is evidence of a *more evolved being,* and that I should not feel ashamed, but here in the wilderness, it is always the fifth great day of God, the day animals were created, and, even in that biblical scheme of things, men are not coming until *tomorrow.*

If there's no sun by which to orient myself and the trail throws in a couple of curves (for example, on a trail that hugs a series of forested mountains—for example, the GR20), I am as confused as a blindfolded little girl at a birthday party, given a whirl and sent to whack at the overhead piñata.

Getting lost on an island is a little less dire than getting lost, say, in Antarctica, because eventually, if you keep walking, you'll come across some sort of human habitation (God, I wish I could still see Calvi). One would think then that walking in the less wild portions of the world would be easier, but it's in the civilized places where I get lost the most, where people are apt to move nature around, alter the course of a road, or block it with something new. All it takes is for some enterprising farmer to decide to plant corn where he had always maintained a service road to his old château, and a walker like me is, as they say, screwed.

While hiking in southwest France with Jean-Philippe, a Swiss friend of both Petra and mine, we came into the vineyards in the Bourdeaux, where is made the "Entre deux mers," the St. Emilion, the Bergerac and Château Margaux; I had bucolic fantasies when entering the Gironne because we were walking among the wine grapes, miles and miles of perfect rows—how lovely, how picturesque! And how could a person get lost in such order, such ancient, stately order?

First of all, there is no shade in vineyards, or if the grape vines are high enough to create shade, then they are like those human mazes, and nobody wants to walk in a human maze with a backpack. Second, the grapes draw all sorts of bugs: wasps and flies and such and such. Two vineyard rows is the perfect width for building a spider web big enough to snare cows (the earthy Jean-Philippe was more philosophical about webs than I: "I would not like to bicycle in France," he said, when I complained about my aching feet one evening, "because then I would not be able to feel the spiders.") And further, the farmer will move his vines, or grow new grapes in new rows, and you will lose the path, or it will not be on a perfect north-south perpendicular to the sun, so that you slowly walk away from your goal until you have accumulated kilometers of overshot or mis-shot distance.

Fellow walkers once convinced me to take a "night étape," a step of the journey in the dark. We stopped at dawn, after an evening of stumbling over the tiniest rocks and sapping our flashlight batteries, in a village seven kilometers to the south of where we wanted to be.

I made plans, some years back, for a walk in Spain's Picos de Europa, where they make the cheese called Cabrales from the milk of goats and sheep and cows blended all together and then aged, wrapped in grape leaves, buried deep in the warm steamy caress of decaying manure so that it is such a stinky blue cheese that it is purple. My partner and I needed maps, and on the way to the walking, we purchased some in a shop in the town of Oviedo. They were not so much maps as charts that were drawn up by Franco's military in 1954. Not so much charts as wish lists for Santa Claus. The charts were very picturesque; we liked them as potential souvenirs, and we had no guide for the Picos. Even the shopkeeper warned us that they were out of date; yet we were swept up, I think, in the romance of using old maps, of making do.

What we found, far too late and deep in the mountains, was that the maps depicted villages that no longer existed (think: Guernica), and also villages that the regime dreamed would one day exist in its new world order; roads, too, and vice versa. The problem was that there was, in one particular portion of our hiking trail, a network of paths that the grazing ingredients of Cabrales had worn into hillside, so that it was easy to believe we were not lost but that these old charts were perhaps a little off without modern GPS surveying. And we continued to follow trails that didn't exist and made ourselves believe that two or three stones, more or less arranged in a triangle, were another hiker's sign for us to go this way or that, when in fact they were just two or three stones sitting around, more or less arranged in a triangle.

Waist-deep in brambles and realizing that even sheep had not come over this path in a few months, a very large creature, which, for now, I will accept may have been a spider and not an animal with bright yellow fur (but I want this argument to remain open for future discussion), crawled up my pants leg and into my pocket. I screamed something like we are going back we are going back, and I was already going back, no open arguments there, and that is, I believe, the only reason we did not disappear forever into the wilds of the Picos de Europa. Today, the old Franco charts are locked in a box with some snow globes and collector spoons and other useless souvenirs.

And there's more than just my bad sense of direction to reckon with. Between my guide to the GR20 and Petra's German guide, there are thousands of discrepancies of distance and direction. It reminds me of how guides to the Camino de Santiago in French, Spanish, German, Dutch, and English never agreed on the number of kilometers to the next place. Each day, we multinational pilgrims would pool all the numbers together and average them out. All charts for ocean travel come with an advisory emblazoned in the corner: "Note: the prudent mariner will not rely on a single source of information while navigating."

And sometimes, misinformation and misapprehension are handmaidens to success. My friend Marta told me a wonderful story about how, in Nepal during World War II, there was a soldier from Ghurka who escaped from a Burmese prison camp. He stumbled out of the greenery into the British headquarters at the front one day, covered with running sores, filthy, weak with hunger and dysentery, but miraculously alive and, as Marta put it, *"there."* He saluted his commander with a feeble arm.

You can just see the commander straighten to attention for the survivor, after bending fruitlessly over his charts. "How could you possibly escape the Burmese?" he asked the Ghurka. The soldier didn't speak English, but little by little, through an interpreter, he explained that back in the prison camp, a dying English infantryman had given him a map.

Now you can just see the commanders eyes narrow with disbelief and hope. A map of the jungle? See the officers look at one another. As far as they knew, there were no maps of the impenetrable Burmese jungle, just as there are no real maps of the maquis. This had become quite a problem for the Allies as they tried to plan their maneuvers. They grew excited; a map was just what they needed to turn the tides in a campaign that wasn't going well.

The commander asked the soldier to show them the map. The Ghurka pulled it from the inside of what was left of his shirt and unwrapped the dirty cloth that protected it. He squatted down and began to unfold the stained, fragile paper on the ground. One quarter had come loose along the folds and had to be placed like a puzzle piece where it fit. One corner was missing entirely. The officers looked with anticipation over the shoulders of the small Nepali man.

They squinted at the blurred tangle of routes and rivers. And suddenly: *Piccadilly,* someone made out, *Buckingham Palace, Hampstead Heath, Wimbledon.* They were looking at a map of central London.

Now where was I before that long digression? Oh yes: lost!

And so I flounder about in the weakening Corsican light, getting farther and farther away from where I want to be. I continue to take trails that are obviously not the right ones, because I am devoted, even to my mistakes. My big Michelin maps of Corsica are folded incorrectly, and I'll continue to fold them incorrectly in the same exact incorrect way until squares will come loose, like the squares of the Ghurka soldier's London map. Getting lost is like using the wrong theorem in a geometry proof but proceeding anyway.

I know I shouldn't panic. I'm not really lost in the way one might get lost in the tundra, but it's an annoying kind of lost, a walking through spider webs lost, a did-they-say-there-are-poisonous-snakes? lost.

And then I hear cars. Oh, the sweet sweet spiritual "ommmm" of auto wheels on pavement. I follow their sound, and tumble out onto an incongruous highway, and I am sweaty, bug-bitten, those spider webs in my hair; I smell of goat, and a shot of adrenalin mixes in with the rage and fatigue for a heady soup of emotion, yet I'm following a road clearly marked to our next stop: Castel de Verghio.

But another big thing about being lost is that one loses confidence entirely, and every bit of proof of not being lost is disbelieved. Even a highway sign will not convince this lost wanderer that he's been found; I am sure that the signs are directing auto travelers to a *different* Castel de Verghio than I am going to. A hiker seeks the mountain called Castel de Verghio, while a motorist is looking for the restaurant called Castel de Verghio. Instead, I find the hotel we had called back at the dilapidated bergerie. And I still feel nervous. In fact, it matches the description in my guidebook, yet another defunct ski resort that looks like it had been run by a Soviet bloc country, and when I can't find Petra, I decide to ask for a room.

This does not help belay my mistrust in being found either— because they give me a room.

I worry, even as I shower, drink a beer, finish the leftover brebis we bought from Paulo. Perhaps this is not the same place Petra called on her cell phone. I am still lost! As the sun sets and the dinner hour approaches, I don't quite know what to do; I figured Petra would be here, and she is not. Is she so angry with me that she walked farther on? Where would her energy come from? I worry, then drink another beer on the veranda, hoping to see her pass along the road; she'd have to pass along in front of the hotel. There is a tent village behind the hotel, but I carry our tent in my pack. I poke around back there anyway, say a sheepish hello to the Pyrenees couple and Lula the Lab, see only one of the two mustachio'd shirtless macho Rooster men (if they annoy me, they must make each other miserable and avoid each other as much as they can while still being considered "together," guarding one another's safety), spot the Scottish military man smoking a pipe on a rock, and voilà!, not Petra, but the three missing French boys who were last seen in Carrozzu. Forever turtle-eyed with hangover and taking forever getting across Corsica.

"Allo!" they say, almost in harmony, like stooges. They are happy to see me, and I know why: I am the companion of Petra, who is something to look at on the road besides rocks and trees. But they are as indirect as American boys: "Do you have our cooking pot?" Oh, the French. Always thinking of girls with their stomachs.

"Petra is carrying it," I tell them. They moo and chide, for how could I have left their cooking pot and its attendant unattended?

I worry, but drink another beer and wash some socks. And then, under the buzzing sulfur lights of the rusty ski lift, I see her, trudging up the trail, me fresh and scrubbed, she covered in red dust and so pissed off, I swear I can see steam shooting out of her ears. I run in and practice in the mirror, trying out my "upset" face, the one I truly had while lost deep in the woods on a goat path. I hope this face will eclipse or nullify her anger. I run out and meet her in front of the hotel.

"There you are stupid German girl I got so lost it was horrible but I got us a hotel room and it's my treat want a beer?"

She is silent for a couple of minutes, sticks out one hiking boot for me. She allows me to unlace it for her, and my quick fingers turn red with the dust. To show me she is going to forgive me, she says, "The Damenkarte hotel room?"

Sure, you betcha.

I lead her into the Hotel Castel de Verghio and insist on carrying her backpack up the stairs. For a place that is the source of great luxury and relief, the hotel is hideous, and critiquing it is my odd way of cajoling Petra out of her righteous anger. There is a Corsican man at the front desk with a face that looks as if it has been folded like cardboard, creased, and unfolded again in several odd places, and this is his hotel, his kingdom. He had, it seems, rerouted the GR20 so that walkers have to come to him. He has painted over the signs in the woods (and this is why I got lost, I think) and makes his rundown ski lodge an all-stops. Downstairs, on the veranda, four guys—perhaps from Flanders?—speak a wacked language just ever-so-barely Romance in root, and it makes this place feel even more strange.

But the mountains are always nice to look out upon, even if our balcony is ugly, and if I position my chair at a certain angle, I can't see the beat-up rusty ski lift or the water-damaged industrial carpeting that curls at the corners of our room and shows the dry-rot floors beneath. A shower nozzle, even a European shower nozzle, and a fridge-cooled beer is luxury enough. Another reason why I walk: lowering the standards of what is considered luxurious.

I buy two more beers and bring them up to Petra. More placating salve. She steps out of the bathroom scrubbed clean of the red dust and accepts the cold one. "We have to be nicer to each other," she sighs, and drinks.

I think of the crafty hospitalero of this hotel, trapping walkers in his socialist-realist shack, and I think of our rather unsociable fellow walkers frowning as we skinny-dipped in the Golo, and then I nod to Petra. She is right: I must be nicer. She is not the enemy. The enemy is—what? Who gets me lost? Who makes me eat salty cheese when there is no water to wash it down? Who makes me sing "I know an old woman who swallowed a fly" over and over and over?

I look from the pretty mountains down to my feet, and to the ugly balcony. "I was very lost and very frightened," I explain to Petra one more time, "but you are right. I shouldn't have stormed off at the goat hut." The Corsican beer is good. It's called Pietra. It's an amber, and both Petra and I prefer red wine, but sometimes you need cold beer. Petra teaches me a great onomatopoetic German word for the effect cold beer has on a furious, bilious mind, minds like ours at this moment. "It is the word that sounds like you are throwing cold water on a smoldering fire," she says, *"zischen."*

On our Soviet balcony, I would not doubt that everybody in the building could hear the zischen.

Castel de Verghio to Manganu

Although I spent nearly as much money on beer the evening before as I did on our room, we decide, in a stridently moral huffiness only a good night's sleep can foster, not to give that awful hotel any more of our money. So we are up early and out on the trail before most of the others. It's not until we have walked for more than an hour that I remember the French boys, looking for their aluminum pot. But the pot is light and Petra is glad to keep it, in case we have to cook for ourselves again.

With our stolen pot, we pride ourselves in being two bandits, as the first hour is a walk through the Forest of Aïtone, famous for harboring refugees.

"What other crime did you commit?" Petra wants to know.

"I killed a pig at the ski resort," I tell her, then add, "and stole a wallet from the Comte du Castel Verghio," when she is not satisfied with my misdeeds. She waits still: Petra loves a wild fantasy. "And I didn't pay my cell phone bill." This, finally, seems to satisfy her, the Siemens employee.

"What did you do?" I ask.

"I blew up a building with a bomb," she says, as a matter of fact. Such a violent woman.

From the woods we can still see that ski resort, the broken-down ski lift looking like the Mad Mouse coaster ride at the traveling carnival of my childhood, the one that always broke down at least once, throwing some child into the sky or cultivating a crop of neck braces for the whiplash it engendered. This machinery here at Castel Verghio looks like it has been half-dismantled after such a terrible accident. The wild pigs sniffing around it do not add much glamour.

Before the sun is too hot, we are able to scale to the admittedly lovely but treacherous Ciottulu a I Mori, the "Hole of the Moors," whose name refers to a crazy pierced stone at the top of one of the peaks. There is a refuge, and many of the walkers have not yet packed up yet. I recognize the bickering Australians, and the French guy who doesn't know how to wear his socks. And mein Herr und Frau Dancing Bear. The only friendly person is the gardien, who slaves away in his shack making omelets for the macho French Roosters who have taken their shirts off again when really, *really,* they shouldn't.

Petra and I are starving from our pre-dawn sanctimony, but the gardien is the only French speaker I have ever met who says "Je suis désolé" without some aspect of verbal irony affecting his tone, "no more omelets."

We look over at the two shirtless men, and it seems to me that they are eating a dozen eggs themselves. "The rooster is tired," the gardien tells us, and for a moment, I confuse his egg source with the shirtless men, and then I see he is making a joke. Petra tells him that roosters do not lay eggs, and perhaps this is the problem. Then we pool our money and buy two Mars bars and two Coca-Colas and we pay ten euros—more than ten American dollars—for them, and we do not complain. We move on, and I smile, knowing that at least the big omelets will slow down the extreme sports guys.

By noon we take our ease along the *pozzines* of Lac Ninu, which runs a little dry, like the promissory illusory springs that gambol through Petra's guidebook. It's late in the year. Pozzines are lush, green, grass fields, the grass so short it looks mown or manicured, kept irrigated by small streams threading just below in winding narrow trenches all around us. We have to watch our step, but it's such a pleasure to walk here, and remarkably striking in contrast to the severe and bizarre gray and orange towers we walked through to get to Lac Ninu.

The walking has been mostly gentle today, but even so, the étape seems a song sung in a minor key, to be sung in a gingerly tone since even walking on soft pine needles and these pozzines, stuff that looks like the greens on golf courses (I sit eating bread and cheese and olives with Petra on the fourth hole and wonder whether there are any gators to exercise my heretofore useless zigzag strategy), reminds me that I am suffering blisters. That it is September, too, cannot be denied: fewer walkers, an angle of light, that drying, dying lake.

Wild horses appear on the shore! And day hikers, a woman with a tiny pack and her beast of burden, a great St. Bernard of a husband trudging up behind her. These feel like air let into a stuffy room—the woman's tiny backpack is a subtle sign that escape is always possible, a left turn can lead us into rooms run on electricity and good wine and coffee. That's all I really need: a subtle sign that coffee *exists*, not necessarily the coffee itself. The woman and her St. Bernard can leave us alone now. I said, you can go away now. Thanks! See ya! They spread their blanket just far enough away that they do not have to smell the two of us.

And as we clear up our lunch and approach the lake, there is an odd optical illusion: the lake seems to miniaturize the closer we get to it. This is the odd effect of the craggy dramatic ups and downs of the mountain peaks at the center of Corsica, which we are approaching. The mountains are not so high themselves, but they look alpine and impenetrable. The lake keeps shrinking . . . and oddly, so do the wild horses.

The horses, as I walk up to one, grazing and ignoring me, are tiny, and I have to bend over to put my hand on its neck. *Lilliputian* tiny. I've seen Shetlands, and these are smaller than Shetlands. Adorable and weird! Once again, I tell Petra that Corsica was once Pleasure Island, a carnival shut down, and these circus ponies, used by midget clowns for some surely hilarious skit, have been let loose back into the wild. They nearly rescue the mood of this landscape for me, which ought to be soft, the meadow on an English estate designed by Capability Brown. But I feel lonesome, and that's no slight against dear Petra. It just may be that "desolate" is easier for me to bear.

The circus animals try to rescue me from the lonesomeness by summoning their pals, a batch of unchaperoned piglets, which appear out of nowhere, not even a ridiculous clown car. It's as if we have come upon some Neverland, with the munchkin ponies and cholo piglets and husbands transformed into St. Bernards and manicured golf-course greens with nobody needed to mow them. And when lunch is finished and we pick up our packs to move on, we turn a corner and find a grove of ancient olive trees, so wizened that their very trunk cores have rotted out, so that they seem, on two long legs, to be striding along with us.

I never quite shake the melancholy all day, my brain turning even the lingering calliope music a shade darker. Perhaps it is because there is a difference in landscape. We'd been in stony mountains for days, and that is a desolate landscape. Devil-presides-there landscapes. This interval of softness (the golf course pozzine, trickle of water, the grazing wild horses), this was a lonely landscape. The difference between one tree and no trees is germane. Imagine suffering in hell for eternity, as Ulysses did so unjustly, and coping, as one would have to, and suddenly a door opens and Dante, one of the living, drops by, a creature of hope and goodness. Desolation can be an easier thing to navigate than loneliness.

At the top of the rather freakish red rock ridge—the French word for these, often in a formation that looks like the head of an Indian or bunny rabbit or, what? a spooky goblin, is *calanches*—coming down to Lac Ninu, we rest for a minute at the Col de St. Pierre. An unpicturesque chapel to Saint Peter constructed of mortar and granite blocks, it is something to lean upon and get the view below on both sides, but there is a single tree, one of those pines buffeted all its life by a one-way Mistral wind, that has been deformed into a grasping, cowering scrubby thing. Yes, it has shade to offer, but to take advantage of that shade seems a crime—all of Ruskin's warnings about the pathetic fallacy notwithstanding: this tree suffers.

But we don't have calanches and scraggy trees for long. In the lusher woods into which we descend grow lamb's ear and big white tree fungi. And hellebore, my nemesis! Every time I see hellebore, it seems, something bad happens. I'll lose Petra around a corner, or I'll twist my ankle, or I'll find no natural spring where my guidebook promised a natural spring, or I'll run into one of the two shirtless Rooster men who devour the GR20 in great gulps, exhausting themselves by quick-stepping up a mountainside and passing us by in a whoosh (then collapsing exhausted somewhere, adding an even more unphotogenic aspect to the chapel of Saint Peter, say, so that we'll overtake them and have to be passed again, over and over, all day, always with a sense with the overtaking of big red tail-feathers in our face. Their French is an inscrutable patois from somewhere, and I enjoy not understanding a word of it, although I'm sure they are saying things to me like, "Your pack is too heavy" or "Those are the wrong shoes" or "You're breathing in the wrong way."). Or perhaps I'll begin to admit to myself that I have finally, after all these hikes I have taken, bitten off more than I can chew. But I've thought of this before; I didn't need hellebore to give in to that weakness.

There is this lovely pink mountain flower, wild cyclamen.

Yes, a minor key. The song I keep singing all day is "Blue skies, shining on me. Nothing but blue skies." Nothing. A C chord, just about the only thing. "Do I see."

And when we arrive in Manganu and settle into our tent (relatively) clean, a little bit of that lonely minor key in the bridge of "Blue Skies" still lingers. The next day's walk to Petra Piana will be difficult though pretty, but there's no reward at the end of that étape, according to our guidebook, not the sort Petra and I prefer. It's all hardtack and tea bags. Petra is losing steam, and if it rains, we will be kinda fucked. What revives us is another nudie dip in pools of fresh mountain water along a string of rocks. A little chilly but so delicious. You can pretend there's no refugio around the corner full of macho shitheads (mostly, they're French and Dutch macho shitheads) slapping each other on the back because—why?—they can still shovel meat down their throats?

I feel that if my identity as an American is revealed I'll be descended upon. Time was, when I met Petra, I had a little social curiosity to me, and the jibes I'd get about my country and its activities in the world would be endurable. But that was Love During the Clinton Administration, and this is a time to be so still, like a frog in a winter stream, that they can't even detect your heartbeat. I beg Petra to continue identifying me as a Canadian. She agrees, as long as she can tell everybody that she is Austrian. Two amphibians.

I think I'm also more and more disturbed about Corsican autonomy, which goes beyond the violent and gets childish. The more I know, the more I have no right or power to say anything at all. But if the subject of nationalism is approached from a stance of weakness—saying I don't feel part of the ruling party either, and then saying to myself, "Darling, you must force yourself" to feel part of it—may I be excused?

The night before, at the Soviet ski resort, three Corsican gentlemen watched Petra and me make a mockery of the crossword puzzle section of *Le Corse: Votre Hebdo* (Corsica: Your Weekly), and they used this to strike up some kind of conversation with us. "Where's this guy from?" they asked Petra, when it was clear that she was in charge. It is my burden to explain, every time, that I am not much of a friend of George Bush. What is the best way to diffuse this issue? It makes me sleepy. But we chatted at length with one of the old local guys, and Petra heard that there are millions of Corsicans living in other parts of the world. "In exile," it would seem. Would they ever come home if Corsica were made an independent nation? Petra asked what some of the typical names were out there. He said Santoni, Rossi, and the like. In the villages, they call after each other with an "O'" at the beginning of their names—"O'Doni!" "O'Ma!" (Marie, a common name in this Catholic country, as is "O'Jo-Bate!," short for Jean Baptiste). Rossi, Santoni—these are names, I notice later when flipping through my guidebook, of very active, if dead now, patriots of autonomy.

If I were to stand up for what my own country has been up to in order to protect itself, this would seem more inexcusable than waving the Corsican flag with its blindfolded and perhaps decapitated Moor waving in the air. Patriotism. I have an odd rule about naming towns: if they're big, like London or Rome or Paris, then I call them the name my own language gives them, and let the others do the same: Londres is fine, Roma will understand when I call it Rome, the people there in Paris will recognize themselves when I do not say

Pahr-ees. But the French call Ascu Stegnu "Haute Asco," and in my journals and photobook I am careful to use the Corsican spelling. Those names need more protection, lest travelers destroy what they seek. I like to see the Basque and Corsican and Catalan flags fly: Go team! But the poet Browning said it best for me: "Patriotism is the easiest virtue for a man to acquire."

Tonight, in Manganu, in a tent, there are no lights to read by, no bar to have a nightcap and chat with the locals. We go to bed early. It's a place in the crevice in the rocks. We see a cow, alone, high above us while swimming in the pool, and worry, but he isn't worried. Nor is the black Lab, missed last night, but camping next door, on the other side of the aspen. In front of them, the Dancing Bears. Seven French ladies with little silver packets of freeze-dried dinner have hit upon the brilliant idea (and by brilliant, I mean pretty brilliant, since we have no unstolen utensils ourselves) of pouring boiling water directly into the packets. Last I saw, they were sitting at a picnic table, packets all in a row, waiting expectantly. The Dutch guy has generously offered to wear his shirt in the kitchen. Two Dutch guys who may be gay (Petra saw matching rings) play a complicated role-playing card game. The lone French guy who always passes us and we pass him back is wringing out his socks. The three Australians (or are they Kiwis?) still bicker. A breeze blows through and puts out the feverish little sunburn fire in my face. From somewhere on the other side, a gleeful chorus of "Happy Birthday"— "Bon Ann-i-vers-aire!"—by French girls who aren't tired at all by the long walks. Pipe smoke, just a little, from one of the old (definitely, them) Brits. That, and a green lawn smell, and that cow groaning up in the mountainside: maybe he *is* in trouble!

On my tent, hooded like and called a Cobra, hangs a zappy "sale" tag that proves we paid the six euros for the site and use of the showers and kitchen. My clothes dry on alder. Ancient alder and beech trees full of burls and fright-wig branches rustle.

Somebody is laughing at all their own jokes, a zipper on a tent goes—up; somebody is up. Clouds pass over, threaten rain, then change their minds. There is a slight French guy with legs like logs and a voice that could be mistaken for thunder.

The Dancing Bears are making amorous cootchie-cootchie noises in their tent, but what do they think will happen? What kind of energy do they have? And what will they do when I take a whiz just to the right of their tent? My tent flaps are full of clever toggles; the space age has been applied only to airplanes and super-lightweight tents that break down to the size of a playing card. Everything, including you, must be clever when camping: the order in which you hang your clothes on a single peg in the shared shower stall; the way you arrange the rocks outside so water, if it rains, flows around your tent and down the hill; the timing of the Sleepinol so that it hits your blood and takes you away at the end of a page in your journal, the end of natural light.

Manganu to Petra Piana

This is the chapter in which more wild pigs start to show up. Or, as the Australian guy in the tent behind the scrub alder says when the stray dog begins chasing the two pigs through the tenting section, biting them in the ass and making the squeal of, well, a pig: "Chroist! Eets a peeg een the bivouac!" And the gardien comes tumbling after. Petra says that Frau Dancing Bear in a tent down the way is complaining in German to her boyfriend, "But you assured me there would be no more wild pigs!"

But I am getting ahead of myself.

Earlier, after nightfall in Manganu, we have been given up to one of the famous flash thunder-and-lightning storms of these mountains. The farther we go down the GR20, the more we hear about and see ruined things, both man- and nature-made, zapped by

Thor's hammer. With so much damage done selectively by the trained finger of forked lightning, it is possible on Corsica that damage, too, be both nature- and man-made, and it wouldn't take much college training, I think, to become a rather effective arsonist, given the natural way the lightning can single out an item in the landscape.

Who could prove, after all, that it was a human, not nature, who incinerated that private refuge built to compete with your monopoly on the trekking business? There is a lot of this burning business running around Corsica. Later on the trail, we will find one such site of the remains of an unlucky private enterprise, a hut built to shelter us walkers and a complete suck on the local bergerie's business, sadly bumped off by a sharp fork of lightning, or perhaps a contract fulfilled by Penelope "Pyro" Perkins. But again, I am getting ahead of myself.

Our guidebooks carry specific extensive instructions on what to do if caught in a sudden lightning storm, which include jettisoning anything metal and avoiding close contact with fellow hikers. Petra's book also includes a sketch of a hiker assuming the flash-lightning safety position, which looks very duck-and-cover, and about as bootless.

Besides the lightning, there is also, of course, rain. It's fun to hear the merry rhythm of raindrops on a tent roof when you're snug in bed; but eventually you have to go out, and on this morning before the pig incident, we take the tent down even though it is still wet and the grooves in the stakes are caked with mud, and we plod into our day's hike crabby, unfresh, and even exhausted. Lucky for us the rain never returns, and we are able to enjoy the spectacular views promised to us in the guidebook. In fact, the overcast drab enhances some of the landmarks, clouding out the pesky nuisance and distraction of *other* lovely landmarks drawing our eyes into the distant background.

One set of toothy mountains, stately and severely imperious as

mitered bishops or organ pipes or Klansmen, create a protected surround, much like the place where Brünnhilde sleeps, waiting for
Siegfried's wake-up smooch. When I get pictures developed and
show them to friends back home, one will remark, "This looks like
the place where you made an appointment to see the Devil." But I
am getting *way* ahead of myself.

"If we climb above the clouds," I tell Petra, "they can't rain on
us." I am speaking of the clouds, not the Klansmen. Mostly, we
climb into the clouds, and clouds are cold, clammy and cold.

This also makes it possible, by some twist of nature, for me to be
able to smell myself, smell any body odor when I sweat and exert. It's
an odd thing, disconcerting, like hearing your own voice on a tape
recorder. I think of this to tell Petra: "Cavemen never heard their
own voices on a tape recorder."

Petra is still grouchy, thinking about the wet tent. "You don't
know that for sure," she tries. I try to josh her into a better mood by
telling her that our next stop for the night is named after her, and
her amazing abilities on the keyboard. My jokes are lost in translation and cloud cover.

When we arrive at Petra Piana, we, Petra and I, are tired and dirty
living among the pigs. I blow some euros on a big hunk of *gâteau
de fruits,* a cake with dried fruit in it, a fruitcake, if you will, and a
bottle of overpriced, burroed-in wine, and I'm counting on the first
item to lift us up and the second to knock us out this night. The
French influence on wilderness manifests itself in the officious transfer of planck (quotidian) wine, imported via liter-sized Fanta bottles
or perhaps boxes, into genuine wine bottles stoppered with a wad of
paper. The poor, trusty tent is a thing of clay and wattles made, after
all this dust and rain. Would it were as sturdy as a cabin at Innisfree,
but the weight of our human hornet's nest threatens to bring it
down with its own lopsided weight. Mud slowly dries, cracks, and
flakes into puzzle pieces that I pull off one by one.

I have layered on the Bullfrog chapstick, and it does little to stop the drying-out process. It's dry here, Arizona dry, let's-make-raisins-dry—my nose bleeds, my lips chap.

"They could find us sitting in this tent looking at this map, totally mummified, ten thousand years from now," I tell Petra, after we study the long, long trail blazed for us for the morrow. Without even a smile, Petra leaves the tent. My jokes are the conversational equivalent of "I know an old woman who swallowed a fly." And I am not even able to cheer myself up with lame jokes. The jokes are not even lame: they are unjokes.

And then it is Petra who lifts my spirits immeasurably by coming to the tent with a modest proposal: tomorrow, instead of going on to ugly, inescapable Onda, we stop three hours from Petra Piana at a famous shepherd's bergerie where they'll serve us a fantastic lunch.

"And then," Petra hesitates, because she thinks I am a purist. But hasn't she known me for years? Doesn't she know that I am anything but a purist, or perfectionist? Or lack any kind of discipline at all? And I make a face reminding her of this, and she, emboldened by all she reads there, speaks with confidence and speed, "And then we will take the cute little narrow-gauge train to Vizzavona, where we can sleep in a hotel with curtains and rugs and little chocolates and maybe something salty."

I wish I had thought of it first. This, this gives me hope and joy—the possibility of the three tenets of the Creed of the Knights of Sleepy Justice: Flee! Regroup! Rest! Laugh and run away to the pampering we have earned, earned with day jobs, dammit, and live to charge ahead another day to the second half of our journey, much more to our style of walking.

Perhaps this seems like cheating to purists. I am not a purist, and I haven't any purist friends. Or if they are friends, they are sent to Coventry soon after the stench of continence is sniffed from their big baby diapers.

I must say that, this far down the trail, I am feeling overwhelmed. Each day has been so challenging I can barely manage thinking about going on for another week. These frightening climbs up mountain peaks, lifting myself up thousands of feet over boulders and then slogging down through loose scree and whatever else is on the trail—how long can this go on?

This is such a different kind of walking than I'd done on the Chemin/Camino and all the other roads. This is rough stuff. I come down into each refuge with arms as tired as my feet. My feet aren't flattened by long étapes, but various joints—ankles, knees, like that—are being asked to be agile, I am asked for an agility of the head and body. I am getting better at it, but a rest—

"A rest!" I exclaim to Petra.

—and that is when the wild pig runs through the slapdash tent town, perhaps to italicize the very rightness, the sanity, of our decision. Now, by "wild pig," I don't mean wild pig, not the boar they make into delicacies of every salty and stewy sort. Not wild pig, but a pig run wild. The Corsicans tend to let their various livestock run free all summer, hoping that laziness and gravity will keep them from scaling the mountains we seem hell-bent on scaling. This kind of passive farming cuts down on feed and upkeep. *Faux eleveurs,* indeed. The beasts are rounded up later in November for slaughter, fattened off the fat of the land. As a foe of all purists, I am not judging here. I'm just saying.

So these wild pigs, as with the ponies at Lac de Nino or the stray cow at Manganu, they are fairly accustomed to the presence of backpackers and stay out of our way—or plop themselves in the middle of the trail and have to be stepped over. They still startle me with size, and when encumbered with a backpack, the idea of being charged by a feral pig comes as a vivid negative fantasy, a fantasy I rerun in my mind like a little film loop, as incessantly as "I know an old woman who swallowed a fly." They only seem to run away, or run around when chased by a gardien's dog.

I am not disheartened by the possibility of thees peeg een the bivouac knocking down my tent, and in anticipation for a trip into town, I clip my toenails while watching the peeg scramble down the shantytown lanes we've made with guylines and tent stakes. The screams of startled humans is so close to the squeals of near-feral pigs that I can hardly tell the difference. And that poor, poor German Dancing Bear couple—they have to learn how to secure their tent properly when there are wild animals around. And my toenails have been cutting holes into my hiking socks! It is amazing how just a little personal grooming can go a long way in lifting one's spirits, even if it's done on a mossy rock over dried ferns. I look past the mossy rock to our paper-stoppered *vin rouge*. If that pig so much as makes the wine ripple in the bottle, I am going to open up a can of imported Canadian whoop-ass on him. Her. American. Whatever.

"Would you like to borrow my toenail clippers when I'm finished?" I ask Petra, who is also growing bored with the trotting trotters.

She gives me a look as if I were the peeg een the bivouac: how dare I suggest that we share the same grooming implements. Or perhaps she is holding out for a pedicure in Vizzavona. She applies lipstick, her trademark gesture of desperate dignity in high places.

The pig keeps running around, but soon everybody ignores it (Mankind gets used to everything, damn Him!), and as my mother taught me long ago, it does, as does anything ignored (bullies, lovers, teeth), eventually go away.

Petra Piana to Onda

The French Rooster men see everything as a problem along the GR20. If I could speak to them in French (and I can't, not with that accent, and not with mine), and if I could speak to them only as if I had problems to solve, we would get along just fine. I try to be friendly for half an hour by keeping up with them as they stride, this morning, from Petra Piana. I tell myself that, as long as they keep their shirts on, I'll stick to a short career as an ambassador, and since it is cold and we walk in rain ponchos, not only do they wear their shirts but also grandiose, tailor-made rain ponchos that make them look like matching ghosts floating down the switchbacks. They point up at the scramble we are about to surmount and say it is just like the Cirque de la Solitude: "Moo, moo, moo, *même probleme,*" same problem. And so they open their guidebooks that I can see are so particular that every footstep seems to be recorded there, and their maps, amazingly, are marked down to the house and shepherd's hut. What are those little dots on their maps? Are those . . . are those . . . are those *sheep?* I am reminded of the cheat sheets published for major video games, which, a friend points out, are called "walk-throughs." I can't wait for them to study the sheep dots and translate their "Moo moo moo *inutile,*" and so I seek out the poncho ghost that is Petra in the long line of trekkers and resume not being friends with the Roosters.

We have all awakened in the same rain cloud, and for better and worse, Petra and I were able to bring our tent down in a break between showers. As we stagger down the next passage of scree, the rain comes again. No lightning, but a frigid, you-left-the-freezer-door-open-and-now-it-is-defrosting-down-your-back rain. "An elephant is pissing," says Petra.

"Elephant piss would at least be warm," I counter. I've had no coffee: this is the first of my litany of comically hellish details (my epitaph, I would like to declare now, if it isn't "Tends to Ramble" or "Good on the Uphills" or "A Whole New Kind of Losing" should be, I think, "He'd Have Found Something Else to Complain About"). The downhills, it has been established, are not my strong suit, and when the French Roosters, problem solved, begin to tramp down upon us on the narrow switchbacks, and rain starts to come down in sheets, cold, cold forty-degree rain, rain that makes the rocks like ice cubes and the switchbacks an ever-culminating river, I pull my poncho down around my naked knees.

And having a rain poncho that is not tailored to my body and backpack and is far too big for the both of us, and what with me tripping over it when I don't gather it up like an embarrassed scornful lady gathering in her skirts, and while zigzagging ever downward for an hour, two hours, so that the zigzag course is a river near what you think is the bottom but is not anywhere near the bottom: that, also, is also not the end of the trials.

For what we think is the valley bottom is just a plateau with a little shepherd's bergerie and some flatness but, surprise!—the meadow is now a soupy lake of sheep shit! Marvelous! My feet are soaking wet, the Roosters have abandoned us, without a solution to whatever the problem is, Petra is struggling half a kilometer back, my backpack is about five pounds heavier from the water held by our tent and my undried clothes, and—what do you think I am thinking?

I am thinking that we are better off, ha ha, than those poor schmucks up top who didn't take their tent down before the rain came again. But it is I who am an example of surpassing denial to think such stuff, because I always need this feeling of superiority to get on. Is this all part of what the Hindus call samsara?

It is two hours of this slog of displeasure later, and everything is getting more wet and more ugly and more slippery, until we come to the Bergerie de u Tolla, run by a jolly old shepherd who it turns out can't do math but does all the important things quite well (and by the important things I mean that he cures meat and ages cheese), and his wife, who speaks perfectly good English and does fine omelets, math, and coffee in the hut alongside their home and bergerie. These two are so famous and beloved on the GR20 that they show up in all the guidebooks, English, Swiss, German, French, Belgian, Spanish. They are Jean and Michele Castagnoli, and coming to their home seems another kind of enchantment, for the moment we open their gate, a cat chases two roosters out like the nuisances they are (allegory?), and the sun comes out, and we are handed two big bowls of coffee without even asking for them.

Petra and I and half a dozen other wet pilgrims spread our wet things along the barbed wire fence to dry. I see a fire salamander, then two more, said to be rare, with their slick, black, cute, moist bodies splotched with yellow spots, as if they have rested under a ladder while somebody painted a fire hydrant. They are my good luck sign, strength against the serrated hellebore leaves.

A small batch of older Swiss people, probably around my parents' age, settle in. The berger sells us his good homemade *brocciu* from his cool little hut cave, and a *lonzu,* too, the delicious soft-cured smoked filet of pork, and it will make for deluxe picnics for the next week. But he can't do the addition. It's okay: he's gotten on so well in his life without math or English. Perhaps I could, too. Mrs. Castagnoli tallies up, and we come to an agreement.

We dawdle for more than an hour. The sun dries things out so quickly the storm seems a misreading of the guidebooks. The feeling comes back into my fingertips. I frank the whole episode with too many photos, including one of Jean and Michele, and it's only weeks later, after I get the film developed, that I realize that in every shot, Jean has covered his face, superstitious, no doubt, about having his image taken away from him. But I am, again, getting ahead of myself.

Even my guidebooks speak of taking superstition seriously here on Corsica. It seems to infect a person, me with my fear of hellebore and growing obsession with the fire salamander. The father and son shepherds at Bergeries de Vallone have given me a whole amusing list of cultural facts, and by facts I mean superstitions. There are very strict rules about the evil eye, for example, about seeing a weasel and planning on rain, while snow is brought on by the braying of an ox. The father could tell the future in a goat's shoulder blades. "Corsicans do not tell stories on Mondays," I divined through slow translation at one point but never was sure what he meant by that—didn't lie on Mondays? Didn't talk on Mondays? If this had been a Monday, might he not have told me all this? "The priest always gives the pigs blessings before they are rounded up and taken to the market after a divine procession in town." "And when a child is born"—I remember that he pointed to his son—"the husband is the one who takes to his bed for a rest of a few days." I thought of his wife chopping and boiling and cooking in the back kitchen. That son of his, easy with the myrtle liquor and forgiving of the Yankee, all of eighteen years, smiled.

I sat with the Castagnoli coffee reminiscing about the other shepherds, how, outside, through murky windows, a lovely sun set over the fortune-telling goats, Nehi-orange and wild-rose pink. And in those windows, Ziplock storage bags filled with water and hung by a string, in the belief that the flies would see themselves magnified, like big bully flies, and be frightened off.

"More coffee?" Petra interprets the third query from Mrs. Castagnoli. But I was getting behind myself, having nostalgia for two days ago.

"Non," I decide, and strap on my dryer, lighter pack and say goodbye to our saviors and continue to recall that *other* shepherd hut, what I thought I couldn't, after so much of the myrtle liquor. I recalled how the son was eager to explain away his blondish hair and blue eyes. Being from Porto Vecchio, he had told me, where such blonde stuff is common, "I come from Vikings." I was fascinated, too, by the way, on islands, every town is a port town, if it is not a resort.

Why is it that I find myself most satisfied, in all my travels, with these tours of islands? The concentrations of wild superstitions? I have set foot on Madeira, most of the Azores, Eleuthera, Sardegna, Mallorca, Menorca. England, for that matter. For one thing, they seem finite, they give rise to the belief that I can make a visit and see something like all of it, get a sense of the whole thing. There is a coziness to islands, and they put me in a snug frame of mind. And then come the resorts.

The ones who stay on the islands after the resorts move in, they have an edge of island fever, exhibited in the mad way they drive cars down narrow blind alleys. But there's an enviable purity among islands, as if a culture might be preserved without national borders, without an official autonomy, where McDonald's won't find it economically feasible to set up shop and American moviemakers won't film or exhibit. That purity shows itself in language and superstitions and even the way all the dogs seem related—because they are!

Some islands don't seem like islands, while some mainland places seem islandlike. Vancouver seems ensorcelled by water, while Vancouver Island felt to me a continent. San Francisco is insular as a peninsula and touts all the exoticism islands often have. I have made my walks along the lip of a volcano that had erupted inside a volcano in the Azores, and lowered a prepped and stuffed whole chicken into a boiling hot hole in that brewing island heat. I've walked along the elaborate man-made levadas of Madeira, hundreds of miles of small canals built to catch rainwater off the mountaintops to send down to the vineyards. I saw fish swim their way up to the tops of those mountains through the stony troughs. I watched seals surround my rowboat near Norton Island in northern Maine, and a moose swim, ridiculously buoyant.

But all through these islands, I have felt the same ghostly sense, that the whole place might be relatively abandoned compared to previous times. They have more buildings than they need, and all the population seems heading away from home. On Corsica, this is reinforced by a couple of things, starting with the general exodus of its population (260,000 Corsicans dwell on Corsica, but there are over 800,000 living on the European continent, mostly in Marseille, Nice, and Paris), as we had learned at the Soviet ski resort from the cantankerous gentlemen who insisted on buying us drinks. Also, there is a tricky business in the Corsican family law called *l'Indivision,* in which, in order to protect the family holdings, it is forbidden to sell off any land or house or holdings to people outside the blood relations. That's a little bit of the vendetta coming back to bite itself in the ass: because so many family members leave for the mainland, there are, in any given village, dozens and dozens of substantial houses closed up and empty, nearly ghost towns given up for an archaic law.

And there's this other thing that seems to have everything to do with the tradition of vendetta: Corsicans bury their kin "Roman Style," and by Roman Style, they mean pretty much anywhere they want. We walk along the GR20, and every once in a while, we come across an old elaborate mausoleum. Old, but well tended, with fresh paint and tended hedges, and sometimes even fresh flowers, or at least planted flowers. I marvel at it; who is making the effort to tend them? I lift my nose in the air to sniff for a town. It sounds corny, but when you have been out in the wilderness for a bit of time, you actually can smell the smoke, perfume, garbage, and b.o. of civilization. Even without being in a cloud.

On islands, however, I can't. Perhaps the sea air blows it off, like smog. And still we see more graves. They can be found along the sides of freeways, at the edges of towns, in a garden, or by a shepherd's hut. They are lonesome things. Has Corsica, I wonder as I walk by a mausoleum now, half a kilometer past the Onda refuge, become a necropolis?

But then, what intrigues me is the push and tug of this feeling of bereft abandonment and lush possibility. There is the maquis that grows back faster than it can be burned. And walking among crazy riots of wildflowers, many indigenous to just this place, you tend to gasp: anything could grow here, everything fruits.

It is not the first time that we walk precariously along the lip of a canyon on a not-up-to-code trail skirting a cliff. If this part of the GR20 we are walking were in the United States, it would not be in the United States. Park rangers would install a chain-link fence or reroute the piste. But this is Europe, where they weed out the recklessly foolish and ungainly by letting them dance with death, thus. And by the recklessly foolish and ungainly, guess who I mean.

Really, I've had no trouble with these little patches of trail, here or anywhere else I have walked. My guidebook has warned me repeatedly that people with a fear of high places should not consider walking the GR20, because mostly, that's what this is. I have a much stronger dread of walking along freeways, where the recklessly foolish and ungainly are whizzing by in metal torpedoes just half a foot away from me, and watching the way people drive on Corsica, I'll choose Dead Man's Crevass any day.

Nevertheless, what comes over me at a certain point of this segment is what can only be called "a cumulative case of the willies," a lifetime's vertigo all stored up in a lymph node and then set loose by the simple trip over a bit of loose gravel. I look down, I look at the way ahead of me where south-to-north walkers are coming toward us single file and must be reckoned with, and then behind me, where north-to-south walkers press me forward with an urgent need to avoid bottlenecks. There is no way but down, I think, and I imagine myself squeezed over the lip, bone-crusher-bird food. Because vertigo is not so much a fear of height but the mind's feeble imagination conjuring the drop, the doing of the deed.

Sometimes my mind shuffles up to the precipice of any number of bad memories, perhaps in order to get my own attention when I'm feeling overconfident, too much in command. I remember that in the movie version of *The Lion in Winter,* Hepburn's Eleanor of Aquitaine finally gets her son Richard the Lionhearted to admit he is her own flesh by taking a nail and running it hard down her own arm and drawing blood. I do the same to myself with bad memories, or with my bad memory. All the places I've nearly had terrible accidents, all the chem lab spills and near-accidents with cars, they all come to me there on the ridge an hour out of Onda.

I also think of feeble rescues, of falling off this ridge and grabbing hold of, say, a dozen Mylar birthday balloons or, more realistically (more realistically!), those strange hawklike birds that circle above us along the trail, to buoy myself up and finding my solution woefully inadequate to the need, just adding to the vertigo. I've heard about what happens in falling dreams—you catch yourself by waking up, and the superstition is that if you don't catch yourself this way, you die in your sleep. To do this in waking life, to fully imagine the fall from a Corsican cliff (and also the clever subsequent rescue) would be a real success of the imagination. So vertigo, its definition, may be, in the end, a horrifying revelation of the inadequacy of my own imagination to save me. If I could only imagine myself saved from this imagined fall off this cliff, I think as I let a south-north hiker pass me on the inside of the cliff trail, if my imagination were good enough, I could live. And that's the opinion I carry of myself as I get past this little bit of the day's road again, alive.

I can just barely make out, in the distance, two hikers traveling south to north, clambering over a ridge. As if in a Beckett fiction, I turn back to Petra, trudging behind me. "Look, we're not alone!"

"We're never alone," Petra mock-mopes. I don't know whether she's complaining about the Rooster men or me. I don't ask.

"Yes, but these are new hikers! Soon we'll meet them and we will say hello and we will hear about all the news in Vizzavona and perhaps they'll have a little chocolate for you or a little coffee for me, and we can discuss literature and art and maybe one of them will be attractive and will want to date us!"

"You will be lucky if they are not banditos of Aïtone—they will probably push us down in the maquis and take our backpacks."

"They can have mine," I volunteer.

By the time I have finished my long ratcheted-up fantasy, the two hikers, silent, with hardly enough energy to nod hello, pass us (or we pass them) and with algebraic swiftness, are just as far behind us as they were ahead of us. "That didn't take very long," I say.

"They heard you talking too much and now they are running away, stupid American boy," Petra says, but she smiles and proceeds to talk to me for a while; she must know I'm tired of my own head's nonsense.

People say that people who walk a lot are not walking but running away by walking, but you're not running away from anything by walking. You think a lot. You think too much. It's just you, and your thoughts, and if it's not your thoughts, it's "I know an old lady who swallowed a fly." If it's not too strenuous a type of walk, you tend to think. About failures back home, shortcomings, unfinished business. People prefer not to think. They prefer the strenuous walk. Those who show the weakness of thinking are humiliated, or humiliatable, because thoughts are a threat. The solution is meditation, ritual, walking as prayer, which is what it settles into after a while.

Besides, walking puts you in the way of people (often, more in the way than you'd like when walking single file along the lip of a canyon) and therefore puts you in the way of distractions, of story. I was making an excursion with my friend Robert, who taught at New Mexico State University, and he wanted to show me Ciudad Juarez, the great crazy border town, another kind of port city, however land-locked they may be. He parked the car at the frontier and we walked across, so that we would not be subject to deep cleansing levels of official inspection conducted upon cars entering and exiting. On the bridge over an arroyo, we were descended upon by an American guy of the unshaven sort. If he had been on the GR20 I would have considered him an accomplished trekker; in the city of Juarez, I considered him probably homeless: same difference. He began to offer an extravagant story as we walked, his explanations matching the dactyls and anapests of our walk, and it was amusing to us for the uninventable detail: his son had gotten into a bar fight and he the father did not have money to bail him out. Could we make a contribution so that the two of them could go home?

This is a standard story, with variations, I hear from homeless people in the city: they are down on their luck, and what they need is a bus ticket home, and they are sixty-five cents short of that ticket, could I help out? The next day, there he is again, still sixty-five cents short—always, like Dante's idea of Ulysses (or Tennyson's), always heading home but never getting there.

When Robert gave him a dollar and I gave him a dollar too—we were so amused we felt that we had just paid for a performance—he thanked us by staying with us on the walk for a while, regaling us with a certain kind of joke that only men can tell, half-corn, half-naughty ("Did you hear that Suzuki, Kawasaki, and Yamaha are all teaming up to build a super-motorcycle? They're calling it the Sukamakaki!") We fed him dollar bills like a jukebox or a stripper until we had crossed fully into Juarez, and that was the most adventure we had there, except for the part where I decided to get a cheap haircut from a Mexican barbershop.

I take this literary detour into Juarez because this is another thing I love about walking. People, fellow walkers, reduced to the roles of minor characters. Other than Petra, I never see anybody long enough to know much more about them than a few salient character details. Walking is a back-to-nature business, but it also conjures a moving city full of secondary Dickensian grotesques, or the long scrollwork line of figures decorating an Egyptian wall, or a Greek vase, coming to me single file, every one of them with a posture or antic or good joke to tell. They seem immortal that way, those still unravish'd brides of quietness, always on the trail: Lula the dog, the retired British general, the chain-smoking Italian, the man rustling up bail for his bar-belligerent son, the Roosters. They don't change, they are always out there, there on the trail, unravish'd and immortal. More immortal, in fact, than I.

Vizzavona is considered the exact midway point of the GR20. It is the site of a weensy health spa and a big Swiss-style chalet of a hotel. It all seems dwarfed, however, by Monte d'Oro, the big slab of the biggest mountain on Corsica. Because it has a spa, it seems as if a bit of the resort beach has been dragged inland, and it's as big a switch in geographical terrain as the forest is to the mountains are to the pozzines, all those flashy expensive cars in the parking lot and overdressed helmet-haired European ladies with trashy expensive purses mingling with a few hikers. You can't see Calvi from Vizzavona.

So we do not stay at the chalet, and it is there in Vizzavona that the little narrow-gauge train, called by Corsicans "U Trinighellu," crosses our path, not for the first time, but certainly for the first convenient time. Petra and I had planned to book a room in one of the other hotels here, but they are all overpriced, and when we see the schedule and price on the trains, it seems a simple thing to jump aboard and ride away from the GR20 for a few days to do all that regrouping and pedicuring, the washing of our clothes, the drying of our tent, the eating well and viewing the Citadel of Corte, considered the national heart of Corsica. So when U Trinighellu draws up, a miniature locomotive pulling miniature cars on miniature tracks, it feels like we are getting a ride on Santa's train to the North Pole, and we only wish that some avuncular conductor would take our picture on Santa's knee right there at the platform.

Instead, it seems to barely slow down—as if we are running onto the car like hobos or that guy on the border at Juarez (which we probably smell like) and stowing away. It then picks up an unwarranted speed, as all public transportation on islands, especially those with winding, narrow roads and tracks, seems to do, and we speed through dozens of tunnels in the mountains. One feels a little abashed when backtracking on a road of iron in a matter of minutes what one has covered on foot over the course of days. The way we are going? We are going backward, and second times never go well. Unless, of course, you are going someplace new.

The train is crowded. I'd read in my guidebook that there was talk of closing the system down a couple of decades before, due to lack of use, but I couldn't imagine that now; it isn't just tourism filling up the seats, for there are plenty of locals who have seen the spectacular scenery out the windows for far too long to be impressed any more, and have their noses buried in *La Corse: Votre Hebdo*.

Velocity upon velocity: by seven in the evening, we are billeted at the Hotel Sampiero, modestly priced and with reservations for a fine meal up at the top of the citadel stairs.

5

Why I Walk

The Rake's Progress

What is this strange madness, this mania for sleeping each night in a different bed?
Petrarch, to his young secretary

1. I was surprised to find, though now I know I shouldn't have been, Ulysses eternally punished in Dante's dank oubliette of an Inferno— deep down, even, at the eighth circle, among the hypocrites, thieves, and schismatics. After reading this, I remained defensively respectful to Ulysses, who always stopped to have a nice meal, even when his pals turned into pigs and One-Eyed Jack breathed down his neck. I discovered later that there's a reason for this misdamnation, and it's not just because Dante was a man who was only able to spin poetry out of pure cussedness. It seems that neither Dante nor any of his middle-aged contemporaries had the complete text of the *Odyssey,* and as far as Dante knew, Ulysses never bothered to get home to Penelope, and Dante believed Ulysses to be a love 'em and leave 'em kind of guy:

> Not fondness for my son, nor any claim
> Of reverence for my father, nor love I owed
> Penelope, to please her could overcome
> My longing for experience of the world,
> Of human vices and virtue.

Ulysses' journey, like Dante's, is often considered a fable about the soul's journey toward education; the return home is symbolic of the soul's deliverance. To be a pilgrim, then, to have a specific goal in travel, in order to bring something valuable back home, is proof of spiritual superiority. To ramble on, partying hearty and cruising the avenue and shirking responsibilities of family—*that* will put you deep in the bowels of H-E-double-toothpicks.

2. There is a gushing, nearly religious phrase I often read in personal accounts of foot travel to wondrous places: "walking saved me." Well. Walking hasn't saved me. It's nothing so rapturous or dramatic for me. That sort of statement means that the crisis has ended; things just don't end. The stuff that one needs to be saved from, that goes on once you've returned from the road, and after a while I figured out that it's another road, a new wondrous place, and that's exactly what I need to jump right back into. Walking, for me, is not a passion, it hasn't made me happy, nor has it saved me. It is the "and then, and then, and then" of living, of party after party, of longing for experience of the world.

3. It seems a circumscribed, even brief period of time that I will, for the sake of trying to document the undocumentable, call "1988 to 1993" five years, in San Francisco anyway, in which my weekends were spent partying hearty. After all, people were dying. In those five years, science, as usual, got ahead of itself, and had invented ways to detect the HIV virus but had found no way to stop its kudzulike flourishing. What could one do but plan rueful, ironic parties in which entire life savings were spent on rented golden halls and exotic kegs of imported beers? Or publish naughty zines like *Diseased Pariah News,* in which the positive editor bragged about being the eighth in an ever-lengthening line of sick editors? Every issue of DPN featured a poz centerfold model (turn-ons: aerosolized pentamadine, long naps, honesty; turn-offs: Stone Temple Pilots, dementia, AZT), and a cooking section called "Get Fat! Don't Die!" full of high-calorie recipes.

In hindsight, mapping this out on the page, it must seem that we were all cynical. It didn't seem so at the time, although those many fairy tales always had the same ending, and glib begets glib, so why not meet ferocity with ferocity? That valley of the shadow of death was heretofore uncharted, and it was with magazines like *Diseased Pariah News* that we created our own travel guides, since there were no cultural or moral maps to offer direction.

Now, of course, nobody goes to that fairyland, and the maps molder in library archives among the other antiquities: "Here Be Dragons." Those map cases are hardly ever opened, and nobody will speak of these things.

By these things, I mean the things medicine and technology always invent and people call progress, while the moral maps needed to guide them through this terra incognita have not been drawn up, and the old maps become inapplicable. A Sikh must wear his turban but legally needs to wear a helmet to drive a motorcycle. You can find out nearly everything about your baby in utero, but if you find out that the fetus inside you is misshapen, will you keep it or abort it? What maddens me about fundamentalists of every stripe is the way they enjoy modern invention, yet demand that the old laws, conjured when the earth was thought flat and birds didn't migrate but slept through winter under the ice, continue to measure human goodness. We live among choices that, as Petra puts it, cavemen never knew.

A Catholic wants his heart to beat forever, but stem cells are made from undeveloped bits of babies. An Orthodox Jew wakes up each morning and thanks God he was not born a woman, but enjoys the income his wife produces at work. A Taliban man of Islam will enforce his isolated purity of vision with the Kalashnikov, a rifle invented by an infidel. A doctor (and Larry Kramer, for that matter) could tell you that you had a fatal virus in your body, and though there is nothing you can really do about it, here, let me tell you how you should *feel* about it: sad and angry. Don't you dare celebrate.

4. You don't actually die of AIDS, you die of all the diseases that take advantage of the weakened immune system. They are called opportunistic diseases. Opportunity. In a very old Byzantine church on the island of Torcello near Venice, there is a mural with a parable of Opportunity, or Occasion—the counterpart to Fortune, the chance that can be seized. The people in the mural who are seizing opportunity stand on little wheels. The wheels look like roller skates, but a thousand years old, and zooming around on roller skates seems as resonant an image of risk-taking as any other.

When people realized they were dying from opportunity, they decided to ride the flying roller skates as well. They threw parties.

5. That nearly forgotten party world is tinted, in my memory, an unnatural color, a greenish-blue. By unnatural, I mean artificial, *à*

rebours. It's the color you get nowadays cast onto the faces of movie-scene submarine crews tracking radar targets on blipping screens, or the weak light from a dashboard on an endless nighttime road trip, or, as I would have said then, had the memory crystallized as it has, the pallor you see on your fellow hiker when you have pitched your tent for the night and you are inside it and the light has begun to fail. Perhaps this is because everybody was a little sickly then. Sickly, or a ghoul, or standing directly under the disco strobes, or afraid—affected by the artificial. The way I remember it, there wasn't much in the way of sun for five years, and gardeners used certain chemicals to make the hydrangeas blue and synthetic fertilizers to make the grass green. There was a faddish cure people were trying for AIDS in which they burned their own skin with photo developing chemicals. It was supposed to stimulate the immune system, but it just burned, and made their skin look unnatural.

6. This is the carnival tradition: just before Lent, the sun goes down on Fat Tuesday, and the usually law-abiding citizens get into masks and costumes and let the laws drop while it's too dark to see anything. Lawlessness looks close to natural animal wildness when you're in the midst of it, the normal state a human ought to be in, perhaps. The rest of the time, we're wired together with rules and guidelines and inhibition, society's rubber bands and paper clips and used chewing gum, waiting it out. Orpheus went down into the underworld to get his ladylove, and they lifted the rules of life and death for him; it was only upon emerging into daylight that he broke a rule and got punished for it.

Also, there were little indulgences that may have seemed like parties. Splurges, humorings. I had no interest in marrying Jeff, my partner, since nobody had interest in honoring the union either—nobody could see the romance, the wish for a life under law and order. I did it for Jeff, who wanted to get married because he knew he was dying, and he had the great progress of scientific break-through to help him know it. We went to city hall soon after the earthquake of 1989 to pay the government fifty dollars so that we could have a little certificate. There was scaffolding everywhere hold-ing up the rotunda, and inside there were cracks in all the plaster. Too much partying in Sodom, said plenty of the ministers of the country, and you'll get fires, famine, quakes, pestilence.

And this wasn't one of those things that just sprung up; there's been a whole history of bacchanal in San Francisco dating back to the Barbary Coast days. Why do you think they call it the Donner *Party?* I moved to the city in 1985. "Welcome to San Francisco," somebody said to me, "you missed it." But everybody was always just missing a party. The biggest orgy ever in the world, a secret con-vening of the Beat poets, Foucault with his legs in the air at a Berke-ley bathhouse. This was the town of the libertine; that's where I learned the meaning of the word; I had role models. A few months after I arrived, Dan White got out of jail from a light sentence after shooting the mayor and Harvey Milk and pleading the Twinkie Defense—too much sugar, too much fun, which excused him from responsibility. The locals had a party of rage in his honor when the verdict came down—bonfires, flipped over cop cars—it was as if they'd won the Super Bowl. Free and sobered up, and presumably off the Twinkie habit, White soon after killed himself by inhaling car-bon monoxide from his auto engine. My first Halloween bash in the Castro, I saw a dozen people dressed as Dan White, sucking on a garden hose full of make-believe car exhaust. *Commence au festival.*

7. I think of the grand parties in the stories I love. The eating, drink-ing, and being merry, for tomorrow, you may die. Ulysses dining with Circe, lotus-stoned. In James Joyce's "The Dead," the feasting and the singing and the dancing go on all night in that snug warm house, while outside, snow is general all over Ireland. There is a story by John Cheever that I think of often when I think of our own parties,

called "The Swimmer." At a cocktail party in the suburbs, in a neighborhood where everybody has a pool, the protagonist decides that it might be possible to swim his way back to his own home on the other side of the subdivision, and enjoy a gin and tonic or two along the way. The characters in that story are also of a greenish-blue color, and as the hero pushes his way along, the weather grows cold, the world grows strange, the neighbors move away, and he finds upon arriving home that there is no *there* there. When I show "The Swimmer" to my students, all half my age, they are mystified. "Does this story take place in America?" they want to know.

8. It's not really a ceremony Jeff and I had in city hall. We stood in line, and we paid the half-Benjamin at a window, and then we stood at another window and got a piece of paper after we signed a form. I suppose the forms are still filed there somewhere, but I wouldn't know where to check. It was our friends who made it a ceremony. On the steps outside city hall, they met us with big bunches of flowers, and a picnic basket full of champagne. They took their lunch hour to do this, because you had to legally shack up during a weekday. There's a videotape of the event, and so I have a better memory of things—or rather, I am reminded of things. They threw Rice-a-Roni at us as we drove off. I slipped a ring onto Jeff's hands, gnarled with runaway warts and staph (opportunistic!) infections. But best of all, there is a comic scene in which Jeff is untwisting the wire top on another bottle of champagne, and keeping an eye on an off-screen policeman who has chosen to turn away from our drunken party. Turn away, that is, until the cork comes sailing out of the bottle and hits a tourist in the head. Then we are all shooed away. Nothing but party monsters, every one of us. "Move along, move along," the policeman told us, and that is what I have been doing ever since.

9. Those end-of-the-world parties felt like a kind of swimming similar to the one in the Cheever story. One wanted to get home, didn't

one? I did, I'm sure of it. It's hard not to associate merrymaking and wandering with irresponsibility and decadence. The ants are morally superior to the grasshopper. In the book of Job, Satan wanders about the earth and God stays put. The prodigal son needs forgiveness, and gets it only when he returns home. From where you stand—hell, from where I stand—those years must really bother you. How could you? you ask, when people are sick and dying? How dare you dance in go-go cages and charm snakes and flush good money down the toilet?

It probably looked like idiocy, too. My friend Adam found out he was HIV-positive and went to live in India for a while, where every possible germy enemy of the body thrived in the rivers and the food. When a soldier goes into battle fighting for oil or land, we praise his death as an act of courage. When you go to India with a compromised immune system, you are an idiot, and deserve to die. Don't *bother* coming home, Adam.

In times of crisis, what people want is inspiring stories of battling against the odds, loving-kindness for the forlorn, swords drawn, tears shed. And parties don't look anything like virtue, not bravery nor generosity nor duty. But nobody ever really thought of the queer life as anything like virtue, anyway. Why bother to be true to your true love when nobody respected your true love in the first place? Why bother trying to put a romantic face on a love story when there are bedpans to wash out and incontinence to rinse from the sheets? What is hubris if not the single-minded attempt to avoid shame, until it is the very shame itself?

10. Not just a faulty memory mars my ability to map that legendary time. It would be hard to record those end-of-the-world parties, too, because one jotted down the address of that big anonymous warehouse on the back of a MUNI bus transfer, and by morning, it was an unreadable wad, useless as the expiration timestamp on the other side. And another hoedown was just around the corner.

Still, sometimes I found myself, months afterward, in SOMA at a hip furniture shop or that restaurant, Rings, wasn't it called?, the one that made Chardonnay-doused french fries? and I'd suddenly realize: wasn't it in there, that space right across the alley, where the guy hired a fire eater and a snake charmer? It might have been. But the man who threw the party (or am I smushing together two different parties?) is dead now, and most of the guests as well, so how could I prove it?

11. Let us speak, then, of the spectacular austerities I have heard told, mostly through religious channels, of penitents and pilgrims who find that simply walking is not enough, is too much like pleasure, or at least too little like punishment. Pilgrims going to the shrine of Our Lady of Guadalupe, to Santiago, to Mecca and to Jerusalem, to Shinto and Hindu shrines have done so on their knees, or crawling, or via unlikely vehicles—unicycles and the Opportunistic roller skates. I heard of a man who walked to Rome backwards, holding mirrors. Also of the ones who travel only in the coldest months of winter, or go with no money, or take in no food the entire journey, or sleep without shelter. The party boy in me finds this ridiculous, even indulgent. I wager this is calling attention to one's self, the way a mime or a papal candidate cloaks vanity and a need to be noticed in humility and silence. Why not put on slap shoes and carry a bike horn for the entire pilgrimage? Why not swim the whole way? Why not do the whole damn thing drunk? Now that would be a difficult pilgrimage. When people began to revive the pilgrimage to Santiago in the early 1980s, some would go in the old costume, with shoddy handmade sandals and heavy felt capes. I would like to conjure a pilgrim from the Middle Ages and show her the options for getting from home to the beloved pilgrim shrine—the choices in well-made shoes, the toggled lightweight tents, the fleece sleeping bags, the aerodynamic canteens. I bet she would choose a car.

12. Certain things were expected of us at those parties. One couldn't just show up and leer all night. Taking photographs would have seemed indiscrete, touristic. Everybody hates looking like a tourist, especially when one actually is one. Anyway, I wanted to blend in, but I do not look good in a wig, and yet I remember going to a hootenanny in which all the guests were required to step into a walk-in vault in a cavernous penthouse on Van Ness and find a dress, and a bit of garish costume jewelry, and some makeup, and a wig. But sometimes it was only there, after five or six glasses of Chardonnay and a joint, that very handsome men, hidden behind their own wigs and costume jewelry, would hit on me. In daylight, back in streetware, having nearly thought that party was a dream, I was a stranger again, and so were they.

13. There were recognizable regulars. How many times would I see signed into the guest book the name Art deBrix? And yet I can't quite picture him now. What remains is something like the Cheshire Cat's grin, only Art's mouth was more agape—not slack, but available, like the slot on a Suggestions box, or the Mouth of Truth in Rome. He also wore loud ties. What happens to so many of those regulars happened to Art deBrix, reduced to two or three kanji-like brush strokes, a bit of synecdoche: Bruce nothing but the garish broach he wore; Trevor his child-bearing hips; Mick's winning lottery Scratcher, spent on ballet season tickets (*Oakland* Ballet tickets).

If the artist Jerome attended these happenings, it meant, to me, that it was a party worth attending. He could be seen in a go-go cage at Club Uranus, a man already bony-thin and further desiccated by the bug within him, always dressed in something meant to produce a shudder of horror. To apply the word "transvestitism" to his wardrobe would attribute an irrelevant regularity. Oh yes, tattered fishnet stockings nagged up and desperately gartered, so that they drew attention not to his legs but to his protruding pelvic bones. Oh yes, clownlike Wite-Out eye makeup, stiletto heels the girth and height of railroad nails, a tarry black beauty mark applied near the already beaklike nose. But one dusk, I saw him standing in front of the Castro movie theater just as the marquee was illuminated, wearing only a loin cloth, a birdcage around his head; he was running his long nails over a hand-held chalkboard and singing "Nearer My God to Thee," and when he finished the hymn, he went down to one of those knobby knees and opened the birdcage door and applied lipstick.

If you want to call this "drag," go ahead. He seemed quite at home in the stuff. One Halloween, that far-too-sanctioned carnival, he worried me terribly by dressing in Banana Republic khakis and a small brown cap that hid his blond tresses. It was the only time I ever saw him dress in a costume.

14. It wasn't always sex, drugs, and rock-and-roll. Sometimes these sumptuous affairs required black tie and evening gown. I remember a specific dinner party that reminded me of a story written by the French decadent Jules Barbey d'Aurevilly, about a dinner of atheists, all eating the night away before going to watch an execution at dawn. We were served beluga and sevruga on buckwheat blinis, tiny bowls and spoons precariously balanced on peaks of crushed ice. "A pity," the host said, when one of the bowls, filled with more than four ounces of caviar, tipped into the melt and was rendered inedible. But after that came course after course on plate after plate, and the pity was forgotten. For dessert, a Château d'Yquem sauterne from 1956, I think, and at the bottom of each of our glasses, a small gold ring, too garish to do anything with, really, unless you were a starlet or a queen who could pull that kind of thing off. Somebody, for some yucks, swallowed theirs.

It wasn't all sex, drugs, and rock-and-roll, but still. In "The Masque of the Red Death," the nobility parties while the plague kills those outside the castle walls. They will be punished. In *The Bacchae*, after and because of the orgies, women suckle wolves, and the king is rent to pieces like an old garment by his own people.

And further, the fun seemed worth it. Here's Thoreau in his journal about a boat ride from Boston to Portland in May 1838: "Midnight—head over the boat's side—between sleeping and waking—with glimpses of one or more lights in the vicinity of Cape Ann. Bright moonlight—the effect heightened by seasickness." The effect, the intoxication of travel, is always heightened by sickness.

15. At one of those parties, I had too many gin martinis, and the host took away my car keys. I was so plastered I didn't even know he'd done it. I didn't know he'd done it, also, because I then got into my car and put my keys in the ignition and caromed home, no problem. But I couldn't get into my house, because the host had not taken my car keys but my house keys, the wrong keys. I was free to drive wherever I wished, the horizon fading forever and forever from my view, but I couldn't get in my house. The neighbor never let me forget this: I peed in their bushes. Can you blame me? I couldn't get home. Move along, move along.

16. Oh, let's face it: we hate travelers. They slip out of all life's responsibilities. They send you postcards of the sandiest beach under the bluest sky, they bring home useless trinkets that will never fit around your wrists, they are gone, and have taken your heart with them, and if they come home, they are jetlagged and complain about how they are simply exhausted and what a drag it is to be here, back at work, back with responsibilities, back with you, you *loser*. We travelers are always looking away from you, or over your shoulder, at the next horizon. And we are always eager to distinguish ourselves from the others, the quick from the dead.

For a while there, I was like the man swimming through all the swimming pools trying to get home. But when I found what I thought was home, I discovered the door locked and my keys gone. I peed in the bushes and kept going. Hotel rooms, tasteful as Muzak and meaningless as discotheque drug trips, were easy to come by. At a certain point, I got myself a backpack and started walking. I started walking to specific places, pilgrim shrines. But every time I got to the shrine, Jeff was not there, nor Mick nor Jerome; the party was already cleared up. Welcome to Santiago, you missed it. And after a while, I stopped having goals like that. I just wanted to get up in the morning and go, go *away*. Pilgrims are holy men. Ulysses is in hell.

17. Sometimes you didn't even know it was going to be a party. Like that time your friend Will from Texas oil money, under the influence of antidepressants, opportunistic infection, and dementia, went out and bought three different luxury automobiles; he'd finish a transaction, drive the Mercedes or the Lexus or the Beamer around a block a few times, park it on the street, and go to the next dealership. We had to go find the cars: whee!—a treasure hunt! We spent the afternoon rounding up the vehicles, finding ways to explain things to the dealer who—*come on!*—should have known from the start. Poor Will just wanted to get up and go away, or to the next big party, riding in style.

I don't remember well, either, because I don't think I wanted to be there, and hoped to forget. One time, Mick had a party for his birthday and it was a "twin"-themed party. You were to come with some other person and try to look as identical as possible. Reason being that at the time, there was some hope among HIV patients that you might get a complete blood transfusion and become negative again if you had an identical twin with the same blood type. Hope you have your twin, Brian, Mick said to me, and at the time he said it, I was consumed with some combination of anger and confusion, as if I'd been mocked for having a cuckolding wife. I wasn't positive at the time; perhaps Mick mistook me for my twin? Now I am positive, and I am sorry to have spent so much time feeling like a cuckold; Mick wishing me twinship may have been the last thing he said to me.

18. Jerome had a contest with another artist (he was an artist, dammit), Charles. Whoever died first would have himself cremated, and the other would use the ashes as a medium for art. Jerome won the contest. Or did he lose? In any case, before receiving his friend's ashes, Jerome was painting with eyeliner, nail polish, mascara, lipstick. The ashes gave his work texture. His paintings were sometimes done on embellished prayer cards, or little TV trays. There were people— okay, people like me—who wanted one of his paintings, and he began to sell in galleries. His manager told Jerome to "paint bigger." That's why Jerome began to paint portraits on bottle caps, a Last Supper on the inside of a pistachio shell. He wasn't going to do what you wanted him to do, so don't bother asking. And he didn't use any of your NEA grant money, so stop fretting. Also, he's dead, so why are you bitching?

19. Nothing I do any more looks like work. My hands are soft, my clothes are clean. There is nothing under my nails. If I get any bruises, it's from careening among the furniture under the influence of something, or sliding down a scree-slippery scramble on the trail. I have spent half an hour writing this paragraph, which will take you half a minute to read, if you read it at all. Most of that half-hour was spent staring at a vase of wild iris I arranged in a sugar dispenser and changing CDs. My work can only look like wasting time. And when my work tires me out, I go walking.

When I walk with a backpack, I sweat. If there is a dirt trail along paved road, I'll take the dirt trail so as to kick up dust, to make my ankles get dirty, so that I'll seem to have earned that extra-long nap I always need after walking. I love to feel clean after feeling sweaty and dirty all day, a shave, salve on my feet. If I get blisters, I'll show them to you.

20. Two people can be a party. One night I met a man in a bar who scooped ice cream at Double Rainbow. Double Rainbow is gone now, too, but it was nothing but pleasure, that place, and I can't even remember where the shop was, now, on that strip in Noe Valley. He had one oversized biceps from scooping all that ice cream, and he showed it to me. It was impressive, and also bepurpled with Kaposi's sarcoma. But I put my hand on it anyway, and that was his signal to take me home. Instead of getting undressed at home, however, he showed me his collection of sake pons, those lovely rice wine pitchers. They were arranged on shelves, his life's work. He invited me to a last toast: pouring out what I found out many years later was an extremely expensive bottle of sake. Pearls to swine, again.

After the sake vase was emptied, the man surprised me by throwing the pon hard against the wall, and it smashed in shards on the wooden floor. He took another off the shelf and handed it to me: now it's your turn. And that is how we spent the night, breaking the vessels, covering the room in glazed clay chunks and dust, dismantling the world, taking it down with us. Yes, I was drunk at the time, and I took a cab home. I don't even remember what neighborhood he lived in, where that apartment is. In it, there must be, still, the empty shelves, a Double Rainbow uniform hung from a nail, and this little odd detail: *Gone with the Wind* playing, forever, edited for television.

21. I still have the ring from my marriage to Jeff. I have his ring, too. He was cremated, and you can't really burn a ring. His is huge, he had huge farm hands, so I couldn't swallow it, either. Mine is tiny. I don't wear the one for me often because I've gotten bonier as I've grown older, and I'm afraid the ring will get stuck on me. To tell you the truth, I still feel I've cleaved unto Jeff, although he has been gone a dozen years and I've had two substantial relationships since. The marriage was sort of *sort of,* I guess, and there wasn't any sort of divorce or annulment. I was never called a widower, and I was never entitled to an inheritance. There was no closure, as there had been very little commencement—just a party, one that goes on and on.

I am not looking for sympathy, for once is more than enough. At a certain point, if one is lucky enough to be able to grow older, one realizes that one does not want to be an epic hero any more. One wants not pleasure, souped-up, snake-charmed, drugged-out pleasure, but something on a smaller scale. Call it, "Delight." Delight is a sissy word, not manly, not about strength. Jerome's tiny bottle-cap paintings rather than *The Wreck of the Hesperus.* "Delight" is looking into an old Viewmaster for the stereopticon depth of old stories; somebody giving you free tickets to a play they can't attend. Grilled asparagus, maybe. Going barefoot the first day it's warm enough. Poetry that rhymes and yet is also written for adults; the sound of a baseball game on the radio. Like that. Delight is more baroque, but no less radical for it—the stuff served up at the end-of-the-world parties. We couldn't quite figure out the difference between pleasure and delight back then, I think, because we were too young, and nobody was able to grow old enough to aim true. When you're young, you want fighty-fight movies and mosh-pit emotions and Chuck Palahniuk novels. Later, you want smaller things, inconspicuous consumption: winning a game of solitaire on the first deal, being surprised by a friend meeting you at baggage claim at the airport, reading Shakespeare in the bathtub.

22. After a while, the life-saving drugs started arriving. All the max'd-out credit cards, the sold-off life insurance policies, the tossed-up careers, that stuff backfired, and everybody said, "party's over." But by then, parties, la dolce vita, that's all we were trained for.

That, and nursing. I can draw blood with a needle, lift the infirm from a bathtub without throwing out my back, toggle between aspirin and Tylenol for optimum pain relief. But parties, I'm better at that. After all, they call the combination of drugs you take for HIV a "cocktail." The celebrations began in a different tone, and new drugs were added to the cocktail—ecstasy, crystal meth, ketamine, GBH. These, too, seem more in the line of delights rather than pleasures, baroque, rather than romantic, since their actual effects are for the moment rather than for the future, transitory, problematically impermanent. Romance is a story, a stodgy story with mirthless villains and heroes. Baroque is artifice and scheme, setting up dominos in a complicated pattern and giggling like schoolgirls after knocking them down. It's all I know how to do any more. Nothing, not story nor love nor family can take root any more. Here's a man who lives a life of danger. Everywhere he goes, he stays a stranger.

23. There is one more bit of apocrypha about Ulysses. Why not? If Dante had not read the true finale of the *Odyssey,* and imagined his own fitting ending to that lost soul, how many others did the same? In one version, it's told that when he got back to Ithaca, Ulysses became Public Enemy Number One. Not many in town liked him— he'd dragged all the decent men into war, got them killed or turned into pigs or swimming after sirens. Penelope's suitors weren't pleased to see him, and when Ulysses had them all shot, his Gallup poll numbers hit an all-time low. Penelope herself was rather enjoying the peace and quiet. Then Tennyson put him back on a boat and cut him loose again. What one wants from a returning traveler is a little bit of shame, for God's sake. Be sorry for what you did, and be discrete. A hero sees his tragic flaw, and that redeems him. This hubris, this inability to see that what you've done is wrong, wrong, wrong— that will make you pathetic. Ulysses, we have no use for your pathetic hubris.

For me, there was plenty of humiliation back at home, the soiled bedclothes, the desperate arrays of pills in the medicine cabinet, the bizarre recipes larded into each issue of *Diseased Pariah News* in the "Get Fat! Don't Die!" section.

24. I've heard often enough that a landscape, like a prairie, or a mountain, or a fjord, can be a character. Geography can take on a life and desires all its own, speak and love and not love, and yes, that has plenty to do with what I do when I walk. But if I really want to offer a reason for doing what I've done, for walking, it would be that disaster, too, can be a character, or almost one—an animal, say, a beast unbroken, unroped, and ever-stampeding, and while disaster can be awful, it can also free a person, unrope him, thrill him into his own life and desires.

I know these surfer guys who travel the world finding the perfect wave. They become intrepid voyageurs in order to find new unspoiled beaches. The unspoiled, uncolonized beaches are in countries where unstable governments or civil war or revolution have scared away tourism for the next five years. Honduras, Chile, Rwanda, what have you. The coast is clear. They paddle out, ride the surf, make a party out of disaster.

They pave the way for the next set of tourists, a little braver, and so on, until there are high-rise hotels and little huts by the beach selling postcards and snow globes full of surfers. By then, the intrepid surfers have moved on, looking for a new, untarnished beach. So you don't have to worry much about meeting up with these drifter party creatures—they've cleared out by dawn.

25. But now and then, you'll see clues that they've recently passed your way. I know where to look. When I see a miniaturist at work, when a favorite restaurant gets boarded up, when a bus transfer falls out of an old book with a mysterious address written on it. In some

of the less fashionable bars, I'll see an array of men standing about, not intending to get picked up, but to provoke—with blue hair, or a cap that doesn't fit their head, outfits that might have made them look good once but no longer suit the sagging way of all flesh, a shirt unbuttoned to the navel, bling-bling where it ought not be. No ring on anybody's hand. This is delight, rather than passion, a baroque song in the mighty days of shock-and-awe romantic drama; it has its place. It's easy to stay, sure, but it's even easier to just walk away.

Corte

Vizzavona

C' Capannelle

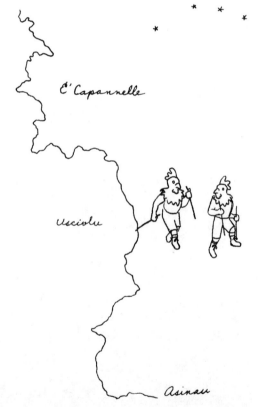

Usciolu

Asinau

6

Lammergeier

Corte

Near the top of the Citadel of Corte, cultural and political seat of Corsican nationalism and the University of Corte, Petra and I, scrubbed, antiperspirated, coifed (her), and shaven (me), are enjoying a late breakfast in a sun-dappled restaurant al fresco while waiting for the museum to open. We look like the day after Christmas (Santa never appeared on U Trinighellu, so we had to make our own fun), the first day of school: there are deep folded creases in our street clothes, since they've been at the very bottom of our packs for a week.

The waitress has disappeared, which happens often in Europe near the end of a meal, just when one wants to pay the check and move on. This is one of those cultural differences that I ought to value—nothing is more aggravating in an American restaurant than to have one's plate whisked away (as it often is in our country, our best of all possible worlds) just because it has been pushed back for a breather—except that the Continent errs at the other extreme.

"Is she dead?" I ask Petra, who has her eyes closed to the sun that has come to shine over her side of the table, a high-mountain warmth that heats up the check wallet and my waiting credit card, as well as the leftover food on her plate, spiced with herbs from the maquis.

"Who is dead?" she asks, without opening her eyes.

"The waitress. Has she been taken away in an ambulance?"

Petra is clearly doing me a favor by opening her eyes, and by means of her particular angle of repose she has created by leaning so far back in her chair, she can see inside the restaurant. "No, she is right there."

My hint goes unheeded; Petra closes her resort island eyes once again. Slow down there, stupid American guy. Petra remains in a state of lassitude, the kind that comes over men after sex, and I am the restless, chatty one; food encourages this gender role reversal. Petra picks up the credit card, sun-warmed, and places it against her cheek. "Mmm," she purrs at the feel of hot plastic on skin. "This is a feeling cavemen never enjoyed." Inarguably!

Nor, no doubt, would they have enjoyed a lasagna in wild boar sauce, our indigenous, incongruous breakfast. By scraping off my plate, I can see that the bottom is cast with the Moor's Head, the indigenous, incongruous symbol of Corsican independence. This black profile of an African Muslim with a white kerchief, a *banneau,* tied over his eyes (or simply around his head?), it is seen everywhere we go, on flags, beach towels, fridge magnets, *banneaus (banneaus, mise en abyme!),* and now the plates, and it itches at my politically correct mind with its disreputable connotations—like the Indian as a baseball team mascot, or the connoisseur of African Americans identifying himself as a "Mandingo Lover."

134

Ironic, too—for the Moor's Head came from Aragon in the thirteenth century, a banner used to celebrate the routing of the Saracens during the crusades, and therefore a symbol of colonial rule. I had seen it quite a bit on Sardegna to the south, where it is more of a decoration. But the Corsicans have found a way to make lemonade from this lemon of a historical fact by spinning a legend, the legend of a lovely Corsican damsel named Diana abducted by Grenaden pirates, rescued by her handsome boyfriend, who, surprise, is named Paoli. The diabolical Muslim king of Grenada, furious as an evil queen, dispatched his best general, Mansour ben Ismail, to get her back. He took an army that performed the standard rape-and-pillage until he was soundly defeated by a plucky Corsican army, hastily assembled. It was Paoli, of course, who personally beheaded Mansour and strutted around the island with his *tête* on a stick.

Nationalistic movements seem to feel this urge to offer corrective service, as if we all live on prison farms, future walk-offs, every one of us. In Corsica, in Catalunya, in Basque Country, and Quebec, I have walked along roads and seen how they use black spray paint to cross out the ruling colonial language's name for the town, as printed on colonial government signage—"Hospidale," for example—and scrawl in the local language's traditional name: "U Spidale." Just as the island seems to be shaped like a scolding finger, there is something in this guerilla spell-checking that makes even the most incendiary nationalist underground terrorist seem, in my imagination, dressed like an aging teacher-maid, hair pulled back in a severe bun, girded with cat-eye glasses, a pointer, and a big red marking pen. And has, after seeing the "Wanted" signs at the Marseilles boat terminal (the other) number 2, been sleeping in a wrinkled, maquis-snagged skirt-and-sweater set.

I think that I am afraid, a little, of this purifying process, the "Francesi Fora!" graffiti, the exclusionary tactics of the independence-seekers rather than those inclusive—the house-proud friendliness I find when visiting these noncountry countries (I recall one afternoon in Basque San Sebastian looking out the window of a restaurant at a bombed and burned bus while the hearty chef offered us big cups of pacharan, the Basque liqueur specialty).

I understand the impulse, to protect and conserve the culture; without borders, what, after all, can save a language, a people? There are more people who can speak Klingon than Navajo; Hebrew was all but dead until Israel was given a homeland. The Palestinians, thus, fight ferociously for a patch of land to plant a language on. Corte, I think, as I look around me, is a big fort on a big rock at what is nearly the geographical center of the island.

"Francesi Fora!" Are you talking to me? I can't help but feel the scolding, especially as a Yankee, especially as a spineless Yankee pretending to be a Canadian. This nation that I'm from, it's far from pure, and far from the model I'd press upon Corsica's Front Corse Nationaliste Liberation.

The waitress, after all, proves even to me that she is alive and well, and comes to take the sensuous hot credit card away from Petra in order to put it to the use for which it was truly made. Petra makes a frustrated noise when she has to let the card go, a noise they'd use to imitate a toddler with their toy taken from them, a German toddler noise rather than an English toddler noise. "Meh," I approximate here.

Still, the waitress recognizes that we are speaking in English and asks us where we are from. I glance at Petra and say it again, though were I hooked up to a polygraph I would pump a scribble the way an 8.0 earthquake would jag across a seismograph: "Canada."

The cock crows a second time.

Lots of Canadians come here, or some, anyway, from Quebec, enjoying simultaneously the ease of language and the fellowship of the un-nationed. It's funny how like seeks like among the French, although Petra and I avoided our compatriots of both language and country. On the table, each of the packets in the sugar rack have little features on special places throughout the world: Quebec, Fiji, Les Seychelles, some obscure island off the coast of Australia—what a coincidence! They are all French-speaking places! If an alien came and grabbed nothing but these sugar packets and pieced together our world, they would believe we write only in long nearly ungrammatical (yet delightfully rhetorical) sentences and think cheese can easily replace dessert.

We get up to wander to the center of Corte to find the grand, if lugubrious, statue of Pascal Paoli, the godfather of Corsica. It is almost a requirement of visitors to take photos of the eighteenth-century bullet holes riddling the walls of the ancient houses facing in on this square, over his shoulder, up where he's pointing, featured and easy to spot, like proud flesh on a horse.

How is it that the majority of my best friends from outside the United States are nationalists of countries that have no borders? Catalans, Welsh, Basques, Palestinians, Quebecois. Each of them has their own language, or at least some dialect to adjust to. They are quick to give me nicknames in their own language, as if they might infect me, too, with the language. In Basque, I'm "Ohinandi," Bigfoot; in Catalan, "La Mangui," The Lady Thief. I love my friends from Northern Spain quite dearly, but getting to know Catalan is like a wearying subplot to an otherwise potboiler of a mystery: how can I improve Spanish when the people to whom I need to speak it are grudgingly listening to me and would rather be speaking to me in English? And what right do I have to complain? I am a representative of the prevailing power.

And as a representative of the prevailing power, there are things I simply can't write, not with any justice. This is a bearable burden, but I want just now to write, "There are things one simply can't write any more." But that is what I wanted to write even more than what I should have written, even more rigorously: "There are things one simply should never have written." The things that shouldn't be written are the condescending things, the generalizations. Corsicans are obsessed with pig flesh! The Germans use the word "stupid" far too often! Ugh, the French, and their . . . their . . . long sentences! And you Americans—you only have one kind of mustard—and you call it French's!

When I pick through the library of books on Corsica, a surprisingly slim collection, there are well-written but wildly reckless thoughts among the pages. In the 1920s, the freewheeling British woman named Rene Juta travels alone to the island in order to meet her giddy artist brother Jan (and by giddy, I suspect she means something else; my father refers to this sort of men, the sort of men like me, as "squirrely"). She is recognized throughout the island villages for her green snakeskin shoes, and hangs around with a fuming D. H. Lawrence and her squirrely artist brother. Of Corte, where Petra and I had now arrived, Juta wrote in *Concerning Corsica*, "Corte, like all the inland Corsican towns, looks like a forlorn hope or a disaster interpreted in mortarless stone. Exquisitely situated over the Restonica river, its gaunt blackened houses tower up into pinnacles of ruin."

Power rises and falls. Seneca hated Corsica, cursed its honey, and claimed the Restonica polluted. Boswell, in his book, "Seneca certainly never ſaw the Reſtonica, otherwiſe he would never have ſaid, that Corſica had not 'hauſtus aquae,' a draught of water." Corte was at another high-water mark when Boswell dropped by. And the Corte that Petra and I encounter is nothing like the ruin Juta encountered in the Roaring Twenties, but considered now the capitol, the spiritual and muscular center of Corsican tradition and dreams of autonomy. Travelers destroy what they seek, and sometimes vice versa.

How strange it was to awaken earlier this morning in a luxury hotel rather than a muddy tent, in a bed with linens like those in a hospital, the sound of cars rather than the tinkling of cowbells. I felt in the wrong place. There were reminders, so that the wrenching wasn't anything like jet lag—the mind could catch up with the body by making transitions. For example, the stone scree of the GR is the same sort they spread under and along railroad tracks, over which the on-board toilets leak freely, various locomotive excretions are also jettisoned. I view all scree with an identical nervous avoidance, and give a nod of gratitude for all transitional material.

Coming into Corte from the train station was a culture shock, and when we walked along and saw the various dorky things everyone was doing—both tourists (taking pictures of nothing from train windows, talking incessantly of nothing, ignoring beautiful scenery reading their own newspapers purchased at the kiosk, full of news of nothing) and locals (not bathing, or roaring wildly through the street in Clios)—Petra said, "we are with stupid people again." Condescending, but true: in the high mountains of the GR20, there are arrogant people, Roosters, annoying people, but they had to have a certain level of self-preserving intelligence.

But it's so cruel to speak poorly of fellow tourists, because everybody can be an idiot when out of one's native element. The other, or another, good reason to travel is to make a fool of one's self at least one time for as many places as there are on the itinerary, so that if one returns, one won't do it twice (and one should never return to the same place; it's foolish). But how can we help it? The contempt one has for other tourists is similar to the contempt a mother has for other mothers' children; those babies are all crap, and mine and ours are perfect.

What I have is more contempt for mistakes people make over and over, en masse. After our unlikely breakfast, we walk up one of the many cobbled ramps that lead to the very tip-top, the belvedere to the south of the Citadel of Corte, where years of teenagers retest the effects of gravity on bottles over the rocks below. Look: two of them are engaged in research right now! At this moment of the test, they are thrilled. "Yes," is the conclusion of the experiment: "Gravity is still working. We can all rest easy. For the moment. We'll be back in an hour to check it again." After the test, we are all in worse shape than before, for, when they leave, bored again, Petra and I peer over to get a look at the base of the wall: an ever-growing garbage heap, very picturesque.

Petra and I go into any number of the cafés to take in big boulles of black coffee and listen to the locals make noise. It reminds us a little of the *gîtes* after ten in the morning along the GR20, full of women, clucking French as if they were in a henhouse, missing the roosters, out scratching at the ground outside some refuge miles from here.

What I want to write is, "Corsica is an obstreperous island, a people voted most likely, if there is a bar nearby, to get into a bar fight." I want to write, "Corsican men will not tell you anything about themselves but will ask you a hundred questions about yourself, and only unbutton their minds with a little drink in them." I want to write, "Corsican women walk behind their men with a sharp stick, poking them forward into deeds they might not likely do otherwise, sometimes deeds that are not wise." I want to write, "The dream of a free independent Corsica seems driven by an idealism that is rooted in male vanity and female superstition." But all of these sweeping generalizations are too general. Based on one visit, one pass through a place at one specific time. And one ought never go a second time.

And the danger of generalizations seems to reside in being too specific. You might say, "The French look beautiful and are prone to moles," which could be acceptable, and then you write, "On the plane ride here, the French behaved like we behaved when a substitute teacher came in to cover our classroom in middle school," and then you start toward trouble; it's just one planeful of French people you're talking about, and one step away from bigotry.

So you retreat to general compliments, which always seem acceptable to any culture: "The French, they sure like to cook!" or "Gosh, but the honey on Corsica is superior!" But even complimentary chauvinism seems dangerous. When George Orwell gives homage to Catalunya, he is as likely to fall into these traps of chauvinism and condescension, a man from the world of power visiting upon the powerless his sympathy—and that patronizing, cloying charity. The powerful and the powerless: this is the history of melodrama, even when the powerful are not tying the powerless down to the railroad tracks with a twist of the mustachios.

Petra makes her own generalizations too, but her scorn is reserved for the Dutch, who often caravan into her country carrying their own water and potatoes, an insult to German cleanth and economy. "The way to keep the Dutch away," says Petra, while flipping through her newspaper quickly—and whatever she's doing when she speaks of the Dutch, she does a little more quickly—walk, stir soup, sweep the floor—"is to introduce extra fees for everything. They won't come if they have to pay extra." She makes me laugh, for she knows about my unsuccessful relationship with the Dutch, or a Dutch, and of my needless and overfunded research into making it successful (Nope, still doesn't work!) while attending a certain Hollandaise Ecole of Hard Knocks. All along the GR20, I encourage her to tell me more of such words of wisdom, and she's happy to share, but while she wraps her mind around her disdain, her body quickly follows, and she may start running along the trail or stir the soup so violently that it spatters and scalds; the finish on the flooring must be reapplied, for the broom has broken through it, she sweeps so vigorously. "Do you know why they have liberalized drugs in Amsterdam?" Ooh, a funny riddle! "It is so they can forget that nobody would ever miss them if they were flooded away." I sink down without a punchline to buoy me up—no wit, just a bit of poison. Perhaps that's how they tell jokes in Germany, or Austria.

A friend of mine doing Peace Corps work on the island of Madagascar got food poisoning; these things happen. They told him that only American travelers come to their island and expect to have hard stools. I must admit: I have this expectation, and when reality falls short of these expectations—not just on Madagascar, but anywhere not on home soil (if you will)—I consider the failure my own, my body's, my good judgment. Does this mean, I wonder, whether in having overly high standards for myself, I harbor lower opinions of anywhere not here, or at least anywhere I don't have a solid stool? Is it secret prejudice, prejudice through condescension?

Perhaps it is this desire to map a place, to set it down in a guidebook of one's own making, and guidebooks require all sorts of sassy judgments and overly broad generalizations. It attempts to bring The Other under control. But it never works.

<hr>

At the museum of the Citadel, I read in the broken but well-meaning English pamphlet that this is "Pascal Paoli, leader of Corsica between 1755 and 1769, an unlighted despot." The history of Corsica in recent centuries is about the Genoans and the French, and several sorts both native and foreign who wanted Corsica to be or not to be part of the Genoan empire. Paoli was one who wanted not. Nobody was very successful in this not wanting.

There is a ferocity in every scrap of history presented to us in the museum. The nationalist movement notwithstanding, there is cast over all this business of the vendetta, for example. In the gift shop, you can buy your own souvenir vendetta stiletto, sleek, cross-shaped, elegant, pearl-handled: aestheticized violence, seventy euros.

I knew about vendettas long before I'd heard of the maquis: blood feuds. It's the stuff of nineteenth-century novels and swashbuckling movies. Vendettas are limned (for me) with a slanted, low-class light through the hillbilly Hatfield-McCoy business but tarted up by de Maupassant and Dumas. The tradition may be as old as the first century, BC, when the Roman historian Diodorus Siculus suggested that the Goths brought it over (first this, then Marilyn Manson and Columbine: the Goths are blamed for everything). By the time the Genoese ruled Corsica, an average of 900 vendetta murders occurred annually—pretty astonishing when the total population hovered around 120,000 (the homicide rate of Manhattan is only a third of this). The member of one family was done wrong by the member of another family, and revenge had to be exacted through an almost ritualized stabbing. And there was that body on the floor, and mama pissed off and ululating for revenge: go, my second son, and set this wrongdoing right by avenging your older brother. You can almost see it as a scene in a minor opera by Massenet: commanding posture, the black-decked diva, the puzzling supertitles—what's *her* problem? And back and forth it would go: payback's a bitch.

Pascal Paoli tried to curb the vendetta death rate by promising to execute the executioners and leveling the family house and placing a "pillar of national disgrace" upon the rubble. Using the shame of "disgrace" was a fighting-fire-with-fire tactic, for a family member was expected, in a vendetta, to commit a murder in order to keep family honor. Usually, vendettas rose up over the honor of women, who, if seduced or raped or carried off and wed by the member of another family, needed to regain their dignity. Lesser things could start the bloodshed, however. Just a walk along the river with a pretty lady without her father's permission could begin the cycle of vendetta.

And there are even more petty causes that would be hilarious if they were not so tragic: the Paolis and the Sanguinettis murdered thirty-six family members because of a chestnut tree. In Castagniccia (the word means Chestnut Town—more than coincidence?), a rooster was stolen, causing fourteen deaths. And one of the longest lasting feuds in the Extrem Sud region began because somebody didn't tie up his donkey.

Is the vendetta a culturally specific tradition that needs to continue simply because it is culturally specific? I don't want to trot out high school anthropology questions about whether a culture is destroying itself with its own rich traditions (African tribespeople cutting the clitoris, not allowing women to attend school in Muslim nations, the Amish eschewing zippers), but am I not allowed to express a value judgment on murder, on self-destruction? Then if not on a specific culture, then on this: a bizarre lack of imagination. Could not the Aztecs, in their incessant use of ritualized blood sacrifice, come up with a less actual, more symbolic, imagined sacrificial rite? Couldn't the Corsican feuding families simply sit down at the table and work it out? "I'm sorry my donkey shat in your flower bed. Please accept this lovely shovel as a peace offering."

Perhaps it is those with wild imaginations that are to blame, however. Apparently, when Dumas wrote *The Corsican Brothers* and *The Vendetta* and de Maupassant wrote "A Corsican Bandit" and Mérimée told the story of Colomba, stories that romanticize the vendetta and add all sorts of imaginative dimension that might not have been there, the Corsicans themselves read these works and took them to heart: this is our tradition, this is what we look like. Actual vendetta violence modeled itself on the art that embellished it. The actual vendetta got a shot in the arm from the metaphorical vendetta.

At least some suffering breeds a bit of beauty, and out of the violence of vendetta grew all sorts of art—the shiny, pretty knives in the souvenir shop, the rich literary tradition, and above all, for me, the music. There is on Corsica a music that is so specific and beautiful that it may be the strongest argument for "Francesi Fora!" graffiti. It has grown, oddly enough, out of all the violence Corsica has endured, from the waves of marauding invaders who brought with them the many layers of cultural tradition, and this, the vendetta. When a man had been stabbed by a pretty stiletto, his bloody shirt was nailed to the family house, and the house's windows were boarded up, a symbolic gesture grown out of rather realistic siege sensibility. Then there would be a funeral, and the women of the family would begin their song, called the *voceru.* They'd gather around the body, and wail and scratch their own faces and tear out their hair and still have the presence of mind to improvise four- and six-line verses that were meant to lament the dead (Dorothy Carrington writes of hearing such a song: "O my tufted cypress! My muscat grape! My sugared cake! My good and sweet mana" . . . "You were my column! You were my support! You were my grandeur! You were my brother! My oriental pearl! My finest treasure!") and anger up the blood of the menfolk (Carrington, again, records a voceru execrating a priest, related to a murderer, refused to ring the church bell for the dead: "May I see in a basket / The entrails of the priest! / May I tear them with my teeth / And rub them with my hands. / In the house of the priest / One hears the Devil! / Infamous priest, excommunicated! / Dog, eater of the sacraments! / May you die in anguish! / In spasms and in torments!"). Nobody messes with my tufted cypress.

How could a man resist with that sort of hectoring going on in a boarded-up household? Well, any man who did resist was a coward, called a *ribeccu,* related to *rimbeccu,* the taunt that commands revenge: "Do it, you big sissy." And those who did not take on the responsibility of revenge were cast out and usually had to leave Corsica. Those who did follow through, thereby becoming outlaws under law, were considered local heroes, the *bandit d'honneur,* Honorable Bandit, and cared for by the family until death.

These days, officially, of course, the vendetta is illegal. The last official vendetta ended near Ajaccio in the 1950s. In certain ways, it finds its outlets in the assassinations of politicos cozying up to the French government and is fueled by nationalism. Political terrorists enjoy a version of the heroic bandit d'honneur reputation.

And the voceru? Primarily sung by women, it has been adapted to the all-male a capella *polyphonie* tradition and become a vehicle for nationalism, as well, and the songs address Corsican independence. Much of it, as late as the early 1980s, was considered incendiary and dangerous. Musical groups like I Muvrini and Cantu u Populu Corsu and A Filetta made music that was illegal.

I must rephrase my wonder—how is it that beautiful things come out of ugly things? There is Dante again, betraying his own personal hatred, his own voceru, until it turned into lyric in *The Inferno.* Picasso's *Guernica* transforming genocide, if not redeeming it. What art, after all, isn't begotten of pain? Could something beautiful come out of all the terrorism, all our military maneuvers? And who will do the transforming?

Because I have been deep in myself while staring at exhibits behind smudgy glass, exhibits describing how Cap Corse is made, that rather addictive aperitif, or how to cure boar meat, Petra grows concerned because I have been unnaturally silent. And so I let loose that string of questions bottled up in me, and now she is the silent one, perhaps trying to translate the complexities, or perhaps pondering: who are rhetorical questions for? Me? Her? You? You, who got smack to the middle of this book thinking you were taking an armchair vacation, just as Petra thought she was taking a nice island resort vacation, and here you are, stuck, up to your neck in a lot of annoying dense prose? (That question was for you, by the way.)

As an American, a part-time Yankee, it occurs to me that I am the most irresponsible when I am merely a voyeur on the world's troubles—disguising myself as a Canadian, and simply recording what I see. I am thinking all of this as I walk around in Corte, and I realize that to be a witness, to record and describe all types of inequality and injustice in the world, one has to be culpable in the business, to get a little scratched up. To answer to my own nation's bad deeds, but also, to suffer from them, as well. I am resolved, right there in the museum: if anybody else asks along the way, I am an American. The cock won't crow again.

Even though we are taking a break from the GR20, we can't help ourselves, for the museums and churches in Corte seem archival, stuffed, mummified. We arrange to drive down for a day to sample one of three other lovely walks in Corsica, the Mare e Mare trails. Had I to do it all over again, I would have planned to walk these as well as, if not instead of, the GR20. They are the Tra Mare e Monti (a ten-day trek that dances around the north part of the GR20) and the Mare a Mare Nord (a cross of the island from east to west with more spectacular mountains and a few less people to dodge). We take our day to sample the Mare a Mare Sud, known for its views of the villages and a curious prehistoric place called Cucuruzzu.

The sun shines on the harvest cork trees so that they are a deep, scabrous red, as if the trees had been flayed, painfully. They *had* been flayed, actually, but they also seem to thrive on this harvesting of their own bark, for when their barks are not stripped from their trunks, they seem to erupt like bad skin. We have a rental car for the day and drive on the twisting narrow roads behind trucks full of long troughs of cork oak, and these pieces, like overstacked dugout canoes, don't seem well tethered to the truck, and we worry that we might be buried alive in the stuff. Pleasure, or one of its heavier storage units, will definitely be the end of me.

We park our car in a village called Levie and feel we have the energy to do a complete loop, which starts out in an auspicious manner, when a sweet woman, whose rather fortified house resides along the road, fills our pockets full of walnuts. This would never happen on the GR20. The crowds that pass by that way are much like the tourist crowds we pit ourselves against in Corte. Here, things are quiet, and it may be the first time we actually experience Corsica as the way it is most true to itself.

After an easy shaded walk we reach Cucuruzzu, the Neolithic ruins of a village. There is a more famous one, considered a must-see in all the guidebooks, closer to the sea, called Filitosa, but this smaller site, less built up and more available for exploration and touch, suits me better.

I have explored in the past some of these mysterious lost civilizations like the people of the Nuraghi on Sardegna, ancient people with very sophisticated ideas about living well and worshiping well and eating well. There is no evidence of dunderheaded blood sacrifices or offerings to fertility gods, just good clean living, tens of thousands of years ago. Except, oops!, we forgot to develop a written language! Stupid Sardinian Bronze Age people.

Here on Corsica, on top of the village, a couple of medieval civilizations built themselves, perhaps in emulation. There are strange menhirs showing prehistoric warriors and ten-ton stones that have been moved around. Layers of pure civilization, all gone. We have little headsets with a narrative of our walk through the place, and that isolates both Petra and me from ourselves. We feel, separately, alone.

It puts us in quite a mood. Some deep connection to Bronze Age people and even the subsequent settlers who built their towns on top of the ruins, layers and layers of town—like Count Bianca in the twelfth century. Those old hoary holm oaks and cork oaks seemed suddenly young to us. The people who built here had no dream, no doubt, of the forests and civilizations that would come and go before we stand here with our multilingual headphones. These were the cavemen Petra and I have been bragging to. They do not seem to care one bit.

There is that wind of lonesomeness blowing through the site, even on a sunny day, that also blows through the Ozymandias poem. It is humbling, unselfing, end-of-summer, sad: a blow to the ego: you'll be as dead and inscrutable in far less time. If nature is the transforming artist, more than a voyeur, more of an involved witness, then this is its artwork—pilings of stone, yes, but evidence of people being able to live together, their own egos not important at all.

Petra and I snap out of it fairly easily, however, when she decides to take hairpin turns back home quite recklessly, and I reward her with melodramatic screams. We dine that evening on the Corsican charcuterie and wild boar, *sangliere* they call that beast, cooked in a variety of ways, so that I enjoy a terrine de Sangliere, a Sangliere stew, and sangliere "a la Corse"; Petra has mussels and a trout aioli. Good food fuels the ego, and I'm a deluded Ozymandias once more. The stew is cooked down to such a pitch that no spoon is needed. We share a great bottle of wine of the tar and roses sort—so thick I can almost feel the benzene molecules roll over my tongue like graphite. The boar is fine, not gamey at all—game does not taste gamey in Corsica, I suppose, because there is something of a blur, as always, between the tame and the wild here on the island. Corsica may be the world's largest free-range ranch. And the wildness is reinforced when every cut of meat is cooked in *herbs maquis*. To cool the appetite, we have a thick dessert fiadone made of flan and chestnuts. And a second bottle of wine, one with even rougher, hairier shoulders.

The surprise of the dinner: Petra orders the cheese plate featuring brocciu, the aged smelly thing from ewes, and a fresh camembert thing. Our clever waiter, who whiles away summers waiting tables and lives for the winters in order to snowboard (I see him arriving at one of the dilapidated ski resorts on the GR20 and finding himself terribly disappointed), as a courtesy, gives us a gift of the compote of figs and local fruit with the cheeses. Everything, the cheese, the cabernet franc-style red wine from down south, becomes jammy in our mouths.

There is an embarrassing moment when I wish our waiter a *Bonne Anniversaire,* to which he says, "What?" and then, "Oh, I thought you were speaking to me in English." Basically, I say, I am. Meanwhile, on the steps of the church on the piazza, two guys play guitars of certain amped varieties while sitting on said amps. They have us singing to "Those were the days my friend / I thought they'd never end" and then one of the musicians comes up behind his buddy and at close physical proximity, the two play, with bravado, the same guitar.

This would be enough; however, as we stroll along the steps to get air and relax, we hear traditional Corsican folk music. I think it is a recording, but then, I decide, with a beer for a nightcap, a recording will be enough. I want to introduce Petra to Corsican polyphonie, this curious tradition of all-male a capella singing that I'd collected recordings of before the trip.

We slip into the bar. To our amazement, we find a live, five-person group that, for about three or four hours, we have, essentially, all to ourselves, a private concert. Here at the center of the island, and journey, and this book, I am having the best time I will have—I don't care if my questions troubled you, or Petra, or even me.

How do I explain this Corsican singing stuff? "Trying to write about music is like dancing about architecture," Frank Zappa said. There is, in polyphonie, the sound of sheets, layers of voice, necessary layers that keep the wind off you—you think you have enough blankets piled snugly over you on a cold evening, and an arctic breeze blasts, and then another thick wool blanket gets thrown on you even before you shiver or realize you need it. And yet you feel completely vulnerable, open to some new truth you've never even thought of before. Corsican singing covers you up and strips you down, all at once.

Just two weeks before, I felt embarrassed and a failure for not being able to describe to a friend the spectacle of the peaks of the Grand Tetons, from which I had just returned (it was a busy summer of walking). My friend had said, "I guess you had to be there." Nevertheless, like the lunky Dutch guy at the next table who tried to tell and then explain a rudimentary and not very funny blonde joke to our snowboarding waiter, I will attempt to describe polyphonie, without your having been there, with metaphor, first, and then rhetoric.

Metaphor: there is a minor episode in the biblical book of Numbers not much discussed in church but relegated to illustrated moments for children's books found in dentist office waiting rooms (a perfect place for corrective religious instruction). In and around Moab, a man named Balaam was a great public speaker (he whom he blessed got blessed; he whom he cursed got cursed). He had a lot of influence. The Israelites showed up in Moab, and King Balak was a little worried that they'd party too much in his back yard. He asked Balaam—for a hefty fee, of course—to shout some curses about the God of the Israelites. Balaam seems to have been perfectly happy doing it, and probably spent that pay-for-pray curse purse several times over in his head. Imagine him standing out there on the top of Peor, which overlooks the desert, and doing his best to belt out defamations of divine character.

But what should come out of his mouth? Praise! Praise, loud and clear. I see it as one of those variety show mime stunts; you blow on a trumpet and out comes duck call. Instead of "God is a vengeful lazy phony," from his mouth, against his intention, came, "God is great, God is good, God we thank you for our food," and such and

151

such (actually, to be accurate, there were some lines about eating up the nations, but the food image is there). Needless to say, Balaam had to give the king his money back.

Now, I must nudge the metaphor along: imagine an unkempt (and by unkempt, for the image of it, anyway, I mean unshaven) shepherd climbing out of his bergerie and looking to yawn, when out comes a musical note, direct, resonant, scaring the sheep. The note bounces off the lichen-covered mountain walls a hundred times. Four other shepherds answer in kind.

Yikes. More rhetoric, now, beginning with questions: Does the human voice rise to imitate musical instruments, or do instruments we make try to do the same for voice? On my grandmother's Wurlitzer "Funmaker" organ, where she entertained me with upbeat renditions of "Sentimental Journey" and "Theme from Doctor Zhivago," she always chose to open up the Vox Humana stop, reedier, more nasal than we like to think the human voice sounds.

But maybe both instrument and voice are handmaids to the music of nature, try to order its many sounds, orchestrate them. Imagine a half dozen or so men, then, crowded together—outdoors, it always must be imagined, at least, outdoors—and one of them, like a mountain beast—always a mountain beast, a goat, a ram, a sheep, a muvra—bleats out a note, Balaam's intended insulting roar, and what comes out is something from deeper below the man's feet, out of caverns or air, growing things, birth, death. When the bleat becomes a word, when the song's subject reveals itself (the subject always last to be noticed, but noticed, like the last deep voice from the three-part harmony that joins in last, to anchor, to secure us to the world before we fall off this cliff that everywhere suddenly is) it is of love, or dying of it, or revenge because it went wrong because, well, this is Corsica.

The main bleat clears the top of that last peak over yonder and takes the top of your head off along the way, without your knowing it, and after his direct attack, he has, like the flying wedge formation in a football play, given space for the other men in the group to join in, fill in, and vibrate. They vibrate, their voices, the notes nearly match and then tremble up and then down around themselves, modulate, ululate, and you can hear every culture that ever put the moves on Corsica, friend and foe—Islamic calls to worship, Tuscan calls to war, Aragonese calls to drink, stuff that has always been out there in the air—and these modulations the men do are actually bringing that out of the sky like radio frequencies on a ham radio set. You feel capable of singing it yourself (but please don't: leave it to the locals), on some level, I think, and that's its attraction, for it seems it has always been your own tradition, although it is specifically Corsican. It's the song you want to sing when you've caught your finger in the car door, or hit your head on a low portal, or eaten too much at Thanksgiving, or accidentally insulted the host. So much for rhetoric; I've lapsed into metaphor once again.

There's more science and history to it all than that, of course. I ought, as a responsible travelologist, to give you the true history of Corsican music with all its categories and theories: the polyphonies are just one type and developed from that voceru, that cri di coeur of a black-clad woman. There is, too, the *chiama e rispondi,* when two shepherds sing sixteen-syllable lines back and forth from one cliff to another in the mountains, or, as it easily evolved, antiphony, calling back and forth from one wing of an organ loft to another in a church.

I forget myself in the presence of such music. That sounds disingenuous, since I've written it, but it's true: there were half-moon marks in the palms of my hands from clutching my own fists in intent distraction. To describe the sound is to describe the Mediterranean, for which there is no crayon color, even in the box with the jumbo assortment.

When I listen to these guys, I can hardly keep myself from tearing up (I slip into the grandiose again, but it's not crying, no—it's weeping), and I begin to blow money: on beer, for one, for Petra, for the band. Then I pay for a request: "A Tribbiera," which is a gorgeous wailing traditional tune that's sung to an ox as it walks in a tethered circle threshing grain in its wake. The group whips it off (all night they leaf through a songbook as if they know the tunes but need to look at the words, a first-time run-through).

Then I see that they have a CD for sale, and then I buy it, and then I run around grinning, after the weeping, and like a dork, I have them all autograph it. Then I think, this music is different than anything and—while the nationalistic tendency seems simpatico enough already, given the discrete land, the specific language (however in debt to the Genoese), the cultural tradition—it is this music that nudges me fully behind the rabble-rousing impulse. But to be clear, it's not a hardcore patriotism I feel, not a clenching of my jaw, but a relaxing: a softness comes, and I know it's soft—and still.

But they're just a bunch of guys wearing jeans and various styles of black shirts. They'd look like a bowling team if they lived in the States, if that's where they were. In this bar they look like bowlers in bad marriages, avoiding the trip home. I remember, oddly, those package-deal gymnasium assemblies arranged in our high school that were required for attendance: a juggler, a comedian, and, oh no! I'm so worried for that stupid band from Corsica! But everybody loved them—so different and beautiful and, oh yes, masculine all at once. They are masculine, though again there's that necessity to sing in close proximity, touch each other, even press cheeks together or put one's arm around another guy. A tenderness. Any minute now, and they're going to start braiding each other's hair. And yet you have to cover your own ear to plug the other guy's sound, to keep your even pitch perfect and pure. That's ironic.

And then, around one in the morning, two rich French twits walk into our private concert with three high-end prostitutes in ridiculous Eurotrash shorts. They prance and grope, but the band holds its own, although I see them look, perhaps even enviously, toward the twits and twats, feeling that softness (of lust, this time) in themselves, wishing they could have three hot babes any time they wanted. The Bad Element claps wildly after each song, apparently not hearing in nearly every politically charged verse some version of "Francesi Fora!": Give us your money, give us your adulation, give us a beer, and then go the hell away.

They are the bad guys to me, the outsiders, the prostitutes and their johns, and heroes to the band, I guess; to the band, I am the dork, running around grinning and weeping and gathering autographs; weeping, yes, weeping. And the prostitutes make it easy to want to go home, continue our journey across the GR20. Softness begets toughness.

We are nearly ready to go back to our hotel, our expensive beers are gone. Behind the band, there is a door hung in space, purposeless, even hazardous. I've been watching the guitarist on the far left, his pure eyes, the expensive beers, and then—and then a stupid little thing happens. A bit of lavender from my sangliere a la Corse came loose from between my teeth. The maquis mixes in with the Pietra beer, the pure voices, and I have this overwhelming sense of being alone with the band (still not fully ruined by the whores)—even the insiders, they themselves couldn't know my pleasure. It is all mine.

Immediately, I want to ruin the moment by saving it. Where's the CD, I want to know, and then think: Let it go! I am so soft to want to shut it down, lock it up, own it. "Stupid Canadian boy," Petra says, handing me a bar napkin: for God's sake, pull yourself together.

"Stupid *American* boy," I correct her, and blow.

She hands me another bar napkin, and I murmur some complaint about their feckless size, but she consoles us both: "Cavemen never got to blow their noses in a bar napkin."

The music, the beer, the joke, they all make me even softer, and each time you read this, I'm as soft as that snake that's lost its skin. I lose it over and over, you, here, watching me now, me, there, shedding it then. It works; I am a viable responsible witness—as long as I write about it well enough and you are willing to take on the burden of believing me.

Vizzavona to E'Capannelle

That deer that ran away from me near the beginning of the étape was not a deer at all, but the ass-end of a moufflon, or "Muvra," one of the "muvrini," as they call these mountain rams and the Corsican band that bleats like them. It was probably as close as I ought get to one, too. And when I stop for a little water and a rest and to look into my guidebook, it turns out I was lucky to have seen it at all.

Sheep dot the hill like throw pillows. The throw-pillow sheep. And they seem cheapened by their rare cousin, whom I have spooked.

Perhaps it was not such a good idea to give ourselves a couple of days of clean linen and fine dining, only to send ourselves back into the wilds. The calluses that take so long to build up on my hands and feet go away within hours, it seems, and setting out this morning from the chalet, I felt soft and, compared to the hikers who had simply stayed on the trail, well-groomed. Even my Wringing Muscles have gone slack in that little time, the ones in the upper wrist that get sore from wringing out clothes after washing them by hand and hoping against hope that they will be dry enough to wear the next morning on the trail.

And the first place we stop is not very inspiring: yet another rusty winter ski resort gone belly-up. If we had not arrived on the train so late in the morning, we probably would have walked farther to the Bocca di Verdi, which we would only be able to find out the next day would have been a perfect place to pitch a tent. As it was, we did not feel like renting another expensive hotel room, and found a semi-illegal corner of the hotel grounds and tried not to look at the nightmare of a ski lift that will take a rider only as far as the Land of Lockjaw.

Sunlight does not so much shine as it does sparkle on a perfect olive tree in front of our tent, and we have decided to "eat in." Petra makes more of the noodles, and I cut pieces of the massive lonzu and the brocciu, too, to go with a day-old baguette. We splurge on another of those paper-stoppered bottles of wine from the gardien, which I find out really comes out of a box and probably costs a buck, even though they charge ten. We eat all this on top of my too-big red poncho, so it's like a picnic. The weather is fine outdoors, but we don't want to be bothered by the riffraff, or that view.

Petra is pleased, for a glass or two of any kind of wine makes her the best dining companion. It's like winding up a tin toy. My companion, my delight. "My cousin is getting married today somewhere in Dusseldorf," she tells me.

"Really? Are you close? Is he going to be disappointed?"

"Well, he's not really a cousin, but we grew up with them, and our parents knew their parents because my grandfather was rescued by their grandparents during the war." I'm always a little tense around these sorts of stories, because what we're talking here is Nazis. Anybody in "the war" from Germany would have been. What are you going to do? Some of them really were foot soldiers, some actually suffered. Patriotism: the easiest emotion. Thinking around it, whether the beholder or the beholden, takes some work.

Petra goes on to say that she played house, she and this cousin, and he was the first boy she ever "touched."

"I used to play house in kindergarten," I tell her, "and I always wanted to play the father, I don't know why. I decided that the thing you said when you were the father was, 'You people are giving me an ulcer.'"

This leads to Petra's discussion of what she calls the "psychodramas" that she participated in during college, including one about the

Nativity in which her role was to say, "No room at the inn!" In all the stories, Petra wanted to play the bad guy.

"Me too!" I say. "Why do you think this is?"

My shoulders are sore from having the backpack on again after three days without. Putting it on that morning, I think I got a pretty good idea what it was like to be a horse, or any beast of burden, and have a saddle strapped onto me: the editor of *Stubborn Pack Mule Monthly*. Why are we doing this? Getting back on the dusty trail to the lonesome Laricios when there is wine and music at the spa down below? Perhaps, I suggest to Petra, it's all about the delay of gratification, the withholding of pleasure. "Or entering pleasure through the side door."

"Through the side door?" She is checking her translation; is it an idiomatic expression she has forgotten?

"Like the church in Corte—the Eglise de l'Annonciation. We couldn't walk through the front door and walk right down the aisle. It was locked. We had to go to the side door to be let in. We were only allowed to enjoy the nice things inside if we came to it from the side."

"What nice things?" Petra wants to know. We were both a little horrified, it's true, by a St. Theophilus in that church, a statue made of wax. He'd been melting for a little while. And he was pretty much the main attraction.

But I still like my theory. I tend to eat inward from the edges of a plate of food, especially if it is haute cuisine and complex, approaching a thing that's a grand marriage of many parts by sampling each of the parts first. Climb the mountain to get the vista, descend the mountain to get some sleep.

Even out here, walking along to the tune of that different drummer, I feel out of step even with my fellow out-of-steppers—there are evenings when I feel the need to drop into a coma when everybody around me seems to have breezed into camp effortlessly. And on this night: vice versa—I am full of energy and jokes, and every-body else seems to have had life sucked from them by the sun and wind. Petra has gone into the gîte to talk to somebody in German for a change. I share the night with Auden—my own game of hackey sack. Poetry books are perfect for hiking: compact, plenty to unpack, designed the way high tech guys design my tent and sleeping bag; they are durable and reusable, although this word "use" is a charged, muddy word, for as my hackey-sack buddy Auden says, "poetry makes nothing happen: it survives / In the valley of its making where executives / Would never want to tamper."

I take a walk with my weak penlight down tomorrow's trail a bit, because, of all things, I'm having a spell of my agoraphobia. They've built a massive bonfire in front of the gîte, a small luxury usually forbidden with so much flammable maquis. I find a flat stone and sprawl upon it, so that I can watch the stars; the spill of the Milky Way wheels above me. If I place myself just right, the only thing I can see is stars. Toby, a writer friend who has spent a life fishing for crabs and other sea beasts in Alaskan waters, wrote once about a rare occurrence when the boat he was in, far out on the sea, encountered a calm under a cloudless night sky, and he had the strange sensation of floating in space, the little craft surrounded by billions of stars above and below. It only took the slightest ripple in the water to end the illusion, but oh, what an illusion that must have been.

I'm perfectly content marveling at the surfeit of stars I get up here, free of city lights and smoke—minor constellations reveal themselves here, constellations I could only memorize before today, rather than observe, for my astronomy merit badge in Scouts. It's September and the summer constellations are slowly giving themselves over to the winter sky, so I get a bit from both worlds—Taurus and Cassiopeia, and Scorpio and even Orion's neck—and there are the made-up constellations from countless camping trips with as many marvelous goof-off friends: The Great Dixie Cup; the Peeved

Elephant; L 7 Major and L 7 Minor, those patron gods of losers past and present. Satellites, those must be, blinking, streaking high and with purpose, and I marvel at the cataract glaze of Milky Way once again, a treasure trail itself that seems to rise from the smoke and sparks of the gîte's bonfire just up the trail I've descended.

I stand up among the familiar and unfamiliar stars and back-track upward, and have my own strange sensation of ascending into heaven, and lo!, how, just at the top of the hill, the Big Dipper shows itself, and I have to laugh at its simple familiarity—a bit of the domestic beamed down to me here, oddly the oldest familiar thing to most of humanity after, perhaps, prostitution and religious intolerance—and I feel at home not only geographically but in time, knowing that its big scoop is twinkling down on Petra in the gîte, Michael in Chicago, on Jeff alive again in San Francisco, Boy Scout Brian at Camp Teetonkah, with just two merit badges to go before earning his rank of "Star," and cavemen.

E'Capanelle to Usciolu

I have a bruise on my left hip, and I don't know how I came to get it. Banging all around I suppose, tearing the skin off every digit against stone and stick. Hiking is like a binge-drinking binge, another sort of lost weekend, a blackout.

We have arrived at the refuge Usciolu, and it is a ferociously cheerful place. The gardien loves his job. He has souvenirs, and a postmark he will stamp on any postcards you may have purchased who knows where, and he will run them into the next village on his energetic burros if you give them to him. He's got a solar powered CD player, and he blasts from the veranda traditional Corsican poly-phonie. He has a well-stocked larder and can even make salads. He has enthusiasm and jokes galore and lots of ideas for day hike excur-sions. He has enough energy to sprint the GR20, damn his hide.

What he doesn't have is room. The gîte is perched on the side of a hill and so there are very few places for all of us to pitch our tents. Petra and I are midlist hikers and we arrive at the étape a bit after the supertrekkers have come in and claimed the choice bunks in the bunkhouse and the best campsites for the tents. We always manage to get something—often something better, because we pitch farther away from the facilities, which some think inconvenient, but listening to tired campers stumble over one's guy lines all night while trying to make it to the outhouse doesn't seem a hallmark of convenience. We often find ourselves a little off to the side, where it is more quiet and sometimes more picturesque.

But here at Usciolu, there aren't any spaces left for us, and again all I can think of are those poor suckers that always come after us, the ones even slower and usually much more exhausted. Petra and I search and search and have to come up with a makeshift place between a couple of rocks, where we can barely hear the canned polyphonie.

Along the last leg of the walk, too, we were chased by black biting flies that seem to have been bred from years of donkeys walking along here, the preferred meat of blackfly. So much of the GR20 is made up of very ancient pathways made by burros and goats and shepherds leading their sheep to the huts we pass along the way, called *pastori*. Very nymphs-and-shepherds, except for the part about the flies. And the dung. And the trails that lead off into the bushes and get you lost.

This is the end of a weekend, although weekends don't mean much when you're deep into a trail. But both Petra and I traditionally call home to our parents, because it's a Sunday, when the rates are cheap, though that, too, doesn't mean much in the age of the cell phone. Petra grabs The Most Powerful Cell Phone in the World, and she calls from our mountainside as if she were using a payphone downtown. "Something cavemen never experienced," she, like my father, points out the obvious, as she waits for somebody to pick up somewhere in Bavaria. We were all such cavemen not fifteen years ago. Everybody is somebody else's caveman.

She ended up talking with her five-year-old nephew at length, told him about the lammergeier and, if I can guess through the German, something about sports-walking.

Afterwards, she explains about her nephew who lives with Petra's frumpy sister in Dusseldorf, not nearly as adventurous as her aunt. He wants to go with Petra, and this causes tension between the sisters. He is all kinetic energy, like today's gardien. He never goes swimming, or at least he does not *just* go swimming, but sports-swimming.

"'Sports' is German for 'extreme,'" I tell her.

"What?"

"You have sports-swimming, sports-running, sports-footballing. We say 'extreme.' Extreme football. Extreme running. Extreme team luge."

"What is extreme luge?" Petra wants to know.

"We use one of the team members as sled runners in extreme team luge."

"Ooohhh," Petra understands. "You are talking about sports-luge!"

Her nephew knows that we are walking across Corsica, and he calls it sports-walking. He is correct. I am sports-writing now. By evening, Petra has fallen in love with the concept of "extreme." She wants an "extreme" cappuccino, made with the gardien's blood. We discuss her nephew's birthday, when we can send him an extreme piñata, filled with molten cheese. What would be on the extreme Damenkarte, we wonder.

"Do you want to have children?" she suddenly asks.

"Oh, no. I am a child," I tell her. I pick up her cell phone, because it's my turn to call home. "How about you? Do you want to have children?"

I call back home, too, which is six hours behind us. The news is under water. My mother tells me that my niece was visiting, and she had found a turtle. Jamie, a quiet foggy cat of a girl, gets on the line. Our relationship is strained; whenever we're together for holidays or trips back to Michigan, I usually interview her, and she responds with simple yes-or-no answers. I keep thinking I'll try to rephrase my questions, but here on the GR20, I fall back on old habits. "You've got a turtle?" I try.

"Yeah," she says—and this is the most loquacious she has ever been with me, perhaps precisely because I am on the other side of the world—"but one of its eyes was gone when I got it." I don't know what that really means, "gone." Swollen shut? Rotted out?

"And the other one is gone now," she adds. "Now it doesn't move."

My mother takes the phone back. "We're going to see if we can't put it out of its misery," she tells me. Such brutality, so far away. I can't help the turtle. Jamie's little brother, my own sports-nephew, got on the line, too. "How is the turtle," I asked him, because maybe a second opinion will put my mind at ease.

"Good!" he says, "I'm killing flies for his food. How many flies do you think he can eat?"

Boys and their "mosts." It must be some version of competition, to pit ideas against each other in contests, objects that would never meet in any sort of arena. There must always be a victor, must always be one thing superior, one thing ordinary. Certainly, I am not fond of the possibility of being ordinary. It takes some getting used to. I recall here the feeling I had when we descended from Petra Piana in the cloudburst, how wet and slow and ill-prepared we were, and all I could think of was the people still at the previous campsite, taking down their tents in the rain; I had to be superior, they had to be ordinary.

It's an international phenomenon, this larval macho stage. I can usually guess what people are asking me from context in a foreign language I don't know; it's all the same stuff: Where's the bathroom?

163

Do you have any more of that wine? Can I borrow your knife? Are you using this umbrella? Have you seen a little dead British boy? and so forth. But boys, they ask things like, "How high is that mountain?" "Who ate the most hot dogs in one sitting?" "How many liters of fuel does this farm implement take?" "Who would win in a fight between Heidi and Godzilla?" out of the blue, for no reason, no context in sight.

In the gîte in Usciolu, I encounter the first American I've seen so far. "How many days have you been walking?" He is full of the same numbers and conquests. After my resolve to come out of the closet as an American, without fear, I say hello to him at the water pump and he introduces himself as "Pete, from Philadelphia." He is eager to let out all the stuff he has been storing up inside himself, being alone with his brain for days and days. He tells me about all the places he has hiked and I am, indeed, impressed. But he is restless and unfulfilled. While Petra and I have dreamed of Tibet and Zanzibar and Crete, this Pete wants to go to the top of Everest and the bottom of the Marianas Trench, the most highest and the most lowest. "Then you can relax," he tells me. "You," I remark: you, meaning, all of us; "you": that should be your goal—highest and lowest. Then we can *all* relax.

Pete uses all sorts of shifts in point of view. He's very much a storyteller that way. "Then you can relax," is, of course, a sort of camouflaged "I," so that he doesn't have to show any feelings at all—not even the feeling of not being relaxed, which apparently he isn't, and won't be, until he gets down there in the trench and up there at the top of Everest. On the other hand, when he offers to show me his cooking equipment because it has proven to be a wonder in lightweight, space-saving technology as well as a maker of a mean can of soup, he proves his authority on the subject by switching over to the third person "they": "Because Pete Knows Food," he says, the way "Bo Knows Basketball." It's a puffed up chest-beating stance,

164

warning the listener of that Hulk-like alter ego just waiting under the skin that *you*, brother, don't wanna mess with. Not on the subject of cooking, no way. It seems to be some version of the royal "we" as well, although it doesn't seem nearly as kingly but more like a dog, barking when it is afraid or on the defensive, a protective stance.

To tell the truth, I don't often walk with this sort; they're a new sort. And by a "new" sort, I mean, of course, a very *old* sort, the ones who wait on me at the outdoor store, who bide their time between extreme adventure sorties by playing their own game of hackey sack near the rack of quick-drying socks when I'm trying to select some, or discouraging hikers from buying soap because it's bad to wash in the river, when I'm trying to buy soap (of course it is bad for the river; I don't intend to wash myself or anything else in the river). They don't seem to think anything I'm trying to buy in their store is the right thing (walking shoes instead of hiking boots, a rain poncho that fits over myself and my backpack, energy bars, rain pants that make the delightful "zwik-zwik" noise when I walk) and wherever it is that I've walked or plan to walk, it is not usually where they have been, so it doesn't really exist.

And by the old sort, I mean the sort I used to hike with, years ago when I was zigzagging my way up to the top of Bridal Veil in Yosemite or to Surprise Lake in the Grand Tetons. It was all a big race for those boys, who chose their hikes not for the views but by the level of difficulty. They may think they're sensitive nature boys, but they are just as macho as the next, shut down to the possibilities of anything other than what they know and are comfortable with.

But every once in a while, our paths still cross, and they are filled with a furious, brittle, haughty, and (dare I say it?) queeny (I do dare!) disdain. The last time this happened was during a walk up the side of Mount Snowden in Wales. I went there with my friends Michael and Marta and their young daughter Rafaela, my godchild. It's a fairly easy day hike to the summit of Snowden, so we packed ourselves a picnic lunch with sandwiches and champagne, and one of us carried Rafaela in one pack while another safeguarded the champagne. We were passed by a team of hutt-hutt-hutt hikers in cleated shoes. They wrapped themselves with ropes and clips for safety. We strapped a baby to ourselves, for safety. They beat us to the top, but there was still a table available for us in the pub at the top of the mountain. Come on, guys, there's a pub at the top!

I can see them size me up here (and by sizing me up, I mean that their eyes started up at my face and sized down to my shoes, always it's the shoes they can't abide) on the GR20, some of them passing from the south to the north, and the first thing they do is ask me all those measurements: How much does your pack weigh? Is your sleeping bag going to keep you warm if it gets to be twenty below zero? What level sunblock are you using? Who ate the most hot dogs in one sitting?

Each morning, they break their camp before dawn, do not bother with coffee but replaced it with tiny packets of charmless caffeinated goo that have to be sucked out of a sealed pouch, and stomp by our tent while we sip tea and fold our drying clothes. They stand in disbelief, a few hours later, when we saunter into camp at the next étape, looking at us if to say, How did you find out my name is Rumpelstilskin?

There were those two in particular, inseparable as lovers, the French Roosters, and we lost them when we left the GR20 for a couple of days. Impossible as it would seem, they were replaced by two *new* Roosters, almost identical in build and carriage, although these two seem to hate, rather than love, each other. They are held together by a single shared guidebook, I think, and not much else. There is one other difference between the old Roosters and the new: these two are noisy. Squawking and crowing all the way down the piste. I don't even have to get the meaning of their words when they speak to know the gist: boasting. They are alike in that they are both suffering an odd version of male pattern baldness in which a bit of hair at the front stayed while the rest receded back and the monk's tonsure took hold. They look as if they have large mustaches that have migrated to their foreheads, the sort that barbershop quartet singers have under their noses.

Compared to them, good old American Pete is not such a bad sort. But once he has told me all about the places he has walked and where it is he wants to walk in the future, once he has revealed to me his master plan to plow the Marianas Trench and scale the heights of Everest, then he can relax. And he does. And has nothing left to say to me for the rest of the GR20.

Usciolu to Asinau

Not that the touristic invaders from the coast haven't had their own effect on the inland villages. The locals, in the villages we walk through, seem to be made up of big lunk-headed stony boys with Harley-Davidson T-shirts and aging women in stretch pants, who aren't afraid to show a camel toe (one that seems meant to match their pointed shoes). They drink in the little bars while we tourists drink outside. There is this restlessness of people who live on islands, even when you can't tell you're on an island, that makes them seem like flies bouncing about in a bottle.

They watch us pass through with our packs and are puzzled that we would bother doing this, especially without a car, or at least a mule. And they are something for us to look at, too, for they are interchangeable from place to place, so that we sometimes wonder whether we have moved at all.

On this day our walking goes through the same wild changes of geography as those we experienced near Lake Nino. There are strange stone outcrops eroded by rain and wind and whatever other sorts of weather these mountains create, and then we enter the moors, a jollier sort of moors than are found in England near the border of Scotland. They could be pozzines, if the land didn't rise and fall so often, so repeatedly, and for some reason, I am cheered by being able to see the Gulf of Ajaccio, where I sailed in a week or so before.

From there we start to walk up, and while Petra doesn't complain, my eye is always on her. We take many rest breaks and resolve not to be bothered by the way other hikers overtake us. Usually they die out on their own, anyway. Our reward for this steady work is another new spectacle, a crucifix planted on a dome at the summit, glacially laced boulders strewn about in a way that makes me search around in my mind to understand how the job was done geographically. And when we look on to the way we go farther, it is a prairie full of maquis, as thick and regular as the poppy field in *The Wizard of Oz*. And farther on than that: the Aiguilles de Bavella, and the Emerald City of aforesaid movie are a pretty good approximation of what those look like. Even with a backpack pulling at us the way it has for the previous four hours, we want to run to the Bavella range.

We have left the forests for a while, and so we'll have no shade, and we won't have any more of my favorite apparitions of the moist shady areas, those fire salamanders, slippery black fellows with flaming yellow spots.

"Why don't you sing the fire salamander song?" Petra suggests, when I lament that we won't be seeing fire salamanders much any more. This song, so it happens, is sung to the tune of "Yesterday," by the Beatles, and its lyrics are rather subject to invention, much like the Corsica voceru. It has done little good drawing salamanders to us, either. By the end of the walk today, I have no energy to improvise lyrics, nor sing even "I know an old woman who swallowed a fly," I am that exhausted. I ask Petra if she will set up the tent herself, and she pushes me over, and I let her, and rest in the dirt, because it's nice to be horizontal, even though horizontal is on something of a slant here. I get up, eventually, because all the blood starts to drain to my head.

The refuge at Asinau has nice views, but we have trouble pitching the tent on flat ground, not the first time this happened. This is what happens when you spend so much time perched on the slopes of mountains. Even when we thought we were level, I'd find myself in the morning bunched at the front end of the tent, having slid slowly over the night. My toes do this in my shoes on the downhills, another reason I dislike the downhills.

In the overused toilets of the Asinau refuge, I read a sign in my own language, a rare occurrence, and so written because the message is more important than all the other map directions, fire and storm warnings, and menus: "It pleased to walkers to leave the toilet clean. Thanks to understand." You are more than welcome.

This is a fairly new refuge and only a couple of years before, walkers would have to take a detour for two hours down to the village of Zicavo, a lovely place we would visit in a car after all our journeys on the GR20 have ended, in order to restock with food and water. Now the gîte purposefully carries all the things we need and cooks us yet another omelette. Always with the omelettes. No, no, it's okay—crack a couple of eggs for me. I am grateful.

While I set up the tent and Petra just watches (my punishment), Petra tells me about an old schoolteacher of hers who made this journey down the GR20 twenty years before, when there were no gardiens, no gîtes to support hikers. He had to drive through the island before he walked and buried for himself metal boxes full of food and other supplies, which he could unearth as he went back through on foot. "That's a lot of work," I told Petra. "I don't think I would do it if I had to do that."

"You Americans, you have no morals," she said. "You are all like midwives." Apparently, the midwife is an effective metaphor of the weakling in Teutonic countries. Staying up all night and helping a woman in labor—that sounds like a lot of work, too. But secretly I wish there were places in the world like the GR20 twenty years ago. Every special place, every camino and chemin and trail, seems to have been fully discovered, picked over. Perhaps I will turn to caving next.

A foot journey, whether to a pilgrim site or anywhere, is a love affair, I suppose; I'd had my chance with this lover. In Corte I went to a quiet morning café before Petra got up. There were six hard-drinking Madrileños who asked me to pull up a chair with them: they were impressed with my Spanish, and I'm easily flattered, although I quickly volunteered that I didn't quite understand the subjunctive. How is it going? they asked, and I told them we had been resting from the GR20 and that I was running out of trails in the world and I would soon return to walk their own road to Santiago a second time. One of the men of the group took a moment from his avuncular, alcoholic happiness to say with great seriousness, "Segundos partes nunca fueron buenas," second times never have gone well. Or Einstein said it another way: the definition of insanity is doing the same thing over and over and expecting different results.

7

Why I Walk

Adnomination

> It is a fact that not once in all my life have I gone out
> for a walk. I have been taken out for walks; but that is an-
> other matter. Even while I trotted prattling by my nurse's
> side I regretted the good old days when I had, and wasn't,
> a perambulator.
>
> Max Beerbohm, "Going Out for a Walk"

I'm better at packing for a trip, now. Any trip, not just the foot
trips. If it doesn't fit in the overhead luggage, it's not going. Every
time I've checked a bag, something got broken: CD jewel cases,
toothbrush handles, a souvenir trilobite fossil. Nothing important,
agreed, but once, when unpacking after Mexico City, I pulled out a
small showy bottle of good tequila and didn't at first notice that it

had broken, and then I noted that it was as if some small animal had taken a small bite out of a bottom corner of the glass, and the agave had soaked into my clothes, so that they smelled of sour yogurt and sweat. After a beach trip to the island of Vieques, I saved a spiral seashell, but when unwrapping it, a hermit crab, shriveled into a tiny fist, slid from its pearly chamber onto the floor. I had to jump back, the body had the shock gag heft of a rubber chicken, a whoopee cushion Bronx-cheered out flat, harmless now, the damage done. I was scared, but it was killed. Better leave things where they are, take nothing there, and bring nothing here. Avoid souvenirs, keep a light knapsack, or plan to carry sorrow.

At the beginning of long trails, I have found many things ditched in the ditch. I have walked along the trail, and they'd be there, a museum exhibition. There have been shirts and extra shoes and pages ripped from guidebooks—after you've walked through a map, it's no longer worth its weight. My favorite item: a copy of *The Portable Dante,* not portable enough. There was a most beautiful new leather jacket left on a grassy knoll, curled like a sleeping animal, delicious as an advertisement for a nougat candy bar split open to show its sheen and luxury. Nobody picked it up, as far as I know, not anybody walking on the same trail, anyway. The gîtes and hostels and refugios, even in the most remote alpen reaches, have impossibly huge, almost mythic libraries of abandoned books in many languages, a library of Babel.

People will make me wonder at the burdens they'll carry for pleasure. The extreme sports boys have invented superflyweight tent steaks as light as a Coke can. Nylon rope, vacuum-packed freeze-dried noodles. All this, in order to make room for a six pack of beer, an elaborate camera, hackey-sack beanbags. They always lecture me when I come in, about how my pack is too heavy and not the right name brand. But when I have pulled out a good bottle of red wine, one properly stoppered and not with a wad of paper nor sold at extortionate prices, the sort you'll get from the gardien at the refuge, I have thought—who will help me eat the cake, asked the little red hen.

After one or two days of walking, a walker knows pain. Pain consumes you, not just physically but mentally (you can't hear a pretty song or enjoy a beautiful view) and emotionally, and even the imagination is consumed; you start to believe that your bones will shatter, your flesh turn to jelly; you cannot avoid it. It becomes a kind of focus, an asceticism, if you want to be vain about it. No wonder religious types see it as a test of faith, a punishment even.

Sometimes the meaning of something changes when you just shift the position, or disposition, of the roots, the context, a little bit. Among words, this is called "adnomination," a kind of wordplay in which the root meaning or phonetic value of the words are similar or alike, but that actual meaning between the two is germane. The only dictionary where I can even find the term listed begins by telling me that the word is obsolete. We get our puns elsewhere these days. But I'm thrilled at the small difference between two words, for the meaning of "restive" is quite different from the meaning of "rested," especially if you are a walker with a pack.

I descend from long-drawn tailings of lumpenpeasants, German, Irish, Polish, Hauserbroad. I was built for work, like a mule, though I hunch over a desk most days. So, when I put on the burden of a backpack, it shouldn't surprise me that I stand up straight, my posture improves. In the Corsican mountains, I have the high peaks as role models, and I try to match them with my own stature. Even the villages on this island are exemplary to a walker—the stone houses stand up tall, seven stories high and carrying their own burden. They swagger while they conserve, these citadels, these defenses like Corte and Calvi. In the bars, I see Corsicans sit bolt upright on their stools, and I am sure they are ready for any attack.

What does it mean, that I am at my best when I am loaded down, respond so quickly to the labor? Despite the softness of my hands, my body sends many signals: it was meant for work. I never get sick on these walks, although I shiver in cold mountain clouds and fry under too much sun. After a few days, the bones in my feet begin to spread, to give me a wider base. I shed pounds, lose that grief, too. After walking a few weeks in central France, I was embarrassed when my shorts fell around my ankles.

Adnomination seems some version, within one's own language, of "false friends," faux amis, words that share the same cognate between two languages that are quite different, in fact. "Demand" in English, "demander," in French: To require of another, to ask of another. "Exit," in English, "exito," in Spanish: a place of departure, a place of success. Petra tells me that when she goes to London, she laughs at the Gift Shops. "Gift" is the German word for poison or venom. With shorts around my ankles, with no water in my bottle, with no bed to call my own, do I stand before God with humility, or humiliation?

Grief has weight. After a terrible breakup, I frequented a deserted Chinese restaurant that did most of its business in carry-out. It was me alone in a room full of nostril-red paint and outdated paneling, the good-luck cat, his paw up as if to say, "Right on!" watching me order plateful after plateful of chow mein, especially the hot and spicy "Emperor's Special," and all that ingested starch was sorrow made manifest. I had to walk it off.

The appetite comes—or goes. Once my plump aunt's husband died, she began to lose weight. But it was more than that, as if the body wanted to disappear itself. Her doctor called it "the dwindlies." Get fat! Don't die!

When my partner Jeff died, he was not much more than a pile of twigs. He could not make his way upstairs to the bedroom, so we had set up a hospital bed downstairs, very close to the bathroom. On more than one occasion, he had gotten up to go to the bathroom, and he'd run out of energy on the way back, so in the morning I would find him asleep on the couch or in an easy chair; I'd have to get him up or carry him back to the bed. The day he died, I didn't notice at first, because he seemed to have run out of energy again and simply slumped under the cuckoo clock. I had been awakened that morning by an early phone call. "I'll have to call you back," I said to a friend who didn't realize the time difference, "I have to put Jeff back in bed." I went over and found him cold. There were, above him, the two lead pine-cone-shaped weights that pulled the gears ever downward, drawing the time through the gears and up to the hands of the clock face. The pine cone rested on his bony shoulder. He had stopped the mechanism of the machine with his body, and I knew exactly what time he had died: 5:12 a.m. He lay pressed down by the clock's weights like that curled up leather jacket at the side of the trail.

It's only precious word play, on another level. Take the "l" out of lover, and it's over. Petra asks me, "Have you ever noticed how 'fashion' and 'fascism' sound nearly the same?" I am not sure whether it is better to be an "invalid," or to be "invalidated." Did the bandits d'honneur that hid for so long in the maquis "give themselves up" or simply "give up"?

When I took the long walking journey through France and Spain to the pilgrim shrine of Santiago de Compostela, I carried in my backpack a stone from home. I picked up the pebble from my mother's garden. "What are you doing in there?" she asked as I poked around. I'm sure she thought I might stomp on a tomato. I explained that I would carry a rock from home and when I got to a place about three-quarters of the way to the pilgrim site, there was a great iron cross, the *cruz de ferro,* and at the foot of the cross, pilgrims over the millennia had tossed their stones. The stone is meant to represent the burden of sin, and after the purification of pilgrimage, one is allowed to shed that weight. My mother picked up a stone. "Take one for me."

Whenever I walked, my mother took care of Grace, my dog. My mother was less strict about feeding my dog, so she'd have to go on a diet whenever I returned. I once made the mistake of reading a book about dogs, what they think and feel. It's all guesswork, but the guess is that dogs are pretty much easygoing. The only thing they hate is being left alone. I didn't want to know this.

———

The Corsican bandit d'honneur is *notorious* to some, but enjoys *notoriety* among his own. Some say he gets by in the maquis with a good knowledge of *craft*. Others think him merely *crafty*. The Maquisards, those workers for the resistance against the Axis nations of World War II were *revolutionary* to those who longed for a free France, *revolting* to the Nazis. As I trudge through the maquis myself, I think it is good to be *outside,* but would rather not be looked at as an *outsider.*

———

Grace once got sick from eating while I was on one of my long journeys. "Garbage gut," they call it. She had to have surgery to remove the blockage of too much food. She was okay for a few years, then the scar tissue around the surgery built up, and became a mass that couldn't be removed. When I returned from Corsica, Grace got sick again. At the vet's, there are four private rooms, each equipped with an examining table. The table is also a scale, so when you put your dog or cat or parakeet on the table, a little readout at the end tells you how much the dog weighs. I put Grace on the table: twenty-three pounds. When I take her leash off, the light-emitting diodes adjusted: twenty-two pounds. The doctor, who had known Grace for years, only talked to her now. "What you got there?" he asked her as he poked around her little paunch. He took her in to be x-rayed. When he returned to the examining room, he left Grace behind for a little hydration, and we put the x-rays into a light board above the weighing table. He leaned forward to show me the spooky shadow of blockage and tumor. The weight from his leaning body was registered on the readout: twelve pounds. "See this mass here?" he asked. I leaned forward to look with him, and pressed my fingertips on the table. Twenty-one pounds. A little more leaning for him: twenty-three pounds. "There's really nothing we can do about it." I stood straight, as if I'd just put on a very heavy backpack. He stood straight, too, looked down at the table as if he might make the weight change with his mind, but it still said: zero pounds. "So when you say there's nothing we can do, then that means there's nothing I can do," I said. I placed the flat of my hands on the table. Seven pounds. He did too—he must have noticed this business himself. It must happen all the time, the pressure on the table. A Persian cat: twelve pounds. A black Labrador: fifty-six pounds. My torso, my head, my arms, as they hung over, realizing I had to make the decision about how much longer Grace will live: about the same as a black Lab, I suppose: fifty-six pounds, then, breathing in, fifty-four, then fifty-six again, fifty-four, fifty-seven, fifty-five, fifty-six, fifty-four, fifty-six.

I know what you're thinking: Just what is adnomination's relationship to antanaclasis? I've anticipated that question, for antanaclasis is the repetition of a word whose meaning changes in the second instance. "If you aren't fired with enthusiasm," Vince Lombardi once said, "you'll be fired with enthusiasm." After a day of walking, I am *enervated*. After a night of sleeping, I am *energized*, or should be, if I had real coffee instead of little packets of coffee goo to suck on. With real coffee, I am *content*. Without it, I am *contentious*.

Deep in the heart of Corsica's "Cirque de la Solitude," we used chains and ropes to scale up and down sheer cliff faces. I felt ridiculous, sure to fall. With a backpack pulling you down, it's as if gravity itself wants you dead. But loose stone is even more treacherous. The word *scree,* is it, perhaps, adnomination with the word *scream*? Somewhere among the gila monster–backed peaks of the Bavella group, above us, three birds soared nearly at eye level over the canyon below. I watched them swoop down to the bottom and come back up with sticks in their claws. "They must be making their nests," I told Petra. "But it's autumn," she said. "Birds don't feather their nests in autumn." Then what were they doing with the sticks?

They were dropping them. Apparently, the sticks were too heavy to carry for long. I saw them break on some rock ledges just below me. The bird went down to retrieve it again. But wait: the bird poked its beak into the broken stick, and ate. That's when I realized that the bird was a buzzard, and the sticks were bleached bones. Later, I'd read about this bird: a lammergeier, a lamb vulture, known for its ability to get the last tender morsel out of the inside of an old bone, hollowing it out, the last dwindle of the dwindlies.

Seeing the lammergeier in action and not knowing the nature of its actions—it's like eating the last ramekin of caramel custard in the fridge and discovering that it's gravy. That sort of horror.

I held Grace's head while the vet put the needle into her paw and put her to sleep. It's so fast, that business, that you can't trust it. On the examining table scale, it still read: twenty-one pounds. Her eyes still open, her body still warm. A week later, I got her back, dust in a box. I put the box on a kitchen scale and it said: three pounds two ounces, but I couldn't trust that: my doctor is always weighing me in my boots, so I can never trust these measures, they are never accurate.

Grief is so strong at times, one tends to forget one's self—all of the mind is deeply engaged with the one who is no longer there. After a while, when the searching around proves fruitless, one needs to find a reason for the loss, blame, and so *grievance* is born. Such an ugly child.

Grace is gone now, and I have no companion to join me on my park walks. In the same spring heat I felt the need to step into the tender grass and watch children play on the jungle gyms. I stood by the fence and watched the kids, giddy in the air, coming out of it in swings and on slides, and I laughed, too, in sympathy. Scaling a mountain and sliding down in the scree is just some grownup version of that feel. But as I stood, I watched a mother, then two, take a look at me and hustle quietly to their children's sides. Weeks before, these same mothers might come up to me and ask me, "Can she pet your dog?" and it would be a way to talk to them. A dog is park carte blanche. Now I am a sketchy single man, a stranger, a danger, with no business in the park.

When you walk among villages in rural Europe, the backpack makes you look funny to dogs. I figured this out years ago when walking out of the city of Pamplona, and two dogs and their masters approached in the park on the outskirts. I reached down to pet one of the dogs, and it went nuts, barking viciously. "It's okay," said the lady, accustomed to this moment because pilgrims to Santiago were always leaving the town at around this hour, heading west, and her dog must have barked at a hundred other walkers, "It's your back-pack, it makes you look strange, like a monster to him." I am a monster.

I do it too, of course. When I walk on a trail and there are cy-clists, they come and go so quickly I never get to know them. Other walkers, I see day after day; they are accountable. I watch my posses-sions around bicyclists. They can be thieves. Where do they go?

If I had *fastened* my superlightweight towel to the refugio's clothesline, it might have stayed put. But a *fast* bicyclist stole it when I wasn't looking. And perhaps then, I would not bear this grievance, this prejudice toward cyclists, in general. My backpack's buckle breaks, and it will not hold *fast*. My aunt *fasted*, and died of the dwindlies.

Sometimes when I walk, I'll kick a stone. I'll see how far along the road I can take it. It's a silly indulgence, an almost childish anthro-pomorphism, but I'll talk to the stone: you're going on a great jour-ney, you're going to see things none of the stones back home have ever seen. And a half a mile later, I'll have a feeling of guilt, because I've taken the stone away from its home. When I was an actual child, rather than merely childish, I would make sure to kick it all the way back home. When I am walking a long way with no real end in sight, which is basically the only kind of walking I do any more, I convince myself the stone needs an adventure. Or I'll simply take the stone back to my own home.

Petra was raised in Germany learning English, so she knows it well, the coin of the business realm. When she was in high school, her first boyfriend was named Matthias just like her husband, a Teutonic probability. The first Matthias was tall and passionate with just the slightest of stutters. He wrote Petra hundreds of love letters, full of promises and declarations and lyrics from American pop music. She kept them in a shoebox, and when I went to visit her in Vienna one Christmas, she pulled them out to show me. Some of them were dozens of pages long. His handwriting was something akin to typesetting. His adoration was far more emotionally charged than any love letter, at least any from a man I'd seen since reading around in the letters of Abelard and Heloise. A perfect balance of the particular and the abstract: "My love for you is like a thousand flames, although our parents might forbid us to light a thousand flames."

How do I know this, since I don't know German well? All of his letters were written in English. The profundity of this did not hit me until I thought what it might be like to write love letters to a significant other in a language I might know well—Spanish, or better, Russian. Making love in a foreign language is like providing for yourself a bit of safety glass between you and a violent criminal; you can say anything and be heard through it, but you are secure in its manufactured distance. Like oven mitts, sun block, or irony, writing about frighteningly real emotion in a second language, however fluent one might be in it, can render it a stance, an artifice. Passion is calmed to delight. Romance is a barely tethered beast; one needs a shield. The fire and music, for one who speaks that language first, however, can seer and dazzle. I think of Nabokov's Humbert Humbert, Conrad's Marlowe. This, too, is the trick of long-distance walking, to get both the intimacy and the distance. I told Petra that our walk together across Corsica was like reading a love letter written in a foreign language.

"Those were written twenty years ago," she said.

Why do we keep these things, the letters, the ashes of your dog, the rings of a dead partner? I am always sacking Europe, but unlike the Goths, I bring back such valueless things—the stone I kicked, the menu from a special meal, postcards I never sent. Broken pieces of tile, the chestnut given to me by a local woman, seed pods. I put them in a box, and after a while, I don't quite remember where they came from, and why I saved them. They accumulate, they gather weight. Only a couple of things are vivid enough not to be forgotten, only because they are emblems of something painful: a bit of thread I lanced through a blister to help it drain, a bit of bone from the lammergeier's meal. The fluids in the blister are kept *flowing*, the lammergeier has *flown*.

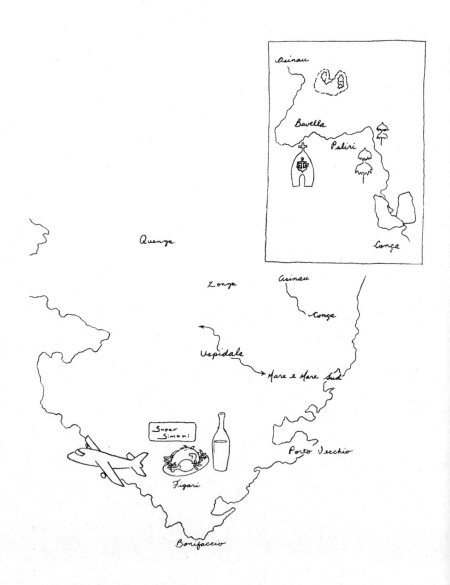

8

Local Customs

Asinau to Bavella

I write in my journal—and it seems important to repeat in print: "I saw a cloud in the shape of a perfect brassiere today." I think I mean that the shape is perfect, perfect for its being in the shape of a brassiere, but the meaning is there.

Many walkers, or so it says in my guidebook, tend to skip the Bavella stop on the GR20 in order to push on and finish the long trek. As I remarked after executing the Cirque de la Solitude, if there has been any regret I have ever had in the walking business, it is that I didn't ramble a bit more, take a side road that pushed on an extra kilometer, or showed me a sight or extra view. Detours are always less peopled, too, and I feel privileged, private.

What we see, then, when we get to the refuge at Bavella, initially troubles us: an excellent view of a large lot full of parked cars steered by day-trippers looking for the beach. Watching cars career up a switchback road in two minutes, one that takes us two hours, dampens the spirit. But what we soon realize is that the tourist types have some kind of respect, or maybe fear, of the extreme trekker types we seem to be part of. They don't come here.

It's at the penultimate stop on many of these long journeys where you also see a curious psychological problem manifest itself: an unwillingness to finish. So many pilgrims to Santiago hold up well, carry their burdens over hundreds of miles, only to suffer a major blister meltdown a scant twenty miles from the cathedral. It's not always purposeful damage, either—old sores will suddenly go septic after healing steadily over earlier walks. Shoe leather will mysteriously fly apart (I'm not kidding: this happened to *me*) when you only need it for one more day.

And other discouraging things happen: friendships of the road suddenly fly apart faster than shoes in a trumped-up bar fight or accusations of theft. And here's an odd one: an Italian woman who walked alone to Santiago was surprised by her husband at the next to last refugio on the road to the shrine. He had come to her as a treat: "I've come to walk the last part with you," he said, with sincere generosity. She burst into tears: everything she had worked for, she told me later, seemed to have been rendered pointless. And so near your destination, the road becomes glutted and cluttered with opportunists, quacks, and sideshow acts.

At Bavella, a man unpacks his backpack and shows he only carries a rain poncho, a bottle of wine, a boom box, and a set of marionettes. He has hiked only two hours from the ass-end of the GR20, in Conça, and he probably won't be walking much farther so well outfitted. Nevertheless, we enjoy a long puppet show with classical music, selections from major French operas: the yodeling alpinist falls in love with the Italian girl dressed all in black. The oaken Cossacks and maple Dervishes do their dances without tangling their

186

strings among them. "He doesn't have any pig marionettes," Petra laments.

There are several new people at the Bavella gîte, those walkers who perversely elect to walk the trail from south to north. These people are having their first hard day's walk, as they are unseasoned—discovering that their boots don't fit well, packs are overpacked, and perhaps it was a good idea, after all, to carry a set of cookware. Their ears are not yet burned purple, not like the ears of serious hikers, such as ourselves. In all, Bavella looks more like a hospital than a recreational facility. The gardien merrily applies moleskin bandages and Bactine. I play Florence Nightingale, because I know how to deal with these things, practicing medicine without a license. I thread a cleaned-up needle and lance a blister, and explain how it is best to leave the thread in while sleeping, so that the fluid has a way to drain out, following the thread out.

You can spot the new ones, if not by their moans of pain, then by their zealously friendly glad-handing. "Bon jour, I am Amadeo, and I am from jolly Gascony," one might as well be saying, buying me a beer without asking me if I want one (I sure do). At seven euros a muled-in beer, I know that by the time he reaches Vizzavona, he'll be as stingy with his beer money as, well, I am. Petra and I discuss an Italian who wore white shorts and a white T-shirt, so that he looked as if he were crossing Corsica in his underwear. A Flemish Jesuit priest, taking a break from his work in prisons. And my favorites: two helpless girls from Sydney, Australia, one plugged into some techno music on her Discman, the other flipping madly through the Lonely Planet Guide to Corsica and saying things like, "What? No Internet access in the gîtes?"

All the lost are found when you hold up a day, as well. The Belgian walkers whose clicking high-tech walking sticks drove me mad for days, until we were motivated to outrun them, have caught up again. So many people along the way, but defined as if they were all part of a two-dimensional tapestry or cartoon with just a few strokes to make them flat, destined never to change but always be: the Italian who chain-smoked himself across Corsica, gathering his energy from nicotine and weighing down his pack with cartons of unfiltered black tobacco Ducadoes (I could smell him approaching for miles on certain days, and wondered whether I might find my own private patch of the maquis up in flames). The burr-headed Portuguese boy and his girlfriend, who once pitched their tent so close to ours that we could hear him grind his teeth through the night until the girlfriend hissed desperately, "Paulo!"

Arriving early in Bavella (it took us only four hours to get here, so we are washed and established by noon) also affords Petra and me a chance to look around. While we feel protective of our mountain hideaway, we feel too that we have full rights to the sights in town, so we walk down into it.

In the church we wander into just off the road from Bavella, there is a nautical theme. Actually, this is one of the few stretches of the GR20 in which we cannot see water at all (except rivers, delicious rivers), so perhaps this is a yearning, a leaning. There are hooks on the pews shaped like anchors, and statues of boats cruising below Christ in Majesty. A buoy buoys up the Blessed Virgin Mary, and even she attempts to capture that inscrutable color of the Mediterranean water, Star of the Sea, in the tint of her robes. The rooms are bright white.

Petra and I are not speaking as much near the end of the trail, either, which is odd, because we will spend another week after the GR20 together exploring Corsica as tourists, from a more luxurious base of operations. Now, we let each other out of our sights along the way, for hours at a time.

I sing more loudly in English. I sing more loudly because it won't matter soon that other hikers might think me crazy, because I have given up on the idea that I am going to scare some spectacular wild animal I have not yet seen (two scissor-tailed kites swoop very close by just to prove me wrong), and because I am determined not to hide my Yankee stripes.

I seem to have broken free of "Island Girl" and other pop hits; I rummage around in my memory's jukebox and come up with an arsenal of folk songs. There are old folk songs that find themselves changed when crossing the wide divide of ocean or mountain or time. In Ireland, a girl sings, "He ne'er will come back til he's rich and can marry me." And we know this will never be. The girl knows it too; it's her life's sorrow. On the other side, the man has been forbidden to marry the girl, and so he is heading west, and won't return until he is the King of California. Or he'll just sing her song, "He ne'er will come back," as if he's talking about somebody else, getting some distance on the pain, and the pain he's causing. Everybody is traveling, everybody is on the move, I think, as I sing.

We are near the end of the high mountain part of our journey, but there is still the spectacle of height and mountain vertigo. The fierce wind off the Mediterranean, the one from the northeast called Tramontana (there are the cold dusty Mistrals from the north, the foggy easterly Levanter, the hot Arab wind Sirocco, the Bentus de Soli from the east that stops at the shore, and the summery, zephyrous Maestros from the west) pulls clouds over the mountains just as I decide to wash my socks. So much depends on dry socks, and thus my knowledge of the winds. I've become nautical myself, at least for as long as I need dry socks.

I am even, here near the end, stunned to have a meal with one of the Rooster men, one of the originals, as they, too, have decided to dawdle somewhere along the trail. I realize, however, that his companion is no longer with him. They've broken up, a macho divorce. He seems vulnerable to me, alone, thrown from the henhouse, perhaps, no longer strutting. Spotting him here, my heart neverthe-less sinks—and he sees me sitting at a picnic table outside the little restaurant and clasps my hand as if we are old friends.

I am dismayed to have to know his name: Michel. Despite my self-reproachful lessons I had taught myself in Corte, I couldn't help but think my terrible, terrible nationalist thoughts. Thoughts like: the men in France are not my type, skinny—emaciated, even—no power in their hands, all in their mouthy mouths, with so many puis-sant frontal labials to pronounce. And their names! Yves! Jean! Michel! What kind of name is "Marie" for a man?

Michel, who is, agreed, not emaciated, sits on a stump as if on a throne, paring his nails with a Laguiole knife. He is nearly sixty, his hands, like his lips, disproportionately massive and once roughed up like quarried marble; now even that quality has been smoothed from the wearing down of age. The nails he cut at seem made of goat horn, like the clasp of his knife. Often, when he talks, bits of spittle form in the corners of his mouth, and he has to wipe them.

He is not emaciated but built like a king, or a butane tank. His head is fleshy but small, and yet his knuckles are as knobby as the knees of a newborn colt. He makes me examine my own hands there under the picnic table, hands that always fascinate people because they are smooth, the palms of a blueblood, or a lazy-ass. Here in Corsica, with my walking stick, I have managed to build up the first calluses I'd had in years, and even a small, curious, painless blister at the tip of my index finger.

Michel has already given up trying to talk to me. What few words I can say in French make no sense to Michel, and because I make no sense to him, Michel apparently decides that he himself makes no sense to me, either. "Un Americain," he says to Petra, and blows out his horsey lips. No, I can't understand that at all.

In truth, mostly I don't understand. Sitting night after night with other guests in these gîtes is like getting clues to a mystery. I listen along, fill in unrecognizable words with a sound (Petra has told me that the sound of English is the sound of a cat chewing gum: Meow, meow meow. In retaliation, I tell her that the sound of French is the sound of a cow lowing), hoping to piece together the meaning later. One person will say, "*Moo moo moo moo* cheese *moo moo* at the market *moo moo moo moo* strong *moo moo* bad (evil?) *moo* down there." And another will respond, "*Moo moo* Roquefort *moo* cloud." Now, entering the dining room, I hear Michel say to Petra, "*Moo moo* Americain Teep," as he tosses back a whole glass of something gold in his own private unmarked bottle. When he lifts his hand, I notice that half of the man's pinky is missing.

Petra, enviously multilingual, says, "Moo moo moo moo?" (Note that the third *moo* I take to be the word *morpion*, which translates as "crab louse," but I'm going to hope that I get this wrong and leave it untranslated.)

Michel answers, "*Moo!* Americain Teep! My country, my family, my religion. Is it true for this Americain *moo*, too?"

Petra turns to me. "Is it true?"

"Bon, Brian." Michel must have realized that he had only been talking to a pretty girl who may or may not be part of a couple, and now makes an effort to engage me. I wish he had not. The only thing worse than not being talked to is being talked to. "*Moo moo* where in the United States do you live and *moo?*"

"Chicago," I say. I am using my tight professional smile, and that makes me mad, because I am on vacation, after all.

"Ah," says Michel expansively, and then, as Petra seems to be looking for an escape from the conversation, he says, "*Moo*, Chicago, Illinois." I nod. "But you know," Michel leans closer, "we call it here in France, Illy-NWAH, moo."

Before I can unscramble this crazy comment, Petra is sitting down next to Michel—she actually likes this guy!

"Petra, tell your new friend that Illy-NWAH is actually the bad pronunciation of the name the Native Americans of my region called the land. It would be like me calling his country Franchise."

Petra is silent for a moment, examines the simple prix-fixe menu next to the door of the little restaurant, then says, "Comment? I mean—what?"

This is the other problem with the language gap; I have only baby talk to convey complex ideas. If they are mooing, I am gooing.

"Excuse-ay mwah," I hit upon it—"But I must wash my hands because the pigs licked them." Both Michel and Petra look at me doubtfully. Still, I flee.

The bathroom is in an unlikely place, built right next to our table. We will hear many flushings as this endless dinner commences. I close the door to the bathroom. It has been all girlied up by a girly hand tired of living in the mountains, with certain odd concessions to tough-minded Corsica. A tiny cigar box made of Lalique glass and framed pictures of hunters matted with exposed cardboard corrugation. And potpourri, even if it is woodsy potpourri. The bathroom is old and damp and windowless.

I look at my face in the mirror, burned purple, then held my hands up to it, as if I can't see properly unless mediated by reflection. I'd read in some men's health magazine that one should sing "Happy Birthday" to oneself two complete times while washing one's hands. I turn off the water reluctantly after the third refrain and dry my hands.

I step back into the dining room. Petra hardly acknowledges my return, for she is back in deep, serious conversation with Her New Boyfriend about—me? She is saying, "*Moo moo* depart from him/it *moo moo moo* early in the morning *moo moo* when we are not seeing each other." What? What? Have I heard correctly? Was she plotting secretly to ditch me along the trail soon? And is this how I am to find out? She says it right in front of my face?

"Ah, quelle déception!" Michel laughs ruefully.

"Deception?" I blurt.

"Brian!" Petra looks caught, surprised I've slipped back to the table without her noticing. "Is it your birthday? Have we missed the celebration of your birthday?"

"No, why?"

"We can hear you singing 'Happy Birthday' to yourself in the bathroom!" Petra repeats this to Michel in French, and they laugh together. But I wonder, if they have heard me sing "Happy Birthday," have they already plotted Petra's ditching me in the middle of Corsica, disenFrenchized?

As if seeing the suspicion in my face, Michel shakes my hand and pulls me into the restaurant. "Moo, moo, moo, and come dine with me!" he invites, slapping the two empty spaces at his table, and we must never offend with a rejection.

He, too, must wash up, and while he does, I ask Petra if she thinks this guy is actually interesting. "J'adore," she says (and I think she is gushing a bit too much—adore!) and suggests he is a tender flower, and we should not do anything to hurt him. But from the looks of Michel, he's done enough to get hurt all on his own, en-joyed too many falls off of mountains, bad skin-care products, for-bidden Armagnac, and unlicensed tobacco. Petra says, "His stomach is very tender, and he may only drink soup and eat bread. So we must not make any miam-miam sounds when we enjoy the dessert my new aunt has made us." *Miam-miam?* Ah—the French word for yum-yum.

This, I can do. I think Petra might forbid me the wine, which I need more and more at these social pit stops, where Petra spends the night jabbering away with the locals while I sit trying to figure out how to eat tiny birds and gussied-up omelets without utensils—or worse, finish my food long before anybody else has (for lack of any-thing to offer to the conversation—and by "lack of" I mean "inabil-ity") and stare at my empty plate while the rest eat like human beings.

When he comes out of the bathroom, he is shirtless again, of course, though he has decided it is suitable, in the establishment, to wear his stained leather vest, since we are having a nice dinner, you know, in a real restaurant and all. The restaurant is the only option for those not cooking noodles over an open fire, so it is packed, and we have to eat "family style," whole tables of total strangers, grouped together, strangers who have no other choice but to dine and talk together.

I hate "family style." If they were to truly eat in the style of my family, Rooster Man would be eating in Michigan while I ate in Chicago. Instead, Michel, Petra, and I are placed together at the same table, as are the two birds from Sydney. It is Monsieur Rooster who begins to quiz everybody at the table; apparently he is from Marseilles, although he claims to have family from Catalunya. When I ask him something in Catalan, it's apparent I know more of that language than he does, and we all slip back into French, which Petra knows well and I know badly and the Australian girls know not at all.

I keep thinking of Petra giving me the slip. She has the good guidebook! And the maps of Corsica from Michelin! And they are all in French: the direction *tout droit* means "all to the right," and I would turn right at every intersection. But *tout droit* really means "go straight." Lost, I think. I'm lost. Little dead British boy's dead American boy.

Michel, that Marseilles Rooster, explains how we should finish the last day, knowing that we have been walking the same road he has walked for the past ten days, beside the fact that he has never walked the last segment of the piste himself, but wanting to make sure that Petra and I do not get lost. The girls listen politely, and one complains about her omelette.

"Is that all this place serves?" she says. They will never make it, I start to think. But then, I wouldn't wager on that judgment. The ones who turn out to be strong always surprise me, the way it always

194

surprised me when I went to Boy Scout camp and I saw the bullies from school flee first in homesickness. I have even surprised myself by making it this close to the end. When you are walking alone, regrets and regretful memories and misgivings (for a week, I really thought I would not make it) open up inside you like sudden holes in the trail. You stumble on and in them, you have to lock your legs in order not to fall into such a flaw in the ground; the mind does something similar to ward off complete collapse under the weight of the backpack of memory, which grows heavier every day, every week, every year.

The Rooster asks—or more specifically, brays like a farm animal, lows the question—do they know French? I translate and they shake their heads.

"But, *moo,* they are in big trouble!" says Monsieur Poulet, which does not keep him from leaning back in our booth and putting one arm around each of the girls in a proprietary gesture. I am up for protecting only myself, however, for his armpits are two dark bushy chapters from a horror novel. "How can they walk and *moo* in this country when they do not understand French?"

"I speak Italian," says the taller of the two girls, the one not plugged into a Discman.

As if to illustrate, or perhaps as a punishment by our efficient waiter, we are quizzed and informed about the menu in Corsican Italian. The Rooster is silent for half the meal, while the four of us speak in boisterous, obstreperous, villainous English. Only Petra has the heart to drag him back into the conversation, taking pity on his weak brothy excuse for a soup, perhaps.

It's almost a competition, the three English speakers versus the two French speakers, and our conversation crosses over each other like badly planned telephone wirings in a gentrifying neighborhood. "Would you like ice cream," Petra asks as I smile across to her, and I fool around with my coffee, putting sugar and cream into it. I like my coffee black.

"No," I say, and think I'll try a little French. When we've called the socialist realist hotel, they lied, saying they were full, by telling us that they were *complet*. I am full, too. I say, "Jeh swee complet."

Petra begins to giggle, then Michel looks down into his coffee and sputters into it. Michel does not laugh but makes a face at the Americain Teep that spoke volumes: What An Idiot.

"What's so funny?" I appeal not to Petra but the Australians, under my breath, as if this were not a dinner for four but one for twenty, and only those closest might hear me ask.

Petra answers, "You just said that you were pregnant."

I stand and go into the bathroom again. One of the Australian girls begins laughing like some cruel girl in an opera, given an entire laughing song to show off her coloratura. She only laughs once I am in the bathroom, however, as if being polite.

I sit on the toilet, not taking down my pants. I feel breathless and dogged. In a basket at my side is a booklet of crossword puzzles, most half-done and abandoned. My mother has such a basket in her bathroom. A familiar sight made strange—the worst thing that could happen. France would be easier for me if there were no samenesses, no cognates in the language, no comparable table manners, as far and few as the Jumblies, their heads green, their feet blue, setting sail daily in a sieve. But no: *crossword puzzles*. And if the answers are any indication, idiotically easy ones, with words like *noir, fidelite,* and *aussi*.

Oh, the French, I think; but what bothers me most is that if I were French, I would be the most insufferable Frenchman of them all. I would have ruined myself on pleasure long before Michel ruined himself.

After I wash my face in the old sink where the hot water boils out of one spigot and the cold comes out of the other, I find the dinner abruptly over; Petra has already retreated to our tent. There'll be walking to do tomorrow, as usual.

In the tent, I step over her body, curled like a question mark in her sleeping bag. To look through the sheer doorway, I straddle her and cross my arms, hoping to get a rise out of her. If I look menacing there, to her, then so what. Outside, I can see, in the perpetual gloaming that seems to be the lux aeterna of Corsica, Michel shooing two other new hikers, two purple shadows. I say, "It's as if he has to know everything or he'll die."

Petra is quiet for a moment, and I think she has fallen asleep already. Then she says, "He knows." It is funny, how I cannot see Petra in the dark of the tent, but I can see Michel just fine, though he is grainy like a black and white photo made from blowing up a negative too much. He taps his shoe bottoms with a stick.

I asked Petra, "Tonight, at dinner, you were talking about something with Michel. What was it?" Perhaps she would admit it. Perhaps I could get her to bring her disenchantment into the open, for once, and I can thwart her plans to bolt.

"About something?"

"About something that was quelle déception."

Petra laughs with her mouth shut. "Oh yes. Last winter, when there seemed no hope that you and I might ever get together, I cheered myself by going to Sri Lanka. On the first day there, somebody stole my camera. Quelle déception!"

I watch Michel plod back toward the gîte. I know Michel cannot see me, not in the dark, but I lie down behind Petra anyway. I took a pleasure in feeling the little calluses at the bases of each finger from the walking stick, from wringing out my own clothes when washing them.

Bavella to Paliri

We just don't want the walking to end, so close we are, and so easy, finally, has the trail become. Either the trail has flattened out, or we have become stronger. One does get stronger with each day, but one never knows it distinctly—it just happens that in the beginning, after only six or seven miles, the body feels like it has been beaten with baseball bats and the feet placed under meat tenderizer mallets. Then, a week or so later, I can stride through fifteen miles and stop only because the place to sleep is the last convenient gîte.

In the Col de Bavella, between Asinau and Paliri, on fairly easy winding wide road, Petra and I are afforded sweet long conversation while we walk, and enjoy endless shifting views of the peaks of the Bavella, towering mountains that look like gherkin pickles, or, as they reveal themselves, no longer Oz's Emerald City but the spiny back of Godzilla, or a nifty device I saw in a shop that grates the skin of a garlic clove right off. Clouds fly over us in sped-up time. We expect rain, then see the sky cloudless, and all things nebulous in between. "The future is cloudy," says the Magic 8-Ball, "Ask again later." Up into the mighty pines we saunter, the view always getting a little better, the road turning into a trail but cushioned with pine needles and the sweet gurgle of brooks, everywhere we go, all heading into the watershed made from the valley that becomes more and more apparent below us. Holm oak, lavender that smells oddly of lamb meat, wild lemon thyme. We name the serrated peaks along the Bavella ridge: "Misplaced Boxcar," "Locomotive," "The Mitten."

And it's always near the end, as the tasks of walking fall away and what is left is the ripe fruit of the task, that we begin to recall home and its routines. The habits of living day to day dull the senses—the ritual of getting up each morning, brushing your teeth, commuting to work, desk tasks, coming home, preparing for another day and heading to bed—so that I often cannot see the small wonders of the everyday world (grass growing, a cloud fleeting by in the shape of a bra, the child across the street learning to ride her bike; all ordinary miracles). It is only when I am removed from habit that I can see a work of art that reveals a new mind's vision, or when I am traveling in a foreign place, or when I fall in love. And this seems a definition of love: the removal of habit, the ordinary world made foreign and wonderfully strange, life as a great visionary work of art.

At a certain point, Petra finds a paradise of clean water and sunning stones with a private ridge, and we rest there. I walk ahead, and as soon as I am out of sight from Petra, such a good luck charm, the trail becomes difficult in that annoying way it seems the GR20 must be at every step: loose scree, wayward winds, wild pigs freaking me out, cows blocking the path, me climbing with my hands again (the word is "scramble," Brian; use the proper trekker word), lots of spiny maquis to fall into and hide the trail.

My quick step startles many pigs, who in turn startle me. They even squeal in French, I swear: "Allors!" "Non, non, Nanette!"

The way becomes ominous. I pass a couple of lightning-blasted dead pines and more serrated mountain tops, deep into a green and yellow valley, and through brookside alder. And then I spy a shepherd and his hut, perched on the hillside. It looks lonesome, almost unattended. The keeper is sitting alone outside, I hardly notice him until I'm right on top of him, and he wants to know if I've seen any pigs. I laugh. I think these shepherds don't give a damn most of the year, but as the chestnuts ripen around this time in September, the beasts need to be fattened for the bloody November slaughter.

I have written elsewhere about meeting Petra on another long walking trip, seven years before our trip to Corsica, on the way to St. James, in Spain. But what had deeply impressed me, being a boy and therefore being competitive, is that Petra had made the pilgrimage to Santiago de Compostela twice, two years in a row. It was her second time down the road when I was making my first journey. The first day I encountered her, we both, separately, chose to part from our companions to walk alone on a detour that added two miles to the day's walking, with only a Knights Templar church as a reward. We walked alone, together. We had the trail to ourselves, and we got to be fast friends, fast.

"Is it easier to walk this way a second time?" I asked her then, thinking I already knew the answer—knowing where you're going, after all, you know what stones will trip you, what house will throw boiling water on the hobos.

"No, it is much more difficult!" she said. "In your mind, you know what the next town looks like, and in your imagination, you are already there." I imagined her imagination, the map of the world collapsing, time taken out of the equation, destination the only goal for each day. Think of the way you're a character in a play scripted to be slapped, and you telegraph a wince before the actual slapping.

I wonder about myself sometimes: must everything in my life be so flinty, so difficult? I am the one who reads the guidebooks only after I have made the journey, to discover that the sarcophagus I stood before was a great queen, or the ground I walked on was bloodied by Roland and his men. Only after. I read the guidebooks for nostalgia but find instead that I have missed a thing I should have seen.

What is nostalgia but this picking through the ruins of living—not living, but *remembering* living? Walking among the renegades in France was the adventure, and after entering comfortable, stomped-over Spain, it was as if I had entered the gift shop and never left it for a month, selecting souvenirs, when I had plenty of that back home.

I want to go back. I always want to go back, but I did go back once, and it wasn't a smart idea. I returned to the pilgrim's route to Santiago a second time in order to walk a new stretch of it, and because I wanted to meet new walkers on that way. "Segundos partes nunca fueron buenas," Spaniards told me all the way to the end: "Second times never go well." And that's the truth. If there's something to walking off from the prison, of escape, of every theory I've ever imposed on myself, I should have seen that the Spanish *dicho* warned me from the first. Think of Orpheus going after Eurydice, or Lot's wife's botched rescue from Sodom and Gomorrah, or Stoker's Dracula climbing out of the coffin in order to find his love again— second times never go well, Count. Nostalgia scares me, for it seems to turn gladness into ghosts, and grief into grievance.

What does it mean to say "betray one's feelings"? It seems to have too many, and conflicting, meanings. If you betray a feeling, for instance, by showing it, especially when it is threatened unless hidden, then the feeling is destroyed by its revelation. But if you betray your feelings by *not* being true to the feeling, by abandoning it, by not being constant to it, then the not showing of an emotion destroys it. Staying true to a feeling can be either noble or destructive. These opposites, like building a sand castle on the beach that will be both a conquering and ordering impression on the chaotic surf, is an effort made knowing full well that the chaos will reclaim it.

Paliri to Conça

For all of my experience in walking, I think there is part of me that expects foreign travel to be much more foreign. When I am far from home, I'm surprised to find that clouds don't form differently, that trees don't have stranger leaf formations, that people haven't invented languages constructed of something different than subjects and verbs. That there isn't a new color, one not found in that crayon box.

More pines like beach umbrellas, more humorless trekkers on that race, always it is a race. "Then you can relax." I think of American Pete for the first time in a couple of days. He probably sprinted over this ground hours ago. I, personally, love to go a-wandering along the mountain track. And as I go, I love to sing, and please God make it not be "I know an old woman who swallowed a fly."

There are long strings of Lavicia pines but standing lone instead of bunched into forests, so that for the first time, I notice how they are like big Seussian umbrellas of trees, which Edward Lear, Seuss's patron saint, loved to draw when visiting Corsica. Also, the strawberry trees are full of their eponymous fruit (the botanical name for strawberry trees is *Arbutus unedo,* which means "eat one," even though the berries taste awful, for nature is red in tooth, claw, and irony). Easy walking, too, a meandering flat trail. I pass hikers heading in, just a few, because they are mostly well on their way by now, those who start from Conça, and I'm a little worried about these stragglers. Apparently, I am not a welcome sight to them, either, a finisher, an all-but-done, carrying swaths of myrtle, the dove that nobody on Noah's Ark wanted to see. La! Shall I wear black to make it easier?

And then we step through a V in a wall of orange-red rock, the Bocca di Uscida, a little pass that seems like one of those portals in a science fiction film. On the other side, there is nothing of the great granite panorama, everything is brought down several sizes in scope.

And we realize: that's it. Okay, okay, the guidebooks tipped us off, but still, there's a definite sense. We have officially completed the GR20, although there's still another forty-five minutes of walking down into the village below. And after that clear ending, we endure the sputtering, half-hearted way the trail trails off (and a rather unsightly garbage dump picked at by life both wild and tame), and it is something of a fizzle. Now it's over. No, now. No, uh, *now.* Wait. The last double-bar of red and white stripes is painted on a telephone pole. Petra takes my photo next to it, a telephone pole for a trophy. There is no other walker passing near us to take a photo with the two of us together. We are quiet for a little while and in fact do not even discuss the decision to walk to the first bar we find.

We drink beers in that bar at the end of the village of Conça. No welcoming party, just amber Pietra and a rack of postcards with sayings on them like, "GR20: Salut Les Forçats!" Civilization intrudes as well—Conça is spitting distance from all sorts of touristic haunts, and two ill-behaved Corsican boys are fighting over a video gambling game at the corner of the bar, which I don't think they're old enough to play. The worse of the two boys, the smaller one, whips the older brother with a jeweled rosary he has, or the remains of one. When the bartendress admonishes him, the boy whips her, too. "The rosary belonged to his poor grandmother," Petra says, not cracking a smile, "and he has broken it." We move out to the veranda with our beers. A rosary hurts. The Marquis de Sade is smiling in heaven, satisfied.

On the veranda is the startling silence we wanted all along. A zephyr off the nearby sea lets us smell everything that grows here. Figs, prickly pear cactus, myrtle, locust—flowering locust?—rosemary. A scolding bird hidden away with a tone of hollow wood sounds like the feckless bartender inside, as the boys continue to squabble. Congratulations, you have just walked the entire Grand Rondonnée Number 20. Salut les Forcats.

When we have finished our beers, we have no interest in walking. Petra wants to hitchhike, a common pastime in Europe. I think again of the signs surrounding my hometown, of the prisoners who debone their wives, and then walk off. At first I try to sound as if I am, actually, still interested in walking. I give Petra this weird, obviously insincere lecture about walking. "This is another significant difference in travel by foot as opposed to other forms of transport—places that would otherwise seem dull or even ugly are lovely and strange and even an indulgence for a walker," I tell her.

Petra says the German word for bullshit, I think.

"No, really!" I tell her, and put my pack on as if I'm ready for another five kilometers. "You get to see it all when walking: the graffiti on walls, for instance." I tell her that in the Spanish city of Leon, I came across some graffiti that was meant to bait skinheads: *Yo Soy Un Yanki Rojo Maricon Judeo Negro.* "I am an American Communist Gay Jewish Negro," with all the glib nasty words used, as if I were a better translator, I would offer: "I am a Yankee Commie Faggot Jew Nigger." In Europe a "Yankee" is as marginal as a faggot or a commie. Graffiti is a part of the whole exhaustion of cities you witness when walking all the way—the exhaustions of cities at their outskirts, the sputtering, the self-unraveling, the petering out. There are death rattles: a half-finished factory, a promissory pile of cinderblocks, then freeway or dirt road, then trail again. "We are here on the outskirts of Conça, and it would be a shame to miss out on this anthropological wonder," I say. Even I'm not believing myself now. Still, I don't want to be deboned.

We walk for a kilometer, and Petra is using the Killing Silence again. A shiny Renault zips past us on a stretch of asphalt we have to pass over. It slows, then stops. I have a moment's panic: we're going to get deboned anyway. I can't really run quickly if this is foul play, not with a backpack pulling down on me. But as with any suspected instrument of foul play, it turns out to be beneficence: a priest in a white cassock, a Père de Blancs, as Petra explains to me as he approaches us, his hazards flashing, his car door agog. He speaks to Petra as if he knew I can't speak a word of his French. "I see you are finishing the GR20," he says.

We nod—you caught us.

"Have you had the communion yet today?"

Hell, we hadn't had communion in years! So we say no. And right there along the side of the road, with cars other Renaults and Clios whizzing by and people staring at us, on our knees, backpacks still over our shoulders, this priest gives a mini-mass and offers us communion.

Thus fortified, I feel bold. "Let's hitchhike!" I tell Petra.

"Yes, before somebody else tries to feed us communion," Petra says, and sticks out her thumb.

We have walked enough. Now is the time to relax and sleep on feathers instead of stone, put down the pack and pick up the flagon, and cook with the maquis rather than walk in it. I stick out my thumb, too.

It doesn't take long; there are no prisoners walking off here. An aged couple see us, recognize us well for what we are, and have probably done this dozens of time. We climb into their car, and the seats and floor are full of big white vats of—honey! They are taking their honey to town to be bottled and sold to tourists. I have to put my feet up on one to fit in, but I'm grateful for the ride. Honey leaks out of all of them, and my backpack, my shoes, my hair, are slathered in honey. Take that, Seneca!

Although the villages are pretty, we zip through them at comparatively astonishing velocity, and I fall asleep, in honey, for who knows how long, and I have to be shaken awake when we arrive in downtown Porto Vecchio: we're renting a car. Petra is in charge, and I am the sleepy boy too tired to be of any use to her.

Bonifacio, Figari, and Porto Vecchio

Here is the afterlife: the natural tall tale of walking forward sputters, reduces travel to vignettes, tableaux vivants. Bonifacio had been our original after-trek destination, the too-famous town perched on cliffs over the southern tip of the island. It's very spectacular to see it rise out of the chalky stone and shape itself, almost before your very eyes, into tall towers in which people live. Some say that this is the home of the Lystraegonians, the cannibals who chased Ulysses off in the *Odyssey*.

Today, they still seem to be eating tourists for lunch, because for Petra and me, Bonifacio is a shipwreck. We rent a car without a problem in Porto Vecchio (though the man at Europcar growled "this is a serious business!" as we leave, because we are amused at the unserious way he runs things. He made us follow a treasure hunt of telephone numbers to get through to him, and while we waited for him to show up at his shop we watched how he made two boys miss their train waiting to return their car. Quite serious. And did he mean, Mafia on my mind, *legitimate* business?).

Aficionados of Corsica, including its natives, would be stunned at how little time we spend in Bonifacio. Its touristic quay below is a good place to get groceries and ship off postcards, but other than that, there is nothing local about the place, even this close to the off-season. In the souvenir shops they make available license plates for children's bicycles and mugs personalized with names that will do me no good: Celine, Chantal, Chretienne, Clemence, Colette, Coralie. To an American, it seemed that the entire French-speaking land were populated only by little old ladies.

Petra and I spend a few hours poking around the maze of streets, full of tortuous curves down which cars and people careen, and find only more gift shops, more tourists, nothing genuine or local but the buildings—all, again, abandoned, a ghost town, only with people in it, people who don't belong here, like me. Travelers destroy what they seek. I would welcome a cannibalistic Lystraegonian.

Petra leads us into the bureau of tourism to try and get us a place to stay in or near town, and the bureau workers are as unhelpful and unseeing as a lightning-rod Laricio pine. With all the mooing and lack of negotiations, I leave Petra to it, and I sit on a bench out on the street, one relatively less busy with tourists, and a long ostentatious sedan drives up, barely able to negotiate the narrow chalky streets, and it is blaring techno disco. A freakish sexed-up Corsican chick sashays toward the car with two fat Spanish men in tow, both very drunk. One of them wants to talk to me, but I am terribly embarrassed for him. "Que tal?" he says, perhaps mistaking me for a Spaniard, but yo soy un yanqui maricon. I can't help thinking: earlier today I was hiking along the last bit of the GR20 near Conça and took in the Peak of the Damned Soul, a small mountain shaped like a witch's hat, and stepped through the Bocca d'Usciolu, and

I am still wearing the same clothes I did it in. Can't this man smell it? Can't he smell the outdoors?

But he is too ecstatic and wants to share the feeling. The girl had probably fed him Ecstasy. "Que tal?" he presses me, and I tried to escape intercourse with "No hablo," but he discovered my accident and shouted out to me in English, "Corsica is *different*." He gushes, "You can feel the *sensation*."

They drive off just before Petra storms out of the tourist office, so that the men and their moll seem an apparition. "Come on," she says. "We're leaving this stupid town." Petra loves the word "stupid." It's one of those words that sounds good to the Germans. I personally like the German word *Schwarzebadehosen,* "black bathing suit."

Down the road from Bonifacio, however, I would be spending many a day bathing in the shadow, sun, and sea of the "Lion of Roccapina," a great natural stone formation that looks like said cat, couchant. I am more impressed by another rock that looks like an elephant. There is said to be a pirate treasure buried somewhere in the vicinity of the lion, and I suppose any traveler who knows this fact spends a few minutes poking around. Maybe I'll be the lucky one to recover the lost doubloons. But as we drive over the unleveled roads down to the sea one afternoon, driving as if we were in an off-road vehicle rather than the mild-mannered Clio clone, we are able to watch some hunters create something of a noose around an unknown quarry in a brambly, maquisy (but not quite) area, perhaps looking for wild boar or what have you. It strikes me that if there were treasure here, it has been found.

Also, how is it that the beach for pleasure is also a city for the dead? We see more Roman-style mausoleums right up to the brink of the sea, "Right on prime real estate," I can't help saying, in my most American voice, to Petra.

Petra can't be bothered: the tanning opportunities are just as good in the Ash Grove as they are seaside.

And in any case, you can't put a tombstone directly in the Mediterranean, and that's where I often find myself snorkeling on the days after our march across the island. Nothing as spectacular as I've seen swimming among the live coral on Eleuthera, one of the outer islands of the Bahamas I once frequented, but plenty of schools of pretty fish and little loners, the occasional trio of three different kinds of fish, some kind of children's story going on right there in the shoals.

Swimming again in the sea, the sand is softer here than it had been on the northern, Calvi side of the island. Nothing to scrape the skin off me. It's a soft lapping, healing our feet and shoulders after the walking. I go soft, once again, in the course of an hour.

Instead of staying in Bonifacio, Petra's strength and fortitude leads us to inquire at a bar with flocked wallpaper in Figari. Figari doesn't seem promising to me, at least in my mind. It's the airport town, though the airport is over a great hill and in a valley out of sight. I will see that place only on the last day, flying out, and it has that sort of abandoned feel that so many island places have.

In the bar, the bartender, after Petra inquires, says no, there's no such stuff, no house to rent for a week in a residence. But wait, he pauses, when Petra does not move. Let me ask Monsieur Simoni.

All of this, I watch helplessly. Monsieur Simoni, I figure, is the guy sitting outside the bar sunning himself like a lizard. "Monsieur Simoni," says the bartender, a great hairy beast of a guy.

Monsieur Simoni waves his hand without looking in, to indicate that he can't be bothered, and the waved hand makes the big gray ash on the tip of his cigar, which matches the color of the hair on the little poodle dog he molests in his lap, fall away into his empty beer glass.

"D'Affaires," presses the bartender. "Business."

This gets Monsieur Simoni's attention. He motions us with the cigar to come sit down with him. He wants to speak to me, of course, because I am the man, but Petra's French is impeccable, or good enough for Figari. There are negotiations, explanations. I order a Pietra. I look across the street from our table to the grocery store. It is called "Super Simoni." In the days to come, I will find there are at least six or seven other Super Simoni's in the Extrem Sud region of Corsica.

Suddenly Super Simoni Himself is on his cell phone, calling his wife. She must have been two doors down, because she shows up, with a small child in her car, and he, without disturbing his own pet, shouts out some directions for her. She motions to us: get in your car and follow me.

So that we won't get lost or mix her up with any other car, though there are no turnoffs or many other cars on the road and she, for a change, is not driving a Clio, she turns her windshield wipers on to make herself conspicuous. "Figari," Petra muses as we drive behind our hostess-to-be. I tell her it is reminiscent of Figaro, as in the marriage of, and also Figo, figs, which are tasty, and also the source of "the fig," one of a dozen obscene gestures for Italians. "Fichten," said Petra, German for "to fuck." So, overall, we are predisposed to liking Figari.

We follow Madame Simoni up two more back roads and find ourselves at a lovely little villa set off the road by a tall stone fence and a grove of well-harvested cork trees. She leads us up the steps and has in her hand a plastic Super Simoni grocery bag full of a hundred keys, all on various souvenir key rings, this one for World Cup football, that for the Super Simoni, another with a crucifix. My heart sinks as I look over the pristine stone villa and think: she will have a key for every house in the Extrem Sud but the one for this door. She grabs up a keychain with a tiny flashlight attached, and tries it, with a "non." A little rubber baby: "non." And over and over. Exasperated, she dumps on the patio table a big bag of keys. They scattered all over like toy parts to something sure to be a cool grand model. "La?" she grabbed at one with a different football insignia of the Marseille team, but no, not there, not la. "La!" again, to a decapitated Moor on a chain. But nope, la, nope. I get nervous—the whole sequence of negotiations makes me grit my teeth the way a good work of art makes me bare my molars in response. Then Petra whispers, "Madame," and points to the entry. The key is already in the door.

And then: "La!," the door falls open, and inside: la, a perfect paradise. Two big bedrooms, a fully equipped kitchen, a patio, a dining room, more room and privacy than we had ever dreamed of. My heart sinks again: how much could such a place cost?

"Ask her," I press Petra.

"Five hundred euros for nine days," Petra responds: it has already been mentioned and I was not listening. This will cost me about forty dollars a day. I try to maintain what might be called a poker face, though I think of those mirthless guards at Windsor Castle baited with jokes. Petra and I converse in serious, low English. We cannot look too excited about the thing. It is a better deal than we would ever have anticipated. But Petra gives me The Sign: she pulls lipstick out, applies it, blots, and turns to Madame Simoni, ready to descend into a new chasm of solitude. "I will need it for a tenth day because my flight leaves a little later."

Madame Simoni nods. It's a deal.

She gushes about the location a bit more, promises to return with a few cleaning supplies in the morning, tells us that the family bar serves a nice meal if we are too late to shop at the Super Simoni grocery store, and if there is anything, *anything* the Madame can do for us, or Monsieur, for that matter, please let them know.

I think that if I ask Monsieur Simoni to rub somebody out for me (and I do have a specific target or two), he might be able to help me. "D'Affaires!" We see him a few days later outside the Super Simoni and Bar U Puncinu shaking hands with the Moroccan boys we'd observed buzzing by on scooters, otherwise notable only for being overly sartorially and tonsorially achieved, and I've decided that they do his dirty work, although I can't fathom what that would be.

But for now Petra and I wait until Madame Simoni's car has pulled out of the compound, windshield wipers still brushing away the Corsican sunshine, before grasping each other at the shoulders and jumping up and down with joy. When we embrace, lipstick smears against my hiking T-shirt, and it is the only stain I am never quite able to wash out from our travels.

Zonza, Uspidale, Quenza, and the Mare e Mare Sud

And as if we have done it all our lives, we find ourselves in a daily pattern, sitting each morning on the terrace with bowls of milky coffee ("un nuage," you ask the French to get them giggling, for the British always ask for just "a cloud" in their tea or coffee and the French like a one-to-one proportion). It is a change from the Corsican tradition of opening an uncooked egg and beating it into hot coffee to make "brodetta," a little broth—not as awful as you'd think—another pattern I've established.

Petra slumbers late up in her room while Grisette the cat hunts in a garden of pines and cacti and dozens of cork trees stripped to the tits to stop up bottles of the D.O.C. Figari wine—the rough stuff (and by the rough stuff, I mean the wine) I'd enjoyed in Corte and Calvi. We haven't actually seen vineyards in the Figari neighborhood, but there are all sorts of fishy things about Figari, and since I do nothing but benefit by them, I won't make trouble.

Basically, it would seem our hosts own the whole town, from bar to villa, every church and restaurant and, if there is one, vineyard in between. Monsieur Simoni is the name, and when we ask why this dreamlike villa we've procured wasn't listed in any guide, he explains to me (though only Petra understood), "We don't like to advertise."

It went something like this: after we had had our celebratory beers in the anticlimactic bar of Conça, we got ourselves our own Clio, and headed farther south. In the mountains we floated among the villages, more suspended off cliffs than built on any sure piles. The radio kept getting and losing the signal, so that the readout would sometimes tell us we have Radio DeeJay (88.9 FM) or Radio KissKiss (97.9), Tam Tam (93.9), and our favorite, Radio Nostalgi Corse, featuring those nostalgic Corsican oldies, Michael Jackson, Ray Charles, and Petula Clark singing "Downtown." There is nothing in the world like slaloming through the mountains of Corsica listening to Petula declare, "The lights! Are much! Bright-er there! Youcanforgetallyourtroubles! Forgetallyourcares and Go! . . . DOWN-TOWN!"

As we got closer to the southern tip of the island, we saw more glammed-out Italian and French traffic with the "Corsica Ferries" sticker, and the locals got more and more hostile with every kilometer. We stopped at a wine shop (where are the vineyards?) and they wouldn't let us sample (another front? But later, a year later, I will discover that there was, in this area, a great wine scandal involving the use of all sorts of fortifications in the wine, both distasteful and, well, distasteful). The office of tourism was downright vicious, and we left Bonifaccio in a huff. I was despondent, but Petra had strength and fortitude and, possibly, Mafia connections. We were just half a dozen miles up the road from the shore and found ourselves in Figari, the garden paradise.

Now, here at the villa, I can relax and regard the new geology, which is whiter, made of soft sandstone out of which people have carved troglodyte garages and shops. At the south slope of Corsica, at the beach, I note how stretches of mountain seemed to be crawling out of the Tuscan Sea, as if it were Sardegna trying to escape itself, a little sun-bleached for its swim, dressed in tufa.

That I could see Sardegna out there, just ten miles off, made me Radio Nostalgic, having been there just nine months before with my friends Adela and Stephanie. Adela had spent a couple of months as a "woofer" with a macrovegan agritourismo couple who shared their lovely farm in the off-season December month. Stephanie, a food writer, was on a dining spree, and I was happy to indulge her in the meat-eating portion of the journey, since her own partner was a vegetarian and the northern Italians love to make short culinary work of their baby animals—and horses.

While wandering through the ruins of yet another ancient Etruscan town gone belly-up, we sat on a broken pillar and watched a fisherman in waders wading out to some traps. We tried to guess what he filled his bucket with—mussels or langusta or eels. We saw him again up at the souvenir stand flirting with two Sardinian girls, bored in the off-season of their job, selling neither tickets nor postcards. He had the girls take a look into his bucket, and we could crane our necks to see, too, the black-green spiny sea urchins. One of the girls looked at him with joy as he murmured something Italian and under his breath, and she repeated it, in order to confirm for herself and so that we knew what had happened: "Tutti per noi!" All for us! Sea urchin sushi, a favored midmorning snack.

Sardegna, no matter how far we traveled inland that holiday week, seemed always close to the water and to the delectables extracted from it. Corsica, with even more coast and beaches, was more concerned with meat—incredible lonzu, that soft, cured loin made from the free-wheeling pigs. The luxurious night before this luxurious morning, I had lamb chops bathed in a honey and fig confiture with herbs from the maquis. Perhaps I was drunk. Perhaps I am predisposed to pleasure, having fallen into the congenial syndicate hands of the Family Simoni. Perhaps I felt triumphant for snagging a box of coffee filters just as the Super Simoni grocery was closing. "What number?" they ask hurriedly in French (and, *moo*-free, I under-stand!), meaning, the size of the filter. "Je ne c'est quoi," I say, a phrase that, like a broken clock, is appropriate perhaps twice a day, "Quatre?" And it worked! We now have forty coffee filters for eight days in Figari. Anyway, whatever the reason, the lamb was heavenly, and the chestnut fiadone (something like flan) served with myrtle liqueur made it all that much more pleasant.

Only the southernmost edge of Corsica feels nautical to me; the setup of the villages changes the farther south you go. As I mentioned before, families establish their cemetery sepulchers willy-nilly, as if all the ground of the island were consecrated; then, you come across an entire town of tombstones, settlements full of a population more dead than alive.

When Petra gets up, we take a swim in the shoals of the Extreme Sud, and in the late afternoon I slow-cook a chicken in the same confiture of honey and figs from the maquis. We walk into the ma-quis a little and find a twelfth-century chapel dedicated to—who?—St. Quilicus, and discover, too, some stately yet secret graves, and a stone basin, the memorial to a few bandits d'honneur.

Drugged on a single Dramamine pill, I am useless to Petra's driving and navigation except to see and smile. We stop at some roadside restaurant called Passeport for a lunch, and everything we ask for on an already skimpy and gummy menu is not available, until we settle for two plates of cut-up tomatoes with chopped onion over all of it and a coffee. Behind me, the ubiquitous Nestlé Glace hamper, where all the frozen novelty confections slumber. The pictures of the ice creams on the sign, like those idealized views on postcards, always look so fresh and celebratory: cones with swirls and colorful jim-mies, day-glo orange pushups, a leering spumoni clown face. But the Real McCoy has been packed into a paper wrapper, then packed

214

again into a cardboard box, and then again into this cart in a mountain town in Corsica. It's all there, the swirls and leers and jimmies, when you peel back the paper, but they're all tamped down, stuffed, smooshed. Your clothes can be clean and still look bad if they've been packed for a long time in a suitcase, and this ice cream is like that: decidedly not festive. And so I say: no sir to your Nestlé Glace confections.

At the Bar Simoni in Figari, the bartender who had introduced us to Monsieur Simoni looks like Magilla Gorilla, but his ferocity breaks down the minute he asks you what you want. "Nous sommes a bar," is the phrase I learn today. Okay, then: progress has been made with my knowledge of French. This, and what Madame Simoni has said about the southernmost beaches: "un plage au sable fine, fine, fine."

In a bar called La Refuge, outside of l'Hospidale, or, as it was corrected on the street sign, Uspidale, another handsome bartender identifies one of my maquis weeds as "l'herbe du Barbaron." We go next door and buy some supplies for a short day hike along the Sea-to-Sea-South.

After easy rambles with light daypacks, we stop in the woods to pique-nique on more lonzu, bread, cheese, a ripe perfect peach, and a long cucumber. The French are everywhere that somebody will speak French with them. Here, in our perfect lunch spot along a sparkling clean river, there are boulders that look as if they rolled off a mountain, evidence of their angle of repose, except there is no mountain around for the boulders to roll off of, or repose. Glaciers? Giants? Chariots of the Gods?

With a beer and some nuts, Petra unlooses her lips again, always telling me the secrets of girls, local and the world over, heretofore well guarded. "When we jump off high places into the water," she says, for example, "we find our bikinis terribly rearranged in the violence of the plunge, and must put it back to rights before anybody notices and takes advantage."

Driving back from Uspidale, we marvel at the way we can see (and so much of) Sardegna. Dramatically close in clear air. People get out of their car at a belvedere turnout just to look at it, as if a whale has swum into the Mediterranean, or some other rare sea monster. I can see the white stone again, and I wonder at the way two places can be so close to each other, and maintain wild differences.

After a hassled trip to the Hyper U, we see the couple from the Pyrenees with Lula, the black Lab, all trudging up the side of the busy highway. We stop and give them a lift to their campsite. They had stopped for a longer time than we did at the halfway point, hoping that the crowds would thin out as the month went on. They report that the GR20 is still very crowded since we left it. A rueful satisfaction, to hear this. But it is nice to see them, as if running into neighbors at the Dairy Queen—we are at home on Corsica. We know some people there. And that's something of the truth: Corsica is a small town, in all.

We unwind that evening over another Cap Corse, the local blood-red aperitif made only on this island. What is Cap Corse? Bitters, I suppose, that set our mouths ready for heavier drinking. It is Sunday, and on the previous Wednesday Petra had bought the German newspaper, *Die Welt,* so we could find out what was going on in the world while we were socked into the mountains. Now, since she drove into the village to get our bread and more coffee, I think she's maybe bought a new *Die Welt* and has the latest news—but that can't be. "Is that new?" I ask her.

"Oh no, it's the same one from Wednesday," she says, smiling. "I like that the news never changes when I am on vacation." And she goes back to study a piece on Gunther, the man who runs the Deutsch version of *Who Wants to Be a Millionaire?*

I drag my teabag idly through a boulle and realize that only the boulle facilitates this long dragging, like a child pulling a pull-toy; it seems a goof that most of the delights of travel are flimsy and based on all the triangulations of juxtaposed culture, the frictions and clownish contrasts. Hee hee, I'm dragging a teabag through a French coffee boulle. Hee hee, they're playing Da-doo-ron-ron on Radio Nostalgi Corse as we drive by another lone crypt. Hee hee, eets a wild peeg in the bivouac, Chroist.

As the days go by, without a segment of GR20 to traverse, I fall into ridiculous activities, like washing the tent stakes in the sink and arranging bouquets of maquis for gifts back home. A mighty wind blows—is it a Mistral or a Sirocco?—blowing Petra and me, and a line of olive trees flanked by our stone fence, looking like spooks trying to scare us. I fill up a bucket or two of water and throw it over our rented Clio—it has been so easy to pick it out in the Hyper U parking lot among the hundreds of other Clios (the official rental car of Corsica is a Christmas-red Clio)—because there are muddy snout marks on the passenger side from a time when we were surrounded on the road by wild pigs demanding a handout.

Petra comes out to watch me and holds the Simoni family dog lest he drink from my bucket. "Your ride is your pride," I explain to her. She likes things clean, too. She's German, but she tells all the people in the world that she is from Austria.

Petra is no less frivolous with her newfound leisure. She busies herself with the remains of my "Poulet Figari," the baked chicken I dressed with maquis herbs and fig confiture, our feast for the previous evening, by making a favored dish of her own homeland:

Knödel. A la Maquis.

Ingredients

Old bread from the bergerie, cubed
The ground-down stuff from my poulet Figari

Chopped pieces of lonzu and sausiccon (you can use ham)
Chopped shallot
Chopped myrtle (replaces the more traditional parsley and nutmeg)
Milk (hot, because the steam will rise up through the bread)
Pepper and salt (lots, because, says Petra, "the bread is nothing")

———

Let the bread absorb the milk for a while; overnight is best. Then add one egg; taste to see if it's necessary to add pepper. Form into small balls with wet fingers. Petra likes them small, though she says, "Some mothers will make them like the size of the heads of babies. Not me." Then boil the knödel balls in water just under boiling temperature until they rise to the surface.

I love that Petra has made knödel in Corsica. She tells me it could be better with schweinbraten or a salad, but we eat it with more myrtle and maquis seasoning. It is a delicacy, especially with Figari (vineyards? Figari?) wine and olives. But when I take the last uneaten bits of the chicken carcass and other garbage out to the road, I find four pizza boxes from the Family Simoni filling up our bin. Everybody wants something just a little bit more exotic.

Cultural differences rubbing up against each other are indeed the pleasure of travel, but they can also make me feel ill at ease. Freud spoke of the uncanny—that it is not the strangeness in strange things that seem upsetting to us but the familiar aspects of the strange thing. When I was a child, I nightmared for months over the whale Monstro, not because of his ferocious devouring of Pinocchio but because of his eye, a normal eye, with pupil, cornea, lids, whites— nearly human, seeing things just as well as a human could see things. I once watched Popeye on a television in a bar in central Spain. Popeye still sounded like Popeye even in Castilian, but Olive Oyl wasn't Aceite de Oliva, but Olivia. I had to leave the bar. I can feel a wave of nausea, even as an adult, when I see off-brand candy in a store, or knock-off versions of major motion pictures. When bread gets wet at the bottom of the sink, and I have to touch it, I get this same nausea. Or when somebody gives me an anonymous dirty joke typed on a piece of paper and then made into a copy of a copy of a copy, that also horrifies, perhaps when it ought to entertain. If I buy a jacket or a shirt in Europe, I am surprised to find the buttons or zippers switched to the opposite side than I am used, the "girl" side. The French write "miam-miam" when they want to approximate "yum-yum" on the kiddy menu. This sickens me.

I was also sickened at the beach north of Porto Vecchio by the granny-aged woman reclining on her towel, topless and knitting a sweater.

What happens is this: If you are not walking, or otherwise making yourself vulnerable to being designated as smelling bad—as long-distance walkers do—or American, or stupid, you can almost forget that you are not at home. That morning, after the sun came and warmed the yard of our villa and the Madame, from her own house, waved a distant good morning with the reptilian-green garden hose on her roses, I went in and pulled a Popsicle from the freezer (the box saying "Popsicles" because apparently that is a word recognizable throughout the world and even the French Academy has allowed it into France), and I unwrapped it and found it was one of those twin-pops, and I rested it against the counter to break it along its length to give half to Petra, for I had hollered out to the veranda in English, "Do you wanna Popsicle?" and Petra hollered back, "Yes," and when it broke it made that same squeaky Styrofoam peanut sound they made in my hometown, in my childhood. I looked over at the English guidebook while Radio Nostalgi Corse played "What's New Pussycat?" and when I sucked on my half of the Popsicle it lost its color, became snowcapped, or boring, or wan, or whatever you want to call it when it's just ice, just as it has happened always, ever, anywhere, and suddenly I lifted my coffee boulle and saw the word in the bottom of my saucer: "Choky." This is a European brand of coffee. But the word is uncanny, not a word I want to see when I am feeling so deeply at home. The world shifts, I stumble mentally, the way you stumble when you think there's a last step on the stairway and there isn't one, or vice versa.

But the nausea passes, for it's a crisp vivid morning, with postcard-blue skies. The harvested cork trees look as if they're wearing halter tops, old grannies trying to look young.

I asked Petra if she ever felt this discomfort of the travel uncanny. She was quiet for a moment. "Do you remember when I came to visit you in San Francisco?" Petra came to see me after walking along the North Coast Trail on Vancouver Island. I introduced her to spicy food in run-down Cambodian pho shops and burritos as big as, well, Petra's mother's knödel. "You also showed me how the grocery stores were open twenty-four hours a day," she reminded me. I recalled her being dismayed by this, and I thought of how she lived a while in Munich, where, in Bavarian old-school style, the shops all closed at four in the afternoon, and I realized that if I were a single man living in Munich, I would no doubt die, being at work all day and having no help getting a few staples to live on in the evening.

But Petra said, "I thought, you Americans have no morals, always with the store open like that. You shoot each other with guns and run into the forest to hide from the guns but there is no place to hide because you have chopped down all the trees." I laugh, but she is serious; there is, for her, something terribly wrong with a twenty-four-hour Safeway, as wrong as gun violence and clear-cutting.

I travel because Petra is right, and I wonder whether there is a better way to do things. Nevertheless, I like the convenience of twenty-four-hour stores.

I nurse another Myrtle Liquor hangover (will I ever learn?). Because we drove an hour and a half to Madame Simoni's native town of

Zonza, where we ate well at the Restaurant Le Terrace, and, because Petra was doing all the driving (I cannot, or rather will not, drive with a stick shift; it is a deal I have made with my addiction to self-destruction: it is as far as I will go), I graciously agreed to drink the lion's share of the bottle of red from the Sartene region, Domaine Fumicicoli (a rouge that makes the inside of the mouth itch as if it were mosquito-bitten, but fruity, too), and bookended it with beers, liqueurs, and grappa.

I dined on more of the local meat, a veal chop, and a terrine full of a soufflé with spinach—preternaturally hot, that ramekin was, even after half an hour. For dessert, an aged brocciu that also made the mouth itch and burn as fiercely as the work of the wine, and then the sweet smooth crème caramel. Oh, and *then* the liquor de myrtle and its devious cousin, the eau de vie de myrte.

Meanwhile, Petra chose the other menu because Madame Simoni had specifically suggested the trout. The waiter kept saying something about how "There was no trout, *désolée,* but there is trout, if you like." We are still not sure what it was all about, but I'm guessing it wasn't a local trout. Petra said it was fresh.

Petra is such a fine counterpart, maybe too sensible when I am too impulsive. When I found that the village of Levie had a small museum that contained the bones of a nine-thousand-year-old woman and an extinct rat-rabbit—well, who wouldn't want to see the skeleton of an extinct rat-rabbit? Petra, that's who.

And why am I so impulsive? I think that I want to live with the same impressionistic surprising pleasures that memory gives off in blasts, unplanned and pungent. Travel is like that, like the way memory will exhale and puff something strong in your face. Or rather, that is how my memory works. Petra is even methodical in her remembering. My mind is a wonderland of rabbit holes, and so is my reality, I'm afraid. How often I get lost. We laughed at my guidebook, suggesting we bring a compass, but we don't laugh anymore.

With all the zigzags and cols and boccas, when walking in the mountains (and here may be a key reason I love to do all this walking in the wonderland) I get turned around every twenty feet, and the wind changes when bouncing off every mountain wall. It's as if I were a child playing at a piñata, swinging wildly at space, disoriented. If you're lucky, candy will rain down upon you. If not, not.

On the ride home from Zonza, zipping fearlessly around more disorienting curves (and in the night!), we saw more of those corrected signs, changed so much they look absurd: "Sortie de Camions" (Exit for Truckers) has been changed to "Ortie de Mamions" "Please hold hand pail." "El rey es subnormal, y todo del mundo lo saben." Such urgencies to let the whole world *lo* know.

But of the hangover: in Simoniville, we give up at the post office and go across to Bar U Puncinu, hosted at all hours by Magilla Gorilla. Two Oranginas, I say.

Madame Simoni drops by and has an Orangina with us, between errands of mercy. Her first name is Angel, and she lives to fill her titular destiny. Her accommodations, suggestions for restaurants, quiet places on the beach—they are all fine, fine, fine. But then Angel flits off; she can never stay long in one place, ever, apparently. Up and down, up and down, like Puck in *A Midsummer Night's Dream*. Petra and I slump back in our chairs and enjoy the view: of the street. A flock of tiny but multitudinous gray-blue Corsican nuthatches circle around four or five houses like a little rain-cloud on a mission. This is how Petra and I are feeling, plopped between wheeling birds and sprightly angels. There is this terrible problem after a journey of learning to sit still again. We spend the week pacing, dithering, investigating, picking up and putting down, looking behind us, looking.

We have parked our Clio badly, and when the gas truck comes to fill up the Super Gas Simoni, we have created a full-on traffic jam. Sitting in front under a parasol'd table, we watch as cars slow to a crawl, then a succession of caravans/RVs heading into the mountain, then, to our great pleasure, a parade of handsome firemen heading down to the coast, all in a red red row, as if this were May Day and we live in Russia in 1972. "Oh look, something else is coming!" I tell Petra when one of those rigs that carry new cars came trundling through with a brand new load of red red Clios. "What else would you like us to stop?" Petra asks. My hangover is suddenly gone.

9

Why I Walk

Imagining the Maquis

"Useless to ask a wandering man
Advice on the construction of a house.
The work will never come to completion."

After reading this text, from the Chinese *Book of Odes*, I real-
ised the absurdity of trying to write a book on Nomads.
Bruce Chatwin, *The Songlines*

All of my travels end up "mid-epic" in scale. I go away for a long
time. Home gathers dust. Seasons change. Milk spoils in the fridge.
Friends move away. Careers launch and fail. Like the eponymous
Swimmer of Cheever's story, the world shifts radically. Is it possible to
miss away the way people miss home? Wanderlust, I guess it's called.
Walking long distances has given me a better sense of distances,

stretched some out into realistic ideas and made shorter distances seem smaller. I start to torture friends when I come back home by suggesting we walk to the movie theater. "Come on, parking is terrible over there and it's only three miles." There is a sigh that can only be the sound of being uninvited. And yet the task of rounding up sponsors for the March of Dimes Walk-a-Thon, the fee I must pay to join the gym—I can't bear it.

I have long given up the pilgrim's need for a site, a tabernacle on which to offer my suffering feet (and by tabernacle, I also mean the March of Dimes or a fit gym-built body). This is desire without an object; call it longing. I need to be outdoors and indoors. Yes, there may be fleas, and sometimes I have to eat tripe, and is there no bathroom in this gîte? "I have never heard of a bathroom in a gîte" (and by "never heard of it," I mean, if found, "you'll never forget it.").

Or this is what I'd like to believe. But what I wish for is coherent story, for an object of my desire, for meaning or metaphor. A trek with danger and pain, a passage that makes the body and heart sore, such a thing should be a metaphor for something, or it is nothing. And that's why I begin to weep on the plane: there are dozens of anecdotes, dozens of objects of desire, and yet the trip across Corsica, beginning and ending so abruptly, crumbles into fragments; the only thing that feels whole here is the sense that the entire trip was nothing but a digression.

For me, crying always comes as a surprise. Weeping comes to me, who willed a shutoff of the waterworks long ago, only when I am off my guard, overtired, under the influence of bad movies and jet lag. Otherwise, crying, or the impulse to cry, swoops down like the lammergeier and strikes a little terror. It's a cleansing experience, though, an unselfing; I feel satisfied as fully used, bleached bones afterward. I want to pick apart the mess that leads to the weep, the initial anger and frustration, say, at not understanding a command in a foreign language, at getting deep-fried lamb intestine instead of a salad when ordering off the menu, at the way little old ladies will barge in front of me when I am stepping onto a train. Usually, I suppose, the emotion I would express would be mere anger if I were at home, but when I am away, some strangeness rolls it over, this decayed log, and suddenly I can see all the beetles and worms crawling underneath. Weeping is this kind of disturbance.

If there is such a thing as reverse jet lag—the dread anticipatory worry of departure—it is a site of some weeping. The child has had fun at summer camp, and he does not want to go back to school.

My shoulders were sore the day Petra drove me to the airport from the previous day's long snorkeling excursion in the Gulf of Santa Manza. After the snorkeling, I slept in a bad position. I was scheming rather than dreaming: how was I going to get all of the loot home? Besides my own souvenirs, Petra had given me one of her two high-tech walking sticks and, wrapped around it, a roll of Mentos with the flavor of pink grapefruit, a flavor not available in my best-of-all-possible-worlds country. Our tryst was ending for another time. But we were already making plans: Zanzibar! Crete! Tallinn!

And then I was alone at the gate, for I had commanded that Petra leave me. I wouldn't want her to see me weep. Besides, she has to drive the Clio all the way up to Bastia and fly back to Vienna very early the next day. Our goodbyes have always been perfunctory, a kiss or two, but mostly because this is ongoing, breaks between being mostly together. What makes a gay man wish to be straight? A friendship as easy and enthusiastic as the one I have with Petra.

Before I knew it, I was leaning out my window, meditating on the throbbing, undulating barcode of skidmarks on the small airport landing strip.

Or perhaps I weep because I read in the final Corsican newspaper I'll get during this trip that the little dead British boy is—they've finally

227

discovered—really dead. My heart is a cactus, and I weep for that, too.

Driving to the Figari airport, we were slowed by cows, the first time cows ever threatened to make me late for a flight. Earlier, when I planned this trip, I had the choice of taking a ferry or one of those rinky-dink flying operations (in this case Air Littoral), the sort in which the plane is borrowed from another country (in this case Spain) and everybody claps when the plain lands—from relief, maybe? Or maybe it's like a small town putting on a big musical production of *Oklahoma!,* and everybody knows personally the big stars that play Curly and Judd and the captain and your stewardess. And you collect the air sickness bag for your friend who collects air sickness bags, because this is one he can't *possibly* have, but statistically, the air sickness bags of this kind of plane are used 1000 percent more often, making them an even more rare collector's item.

The plane took off. It's amazing to be able to see the shape of the island from the air, a big Michelin map. It's like knowing all the vocabulary, all the declensions, all the conjugations, at last, of a language you've been struggling to learn—and then it's time to go.

The highways and paved roads of the world were once walking trails that kept getting used, known conduits, the devil we all knew. Before that, they were the paths of our domesticated animals, trying to get to food they were willing to stoop for. Before that, their trails were paths of animals not yet domesticated, as yet unstooping, or maybe untameable. Before that, they were arroyos, dried river beds, or the drag marks where natural gravity pulled at matter until it reached its final resting place, inescapable. If it is not all of these things you see in the way between here and there, then we probably blasted it out of rock, or did something equally violent or unnatural to make it exist. In which case, we travelers not only destroy what we seek but destroy the way to the sought thing, too.

I think I saw, as the plane shot out for a minute in the wrong direction and turned around on a steep banking curve, Elba, the place of Napoleon's exile. Not the wrong direction, no: every direction may be exile.

When I came back from Corsica, my bags were full of everything I speak against in my travelogue: a museum of ceramics, liquors, meats, books, and cuttings from the maquis. Travelers destroy what they seek, or at the very least, make a museum of it. I am not hateful toward museums, but I tend to attend the ones in my home town more often than those in the places where I travel. They seem something like ossuaries, a record of something that was there rather than something that is—the half-rabbit, half-rat skeleton, a living stretch of the maquis now dried out and tied up in string, sachet. One of the things I did buy was a collection of essential oils from a little homeopathic shop in Porto Vecchio, reported to be the four main ingredients in the makeup of the maquis. Myrtle, of course, and rosemary, and some mix of several savory herbs.

And still the mind lags behind the body. The mail is still stopped for a few days after I arrive, and I'm too busy resuming the duties of work to call all the people I know to tell them I'm back. Until I do, they consider me still gone. I'm a ghost, have slipped over the lip of the world and disappeared the way a teabag tag will slip when you pour the water into the pot too quickly—and that is a thing cavemen never knew.

Even I consider me gone. I look at my town the way a tourist does, noticing for the first time things that have been there from the first: incredible! My entire neighborhood seems to be made of brick. All these girls know how to apply foundation to their face by the time they are twelve. Gingerbread gets more "cakey" when it is kept in Tupperware. These observations, like the suggestion that we all walk to the movies, challenge my friendships. The Bouldrey we sent to Corsica is not the Bouldrey they have returned to us.

My mind is not with my body but is still back in a village in Corsica. In Sartene, I recall now, a boy hanging out the little veranda over the street with his excited, wound-up dog. What were they waiting for? That is when I sometimes wish I had a video camera, even though the tourists who carry them are international embarrassments. In the museums and cathedrals, I'll watch some dope pan over silver crucifixes, or the history of how the aperitif "Cap Corse" is made (it's made with chestnuts, of course, and quinine, antimalarial and intoxicating), and no doubt that video will never be watched. So too, do they pan over crappy souvenirs, badly lit minor paintings, the wide expanse of the sea and beach. Never over the little boy and his dog, the towering Laricio pines swaying precariously in a wind, an old woman in black peering out her door—yes, I was the one who had them start the vendetta, and watch out, or I'll set one up for you!

I'm being judgmental. I think of the packets of my father's hopeless family vacation photos, of bland open landscapes. They were beautiful places; I was there and I agree, breathtaking to see, but inert, shrunken, even boring in a picture. Buried deep in this inability to see or apprehend or frame beautiful things and places is the longing for it. We did see it, it was apprehended, but how can I show it to somebody else? How do I convince anybody that the aiguilles of Bavella are something brought to earth from another planet and set out there in the Mediterranean? In the phrase "as is," that almost assonantal, glottal-stopping term, it is suggested that there is something wrong with the thing it describes; our task is to find the damage in the thing.

And perhaps I'm asking the wrong questions. Is it natural for every person to wish to apprehend beautiful things, interpreted or isolated or not? I walk with my dog every evening and will now and then witness hallucinatory full moons or the visitation of a barn owl on a low branch, but she doesn't see it. For my dog, beauty is elsewhere. In the smell of vomit, perhaps. And soon, she will be gone.

I watched that little boy on the veranda in Sartene from the camouflaged safety of a café table, watched until the bread delivery man drove up, at which moment the boy lowered his cumbersome action figure on a string down, down, down, until it clobbered the baker, who was not amused, and beat on the door and insisted in Corsican Italian, I suppose, to be let in so that he could exact his revenge.

All the things I brought back—the brocciu and the lonzu and the bundled sprigs of maquis herbs, even the intangibles, the things taken that don't destroy what travelers seek, the journal with all the records of the events, the photos—they are some crystallized, postcard-perfected version of the place, that granite stone along the road without the spray-painted admonishment, "Francesi Fora!" I remember how, while listening to the polyphonie in Corte, some tourists were so moved by the music that they pulled out their cameras to snap a picture of, what?—the sound? Beauty seems only to be mediated through the eye. What will they think when they get the pictures developed back home? What were they trying to capture? Movement, sound, an emotional arc—everything but what is there, frozen, lifeless in the photo. And soon, they'll even forget that music.

That doesn't mean I don't do the same sort of thing. What I miss the most, or remember best, is the smell of a place—Galicia smells like sour milk, wet hay, cow dooky. The Perigord is a great smell of pine and rotting grapes. Andalucia is a spilled Jerez and unfiltered black tobacco cigarettes. Les Landes: railroad ties rotting back into earth. Every once in a while, a wind will tease me with that redpepper-and-cooking-octopus smell, and I am back in Galicia. But I have a box full of mementos of travel—bits of broken tile, sea glass, shells, seed pods from some impossible plant. When we finally got together again, the scentmeister Michael and I mixed up a handful of the various essences I've brought back in order to re-create the maquis. Michael has brought out the little swizzle stick paddles again and a box of ziplock bags. I told him I saw Corsican households with ziplock bags filled with water in order to scare away flies by showing themselves as a distorted, inflated imaged in reflection.

"That's just weird," he said, and I realize he's right even as I tell him about this superstition. But the remaking of the maquis isn't weird to Michael. This, he can understand, or begin to imagine. I can bring that home from my travels, and my friends can get a hint of an explanation.

I get my hint by mixing up various portions of the essential oils—two parts rosemary, one part myrtle, three parts citronella in one bag, then three parts rosemary, two of myrtle, a little thyme, and a dash of balsam and bergamot. By the time we are finished, there are more than a dozen baggies sealed with their attending scent stick, and it is baggie number eleven that seems the closest to what I remember as the maquis. Michael mixes a tall flask with the same measurements, and uses his label maker to tag it: "Maquis No. 11." Later, he makes candles from it for me, and an oil to burn in a censer.

Even so, this is an idealized version of the maquis, the home edition, a Hollywood version. What we lack here is the "uninventable detail": the malodorous alder, or that certain version of thyme that grew out of rocks and smelled like sheep piss. There is no essential oil in the shops for "dust" or "forest fire" or "goats" or "trekker sweat." Still, it does something I don't anticipate: it brings the outdoors indoors, a little of the wild, strange place into my overly familiar living room. It is a little foreign to me. And that is when I start to notice old things in a fresh way. And that is when I confirm that my home has to be just a little bit unhomey, even *uncomfortable,* in order for me to feel comfortable in it.

The outdoors, I realize the morning after my return, has been taken indoors once again. I think this as I pour milk on my cereal and the flat flakes make the milk skiff off and land in spatters on the counter. For if I were outdoors, I'd be throwing flat stones across Lac Nino, and this wouldn't be a mess I will have to clean up.

Days later, even weeks after a walk, I still dream nightly about walking, knowing well that there never will be real meaning in it, that walking is as senseless as violence. And as any perpetrator or recipient of violence knows, it will happen again.

In the city, I can close my window and the world is so quiet—no lovemaking Germans in the next tent, no peeg running through the bivouac. Just the sound of my own pulse when I rest my head against my pillow, the sound of some soft, fibrous cotton rubbed against the hard fact of teeth and bone and my tympanum, rush, rush, rush. I fall asleep to the beat, and I dream of walking to far-off places and it's always pretty and it's always good to walk. I dream a visionary dream one night of a big backpack with long tassels hanging from all its pockets and corners that rotated in space like a backpack satellite. I wake in the morning and begin to pace. Where is my stick? Where is my pack?

The secret thing about travel is that time (namely, the future) is what one travels in just as much as space, and so travelers destroy time with the same intent as the other thing they seek. What keeps me going on into the future, I wonder, if I'm always gobbling it, consuming it, destroying it? A promise, perhaps, made to someone else, or a self from long ago, or one of the future, or God. God may exist to make me be true to all those promises, like the man who built Holyrood in Edinburgh.

I light a candle, scented with Maquis No. 11. In its perfection, it is imperfect. I think of how the travel agencies talk us into wanting a perfect romantic getaway that's picture-postcard perfect, but it's when something mars the journey, that's when it becomes memorable—then we've really done the thing.

This is the phrase: "cherishing something and putting it in lavender." That I like. The maquis will do that to me. For me. For you, I only have my nostalgia to offer, and this book. This book is not for me, after all, but everybody else.

Bibliography

It is rather clear by now that I did not have the wherewithal to execute an exhaustive codex for the nation of Corsica—a comprehensive history, political study, bestiary, anthropological record, and economic analysis of the island—except, at times, as presented in ontological doodads germane to the story. To be honest, the reader I seek does not have the wherewithal for such stuff, either. I did have the wherewithal to read several other volumes both comprehensive and idiosyncratic, and if you're looking for some real tough-minded wherewithal, the books most useful and enjoyable include *Corsica: Portrait of a Granite Island* (1971) by Dorothy Carrington (a writer who, according to Paul Theroux in his book *The Pillars of Hercules,* lives there to this day in self-imposed exile after perpetrating some sort of scandal upon her noble family); an odd-duck volume most in the spirit of this book, called *Concerning Corsica* (1926) by Rene Juta, a sassy sister to a minor artist of the 1920s who seems to have been friends with D. H. Lawrence, reportedly a cranky man by disposition ("What fun we all had! All? I wonder," writes Juta, "D. H., simmering in fury generally, boiling over, hot enough to melt all the snows of Etna. . . ."); James Boswell's dry, sometimes witheringly dry volume from 1765, *An Account of Corsica, the Journal of a Tour to that Island, and Memoirs of Pascal Paoli* (possibly the flattest title for a book prior to *Closely Observed Trains*); and more recently but sadly more scarce, the *Journal of a Landscape Painter in Corsica,* by Edward Lear (1870). This last I got hold of before my trip, and read (perhaps disastrously) more closely than my own guidebooks, so that Lear's vision of Corsica, depicted both in gouache images and pointy-nosed text, colored my own trip in quite a lurid way. Besides being a painter of great ability, Lear was perhaps better known, as can be divined in the limerick that opens the author's note, as the poet of absurd lines (good job, Ed, rhyming "Corsica" with "Corsica"!), and more than once did I find myself, while walking the crazy trails of Corsica, reciting much of Lear's wise nonsense: "Far and few, far and few / Are the lands where the Jumblies live / Their heads are green and their hands are blue / And they went to sea in a sieve."

Abram, David. *Trekking in Corsica.* Surrey, England: Trailblazer Publications, 2002.

Boswell, James. *An Account of Corsica, the Journal of a Tour to that Island; and Memoirs of Pascal Paoli.* London: Printed for Edward and Charles Dilly, 1768.

Carrington, Dorothy. *Corsica: Portrait of a Granite Island.* New York: John Day Company, 1974.

Chiari, Joseph. *The Scented Isle: A Parallel between Corsica and the Scottish Highlands.* Glasgow: W. MacLellan, 1948.

Gregory, Desmond. *The Ungovernable Rock: A History of the Anglo-Corsican Kingdom and Its Role in Britain's Mediterranean Strategy during the Revolutionary War (1793–1797).* Toronto: Fairleigh Dickinson University Press, 1985.

Hawthorne, Hildegarde. *Corsica: The Surprising Island.* New York: Duffield and Company, 1926.

Juta, Rene. *Concerning Corsica.* New York: Alfred A. Knopf, 1926.

Lear, Edward. *Journal of a Landscape Painter in Corsica.* London: Robert Bush, 1870.

Mérimée, Prosper. *Colomba and Carmen,* translated from the French by the Lady Mary Loyd, with a critical introduction by Arthur Symons, a frontispiece and numerous other portraits with descriptive notes by Octave Uzanne. New York: P. F. Collier, 1901.

Noaro, Jean. *Corse Familière.* Paris: Bibliotheque des Guides Bleus, Librairie Hachette, 1968. Photographs by Henry Cohen.

Solnit, Rebecca. *Wanderlust: A History of Walking.* New York: Penguin Putnam, 2000.